NEVER
SAY
NEVER

MY INSIDE STORY OF
THE MOTORCYCLE WORLD CHAMPIONSHIPS

NICK HARRIS

1 3 5 7 9 10 8 6 4 2

Virgin Books, an imprint of Ebury Publishing
20 Vauxhall Bridge Road,
London SW1V 2SA

Virgin Books is part of the Penguin Random House group
of companies whose addresses can be found
at global.penguinrandomhouse.com

Picture sections: Section 1: p. 1 top © BikeSport TT Race Pics, bottom ©
Getty, p. 2 top © Henk Keulemans Archive, bottom © PA Images, p. 3 bottom
© PA Images, p. 4 top and middle © Mortons Archive, p. 5 © Mortons
Archive, p. 8 bottom © Getty. Section 2: p. 1 top © Henk Keulemans, bottom
© Getty, p. 2 top © Getty, bottom © Gold and Goose, p. 3 © PA Images,
bottom © Getty, p. 4 top © Gold and Goose, bottom © PA Images, p. 5 top
and bottom © Getty, p. 6 © PA Images, p. 7 top and bottom © Getty, p. 8 top
© PA Images, bottom © Gold and Goose.

First published by Virgin Books in 2019
This paperback edition published in 2020

www.penguin.co.uk

A CIP catalogue record for this book is available from the British Library

ISBN 9780753553879

Typeset in 10.3/16.6 pt Sabon LT Pro
by Integra Software Services Pvt. Ltd, Pondicherry

Printed and bound in Great Britain by Clays Ltd, Elcograf S.p.A.

Penguin Random House is committed to a sustainable future
for our business, our readers and our planet. This book is
made from Forest Stewardship Council® certified paper.

To Sheila and Sophie – my loving support always.

CONTENTS

CONTENTS

Introduction

IT'S AMAZING JUST how this has all happened. I was just two years old when Freddie Frith won that very first World Championship race at the 1949 TT on the Isle of Man – not that anybody in our house would have noticed. There weren't even any motorcycle riders, let alone racers in our family.

My dear old dad was sports mad: he earmarked me to open the batting and play scrum half for England the moment I emerged into the world at the Radcliffe Infirmary in Oxford. I didn't even open the batting for Magdalen College School second team, although I loved cricket and played for 50 years. And I soon realised I preferred playing football to rugby. Sorry, Dad.

I grew up in the village of Cumnor, near Oxford. I was a happy local boy who suffered from such acute homesickness that, as a teenager on holiday with my mates, I would send a postcard back home to my mum and dad every day. That I ended up with a dream job that took me around the world for 38 wonderful years would seem impossible to that young lad.

Playing sport and supporting the local football team, Oxford United, from the infamous London Road terrace were big parts of growing up. But it was on Saturday afternoons sitting in our lounge watching scrambling on the old black and white television when motorcycles first grabbed my attention. There was a not a family gene in my body that suggested any interest in two wheels, but my love of motorcycles and racing in particular had been sparked. I discovered Speedway at Cowley Stadium, and then, soon after, on a visit to Mallory Park I watched road racing and heard the piercing scream of real horsepower for the first time.

I plodded through my teenage years never worrying about my future and enjoying myself. Motorcycles and football dominated my spare time. Perhaps predictably then, I left Magdalen College School in 1964 with one O level, after two pretty pathetic attempts. And I only achieved such academic honours because the history master told us what questions to revise and he chose the right three. A friend of my parents offered me a job as a clerk in a local solicitors' office, a role for which I was supremely unsuited. I spent most of my time thinking about my next visit to the Isle of Man, ignoring the brown folders mounting on my desk, and was told I couldn't attend meetings with important clients on account of my hair being too long.

My next job, working behind the counter in a sports shop, was altogether more suitable. I supplemented my income working as a disc jockey in the evenings, before I moved on to become the south of England rep for a Manchester-based sports company. Then, out of the blue, at the end of 1972, an offer came that was to change my life.

I'd come straight from Thursday night football training to the posh house of local bigwig Tony Rosser up the Banbury Road. He was starting up a new project, a local free newspaper that was to be called the *Oxford Journal*, and he wanted me to become his distribution manager. I thanked him but said I was happy selling football boots and training shoes. He then offered me three times my current salary and, needless to say, I joined the *Oxford Journal* two weeks later.

We'd always loved newspapers, radio and sport in our house. Years earlier I'd produced my own handwritten newspaper with pictures glued on and would commentate to my dad on rugby matches at Iffley Road in Oxford. I'd never forgotten those early days but, deep down, I honestly believed the opportunity would never arrive. I assumed the highlight of any journalism career would have been back when our headmaster Eric Brodie had pinned my report on the

Cumnor Primary School versus Dunmore game to the classroom noticeboard.

But, lo and behold, it was not long before an opportunity came to write a sports column for the back page of the paper. Just 24 hours after a pretty routine Monday morning for the distribution manager, scooping up wet dumped newspapers from among the used syringes and dog shit under Donington Bridge, I found myself on my first ever jet plane flight, sitting alongside a Scottish international footballer who had scored against England at Wembley. Out of the blue, I was being sent to Italy to report on Bologna versus Oxford United in the 1973 Anglo-Italian Cup. On getting back from the airport a few days later I was met by Tony Adamson from BBC Radio Oxford who asked me if I would give up playing football on a Saturday afternoon to come into their studio to read the football results and make the tea.

Of course I've been so lucky since that first trip. I have often been in the right place at the right time without even realising it, but it's also true that you make your own luck in so many ways. I felt vastly underqualified for the advertised role of general reporter at *Motor Cycle News*, but I went to the interview in Kettering anyway. Being made redundant when IPC closed *Motor Cycle Weekly* led to working with the Rothmans team, and eventually with Dorna.

In so many ways travelling the world reporting and commentating on the sport you love is just about the perfect job. It's the people you leave at home who are the real heroes. When one partner spends over one third of the year on the road in a high adrenaline environment, while the other is at home, bringing up the children, getting the washing machine mended and checking the mortgage has been paid, quite understandably it can lead to relationships breaking down. I have been so lucky to have had the support of my wife Sheila over the last 38 years.

In Austria a couple of years ago, my colleagues and Matt Birt in particular were gobsmacked when I had to borrow a Dorna white shirt because my wife Sheila had forgotten to pack mine. For 38 years, Sheila packed my case – this was the first time she'd ever forgotten the shirts. Another example of Sheila's incredible capabilities was when 'we' moved house in 1994. I left home for the Formula One grand prix in Barcelona from one house and returned four days later to our new home. It was a miracle. I hadn't lifted a finger, and yet all the furniture had arrived and the gas, electricity and water were switched on for my return.

When I embarked on this adventure 39 years ago there was just eight grands prix to visit, and all in Europe. To watch grand prix motorcycle racing grow into this truly massive international sport has given me so much satisfaction. Last year there were 19 grands prix visiting 15 countries on five continents. The average crowd over a grand prix weekend was 151,802 with the new Thailand venue attracting 222,535. When Dorna CEO Carmelo Ezpeleta told guests at my farewell dinner that I was a part of that 70-year World Championship legacy I could not have been prouder.

Happy birthday grand prix motorcycle racing – thanks for such an amazing ride. But the biggest thank you goes to my wife Sheila and daughter Sophie who gave me so much love and support throughout this adventure.

Honeymoon
1949–1953

THE *KING ORRY* gently manoeuvred alongside the harbour wall in Douglas. In Irish Sea terms it had been a pretty comfortable crossing. Half an hour earlier, the passengers had crammed the deck rails of the ferry to catch their first glimpse of the Isle of Man just as the sun popped out from behind the clouds that were hiding the peak of Snaefell Mountain, which dominates the island. Later in the week, many of those holidaymakers would make their way to the top on the electric railway, hoping for a clear day when they could be the only people to see England, Scotland, Wales and Ireland from one place.

It was a surprisingly warm June afternoon, which just about summed up the mood of the country. Food rationing was still in place, and there were still plenty of stark reminders of those bombing raids in cities throughout the country, but a sense of optimism was beginning to take hold. Many of the passengers who spilled down the gangplank of the *King Orry* – whose predecessor had been sunk by German guns nine years earlier at Dunkirk – were there to forget the horrors of war and enjoy their first holiday for over a decade or more. The ferry journey from Liverpool had produced the feeling of taking a continental holiday – one on a giant granite rock in the middle of the Irish Sea, where history was about to be made.

Just four years after the end of the Second World War, the Fédération Internationale de Motocyclisme (FIM), the governing body of Word Motorcycling, launched the World Motorcycle Racing Championship one year ahead of its four-wheeled counterparts. The six-round championship would be held at circuits only in Europe and consisted of four solo classes: 125, 250, 350 and the equivalent of modern-day MotoGP, the premier 500cc class, plus sidecars.

The tracks selected were in Berne, Switzerland; Assen, Holland; Spa-Francorchamps in Belgium; Clady in Ulster, Northern Ireland, and Monza in northern Italy. However, there was no other choice for the opening round than the iconic, demanding and dangerous 37.73-mile circuit of the Isle of Man.

After all, they had been racing motorcycles on the island's roads since 1907. Back then, the speed limit on all British roads was 20mph. The forward-thinking Manx government realised that closing their roads for racing could have far-reaching consequences, and allowed Frank Hulbert and Jack Marshall, along with 11 other starters, to push their single-cylinder Triumph machines into life at 10am on 28 May, and race 158 miles round the 15-mile St John course, at speeds of around 38mph. But those politicians could not have realised the impact that their decision would have on the next 112 years.

In 1949, the British motorcycle industry was fighting its way back after the rigours of world war. Many of the Midlands-based manufacturers' factories had been damaged by German bombs, but the industry was starting to enjoy a resurgence, especially in the export market. They realised very quickly that success in the new World Championship, and especially in the Isle of Man TT races, would help them sell motorcycles throughout the world.

The lack of racing development during the war meant that the change in design and engines was only just beginning. The biggest change to pre-war racing was that supercharged engines were banned. Otherwise, the new World Championship grid looked very similar to those of the late 1930s, both in personnel and machinery. However, missing were the German manufacturers like BMW, who'd dominated the 1939 TT race with their Boxer Supercharged 500, as they were banned from competing in the first World Championship.

AJS spearheaded the leading manufacturers' attack with a trio of pre-war stars: Les Graham, Ted Frend and Jock West, who were joined by Bill Doran and Reg

Armstrong in the 350cc class. Norton fielded Artie Bell and Johnny Lockett on their 500s and Harold Daniell on the 350. Velocette's big threats in the 350cc class came from Freddie Frith and Bob Foster.

The only challenge to the British domination in the 500 class came from Italy and the Arcore-based Gilera factory. Nello Pagani and Arciso Artesiani pushed very hard to bring Italy some much needed national pride. It was a very different story in the smaller 250 and 125cc classes, where the Italian Moto Guzzi and Mondial factories were to totally dominate the proceedings in the capable hands of Bruno Ruffo and Nello Pagani.

The morning of 13 June 1949 dawned dry and clear. The honour of the first ever World Championship race fell to the 350cc machines and the fans packed in around the mountain circuit were treated to the first of a contest that has been repeated so many times over the 70 years that followed.

The race was seven laps of the mountain circuit and a mere 264.11 miles. Riders and machines raced down the Glencrutchery Road before they negotiated the fearsome Bray Hill. Former Lancaster bomber pilot Les Graham – who had been awarded the Distinguished Flying Cross for bravery in 1944 – led the way by 19 seconds at the end of the first lap, but a broken clutch brought his race to a premature halt less than a lap later. The AJS of Bill Doran took over until his gearbox broke up on the mountain at the Gooseneck on the final lap. Later, the ever smiling Shropshire-born Doran had a bend named in his honour on the TT mountain circuit. Frith had no way of knowing about Doran's demise and set a new lap record of 84.2mph en route to a historic first World Championship race victory. Ulsterman Ernie Lyons made it a Velocette one-two with another Ulsterman, Artie Bell, who had honed his trade on the road circuits of Ireland, third on the Norton. Lyons went on to be a top-class motocross rider. It was an incredible day for British riders and the all-conquering British motorcycle industry, their machines filling all 75 finishing places to announce to the rest of the world that Britain was back in business.

Tragically, though, the day also provided a dark reminder of just how dangerous it was to race motor-cycles on the mountain circuit. TT regular Ben Drinkwater died in a crash at the eleventh milestone on the fourth lap. He had been planning to retire from racing at the end of the season.

Four days later and Les Graham was desperate to make up for his 350cc disappointment in the seven-lap 500cc race. It turned into an epic battle. The race was started by the Duke of Edinburgh, and at the end of two amazing laps, Graham, his AJS team-mate and Brooklands star Ted Frend and the Italian Moto Guzzi of Bob Foster could not be separated on time. Something or somebody had to give. Then, Londoner Frend, who was renowned for lapping the legendary Brooklands circuit at over 110 mph on a Vincent in 1938, crashed at Glen Helen on the fourth lap. Foster, nicknamed fearless Bob because of his ability to compete in any two-wheeled event on and off road, had taken the lead, with Bill Doran moving into third place behind Graham.

Two laps from the finish, Foster's Moto Guzzi clutch cried 'enough!' and Graham was back in front looking the likely winner. He held a precious 90-second lead as he raced past the cheering grandstand crowd to start his last lap, but those cheers soon turned to groans. The announcement boomed out that Graham had stopped and was pushing the stricken AJS Porcupine from Hillberry to the finish. The magneto shaft had shattered and for the second time in four days his dream was over, although typically of past and present TT riders he pushed the AJS the near two miles from Hillberry to finish in tenth place.

Bespectacled Harold Daniell brought the Norton home for a comfortable victory to win his third TT, with team-mate Johnny Lockett second and the Velocette of Ulsterman Ernie Lyons third. Daniell had been refused entry to the Armed Forces to fight in the war because of 'poor' eyesight and so joined the Home Guard.

Rather than starting in pairs as they did in the 350 and 500cc races, the riders gathered for a massed start for the very first 250cc World Championship race on the morning of 17 June. Despite their smaller capacity, machines and riders were still expected to complete seven laps, which was a big ask. Italian Dario Ambrosini crashed the Benelli early on at Governor's Bridge leaving the way clear for a Moto Guzzi fight between Irishman Manliff Barrington and English former flight mechanic Dickie Dale.

Once again, it was the heartbreak of a last lap retirement that changed the results. This time it was race leader Dale retiring on the final lap at Ramsey with magneto problems, handing victory to team-mate Barrington, who'd earlier endured an agonisingly long pit stop to replace a broken valve spring. Tommy Wood brought another Moto Guzzi home in second place with Roland Pike a crowd-pleasing third on the British-built Rudge.

The 500cc class was staged at every round of this first World Motorcycle Racing Championship, but the 350cc race only took place at five of the six, the 250cc at four and the 125cc at just three. Three of the classes made their historical debuts at the 1949 TT races on the Isle of Man. The remaining circuits on the schedule were all road circuits, using public roads that closed on race weekends, apart from Monza in Italy which was a purpose-built track built in a park just outside Milan.

The 125cc World Championship riders had to wait another three weeks before their title chase finally started on the 4.524-mile road circuit at Berne in Switzerland. Italian Nello Pagani won the 14-lap race riding the four-stroke DOHC single-cylinder Mondial from the Morini of Renato Magi and Mondial-mounted Celeste Cavaciuti.

Despite his disappointment at that first round, Les Graham was crowned the very first 500cc World Champion after winning the penultimate round in the Ulster Grand Prix at the 16.5-mile Clady circuit near Belfast. With just the three best finishes counting out of the six, it was a comfortable win for the 37-year-old, who is still the oldest rider to have won the premier class world title. He fought off the challenge of the four-cylinder Gilera ridden by Nello Pagani and Arciso Artesiani, but their time would come. Frith, after his TT win, won the next two rounds in Switzerland and Holland to bring Velocette the 350cc crown. Italian Bruno Ruffo handed Moto Guzzi the 250cc title after finishing fourth in the final round at Monza while Nello Pagani, who finished runner-up in the 500cc class, won the 125cc world title after a fifth place at Monza.

How the British public craved a new post-war sporting hero, and he arrived from Lancashire at the 1950 TT races. Geoff Duke just ticked all the boxes – a brilliant motorcycle racer with an immaculate style just made for the rigours of the mountain circuit. Duke was the first rider to wear one-piece, all black leathers instead of the separate leather jacket and trousers, and the helmet concealed a swept back quiff of black hair. Duke had honed his skill on two wheels, riding in the Royal Signals Motorcycle Display Team as a team sergeant before embarking on his racing career. The fact that he had been picked by Norton to ride their 500cc machine with the revolutionary featherbed frame just added to the adulation, and Duke did not let them down. One year after winning the Clubman's TT and the Senior Manx Grand Prix he returned to the island in 1950 to make his World Championship debut. What a debut – he won the Senior on the new Norton and was second in the 350cc race. Geoff Duke had arrived, and the rest of the racing world took notice.

However, despite such a brilliant start, Duke finished runner-up in the 500cc Championship to the four-cylinder Gilera of Umberto Masetti, who clinched the title after finishing second to Duke at the final round in Monza. Masetti also became the first rider to average over 100mph, winning a grand prix race when he averaged 101.09mph in the Belgian Grand Prix at Spa. Duke did bring Norton success in the 350cc race at Monza, and he finished second once again in the championship to Bob Foster on the Velocette. Italy continued to dominate the smaller classes with Dario

Ambrosini and Bruno Ruffo winning the 250 and 125cc Championships respectively.

These were halcyon days for British motorcycling, and 1951 summed up the reasons to celebrate, with Duke winning both the 500cc and 350cc world titles riding the iconic British single-cylinder machines. However, warning signs were there to be seen. The Italian factories of Gilera and MV Agusta were almost ready to break the mould with their faster four-cylinder machines. The all-Gilera podium in the final round at Monza was a clear warning that the challenge to the British domination was mounting.

Duke stayed with Norton to defend his titles in 1952. It was a defiant defence against the might of Italian engineering in the 500cc class. His new team-mate Dave Bennett was killed challenging for the lead in Switzerland and then Duke broke his ankle in a non-championship race. Masetti regained the title for Gilera with that first ever 500cc World Champion Les Graham second after joining the MV Agusta team. Duke retained his 350cc crown with British machines filling the first ten places in the championship. Having been banned from those opening three years of the championship, the German manufacturers who'd left on a high before the outbreak of war in 1939 returned to the fray for the first time with DKW and NSU in the 125 and 250cc classes. It was a long way back for a country whose industry had been almost totally devastated by war but, typically, success in the smaller classes was not far away.

I was sports mad in a sports mad family, even at the age of five. However, while my dad certainly had visions of me opening the batting and playing scrum half for England, competing at the TT on a Norton wearing a set of black one-piece leathers never came into the equation. But even my dad could not ignore the exploits of a certain Geoff Duke. His two great loves in life – the *Daily Telegraph* and the BBC Light Programme – gave Duke plenty of space and airtime. TT winner Graham Walker and his son Murray's commentaries from the Isle of Man often interrupted life in our dining room.

Any visit to the cinema – and there were plenty in those days – featured the magnificent Pathé News. The crowing cockerel and the patriotic music was followed by that unmistakable voice of Bob Danvers Walker describing the evocative black and white footage from the Isle of Man of Duke leaping the Norton over Ballaugh Bridge. It left such an imprint on my young brain, and one that has never disappeared. Oh, for that voice of Bob Danvers Walker and the skill and bravery of Duke.

Televisions were a luxury for the few in those days, but I remember my Cumnor Primary School friend David Betteridge had a tiny 12-inch black and white set in the front room of his house in Robsart Place. We'd already watched the FA Cup final between West Bromwich Albion and Preston North End when we tuned into those early BBC *Sportsview* programmes in 1954 to watch their coverage of the TT. Three years earlier, Duke had been voted Sportsman of the Year in Britain and in 1953 he was awarded the OBE. The sky was the limit for the lad from Lancashire.

Little did I know at the time that there was somebody in my small Oxfordshire village that was hoping to follow in the footsteps of Duke. Dick Madsen-Mygdal worked in his father's dairy next to the Bear and Ragged Staff pub on the Appleton Road and, with a little help from his girlfriend, embarked on a very different journey to Duke's, but heading to the same destination: the Clubman's TT on the Isle of Man. It's a love story that just summed up the mood of the nation in the early fifties.

When Stella popped the question after nearly three years of courting, Dick's response was typically selfish and to the point: I'll marry you if we spend your savings on a honeymoon in the Isle of Man where I can risk my life competing in the most dangerous and spectacular sporting event in the world, the Tourist Trophy motorcycle races. Those hard-earned Post Office savings may have only amounted to £75, but she agreed. The stage was set for an incredible honeymoon and an uncut wedding cake.

Stella and Dick met in the summer of 1950 at the Carfax Assembly Rooms in Oxford, when he asked her to dance. Richard Madsen-Mygdal was the grandson of the Danish Prime Minster and the proud owner of a shining black 1000cc Vincent Rapide motorcycle. Stella only agreed when she saw he could actually dance. After all, she was an excellent dancer herself, and had just returned from a tour of Europe with the stars, including Max Bygraves.

The daughter of an Irish mother and Chinese father, Stella had taught herself to sing and dance while listening to *Workers' Playtime* on the radio in her lunch break from cutting dead bodies and fish out of wrecked military aircraft that had been recovered from the sea at the local Cowley airfield. When the dancing finished on the stroke of midnight, Stella refused Dick's much used line about going to 'see my motorcycle', but agreed to meet the next evening and be formally introduced to said Vincent. She took her mum along in case Dick didn't turn up, but he did, and was on time.

For over two blissful years the pair jitterbugged and roared around the local countryside with their motorcycle-mad friends. Stella was a stunning addition to the gang. A beautiful pillion passenger on the shining black Vincent, she dressed in a split skirt she had designed and sewn herself and an Amy Johnson-style helmet. Oxfordshire's pubs and dance halls had not seen the like of it before and she was soon drinking pints of brown ale rather than her usual brandy and Babycham. Dick was besotted. He already enjoyed a reputation locally of someone not to be messed with. National Service with the army in Glasgow had not only given him his first tattoo, but also a tough introduction to the real world after public school and life on his father's farm. A mere glance or word from an admirer of Stella would often result in a bout of fisticuffs. There was only one winner every time.

A chance excursion by the gang to a former wartime airfield just up the road at Silverstone opened a new chapter for the lovebirds. Dick or Dickie, as Stella called him, was convinced that he was faster than many of the riders they watched in action there. The seed was sown, and within a couple of months he was proving his point. The lovers would ride their beloved Vincent to race tracks throughout the country. After a change of handlebars, seat and footrests, Dick raced their mode of transport with great success before changing it all back again to ride home in time to start work at six the next morning at his father's dairy. Often, one of the gang who could fit a sidecar to his bike would come along, bringing tools, spares and more than a little moral support.

During one of their frequent visits to the Electra cinema with those unique double seats in the back row, the Pathé News highlighted the TT races in the Isle of

Man. Dick was spellbound and as determined as ever to get his own way. The next morning, while listening to those evocative BBC Light Programme broadcasts live from the Isle of Man with Graham and Murray Walker, the TT races became a challenge that Dick realised he just could not ignore.

Following the acceptance of Stella's proposal, with the savings proviso, it was a rush to get the wedding organised. The honeymoon was a bigger priority. Dick's mum and dad did not approve of Stella and refused to attend, but it went ahead anyway at the St Giles Register Office in Oxford. Just eight hours after their date with the registrar the honeymoon was underway as they boarded the *King Orry* steamer at Liverpool docks to start the choppy trip to that lump of granite in the middle of the unforgiving Irish Sea. The Vincent Black Shadow had safely transported the newlyweds on a wet, cold 150-mile night ride to Liverpool, and it was now below them in the hold, ready for its biggest ever test at the 1953 TT. Back in Oxford, the wedding cake remained uncut.

Dick had dreamed of becoming a hero, just like Geoff Duke, fighting against the very best in the world, riding a a British built motorcycle, witnessed by tens of thousands of racing-starved, patriotic fans. It was a modern high-speed gladiatorial contest with the fastest man winning and the losers often paying the ultimate price – 29 riders already having lost their lives since the TT started in 1909.

Despite bad weather in practice, which included plenty of early morning sessions around the infamous 37.73-mile circuit, something that was certainly not conducive to a loving honeymoon in their tiny Victoria Street B&B, newlywed Dick qualified fastest in the Clubman's class.

Race day was mercifully dry. After a special TT race day good-luck breakfast of Peel smoked kippers prepared by their B&B landlady, Dick blasted the mighty Vincent from the start across the St Ninian's crossroads towards the terrifying 120mph decent between the kerbs, walls and houses of Bray Hill. Ahead lay six laps of pure danger and adventure. The pre-race predictions in the press suggesting that he would either win a TT on his debut or crash had hit the nail on the head, but cruelly it was the latter.

Three quarters of the way round on the second lap he was in dreamland. His friends chalked on the blackboard – usually reserved for the darts scores at the Saddle Inn – that he was leading by a massive 42 seconds as he braked for Parliament Square in Ramsey. Dick was still smiling as he raced down the mountain with a view of Douglas Bay below, which was when disaster struck. He could and should have waited but, impatient, Dick tried to overtake a slower 350cc rider at the Brandywell bend. The front wheel of the Vincent slid in the gravel on the outside of the corner and went down the road in a shower of sparks – his dream was over and his two-piece black leather suit and flimsy crash helmet took the full impact of the Manx tarmac as he bounced down the road at over 80mph. Dick would remember little of the bumpy trip in the ambulance to Noble's Hospital, a place that had been a destination for many a TT rider in the previous three decades.

Eight miles away, back at the grandstand, Stella watched the clock that indicated her new husband's race-winning progress around the course with mounting nervous apprehension. When it failed to click, she was worried; when he failed to arrive at the start and finish, she panicked and rushed to the nearby Noble's fearing the very worst. The news was not good, but it could have been worse. Her husband had fractured his skull but was not in danger. The Black Shadow was not so lucky and lay stricken against a stone wall on the mountain road, mortally wounded. Fortunately, that morning, the canny Stella had persuaded Dick to spend their last £5 to insure his trusty steed. Already her steady hand on their finances was paying off, as it would do for the next 65 years.

It was a long three weeks of recuperation on a sedate Isle of Man after the race fans had departed. Gladys, their Victoria Street landlady, did not charge any extra rent and the extended honeymoon had a more conventional feel. Bracing hand-in-hand walks along Douglas Promenade, the occasional trip on the tram followed by fish and chip suppers replaced early morning practice sessions and that silent, never discussed fear about what lay ahead on the mountain course. It was soon over as Dick received the all clear from the doctors to return home, and the very same *King Orry* steamer took them back to Liverpool. With the Black Shadow on its way to Vincent's headquarters in Stevenage for lengthy repairs, the steam train was their mode of transport back to Oxford. At Crewe station the newlyweds could not even muster enough money for a cup of tea. At least they had the wedding cake to cut on their return to start their new life together, along with a lifetime of memories of just what happened on that June morning on their honeymoon on the Isle of Man.

Dick continued his racing on the mainland but never returned to the Isle of Man to compete. His son David took up the baton, and became the rider to gain more finishing replicas than any other in the 111 years of the TT. However, the fine line that road racers old and new tread was never more tragically illustrated than when Dick's grandson Mark was killed after crashing in the Southern 100 road races on the Isle of Man in 2013.

At the start of the 1953 season, Geoff Duke was at a crossroads. Should he display true patriotism by remaining with the aging single-cylinder Norton or carry on his championship-winning ways with the Italians, specifically Gilera? Deep down he knew what he had to do and signed for Gilera much to the disgust of some fans and the British press. Any doubts he had about his decision were dispelled when he regained the 500cc title for Gilera, winning for the first time in the second race of the season on the four-cylinder machine at the Dutch TT.

Tragically, the much-anticipated battle between World Champions Duke and Graham never materialised when Graham was killed in the first round, crashing the MV Agusta at the bottom of Bray Hill on the second lap of the TT. Moto Guzzi made it an Italian double with Scotsman Fergus Anderson winning the 350cc Championship and Germany's return was celebrated by the impressive Werner Haas winning both the 125 and 250cc Championships riding the NSU.

A year later, Duke became the first rider to win three 500cc World Championships when he retained the title for Gilera, while Fergus Anderson's win at the final round in Monza enabled him to retain the 350cc crown for Moto Guzzi. Anderson's other claim to fame was that he was on the Nazis' 'Most Wanted List' (Hitler's Black Book) prior to their intended invasion of Britain after being heavily involved in espionage in the early stages of the Second World War. Half a million fans packed the 7.094-mile Solitude circuit in West Germany to celebrate

NSU's total domination of the smaller classes. Haas, after four straight wins, retained the 250cc title at the previous round in Assen and Austrian Rupert Hollaus clinched the 125cc title for the German factory in front of the massive home crowd. At the next round, 23-year-old Hollaus was killed in practice at Monza to become the only posthumous World Champion.

The British Empire
1954–1960

IN 1954, A certain Soichiro Honda arrived at the TT races in the Isle of Man without so much as a sideways glance from anybody in the paddock. He announced that he would return with a team to compete at the TT because his dream was to take on and beat the finest motorcycles at the most famous venue in the world. Soichiro was shocked at two things on his visit. First, at the anti-Japanese feeling of the British people, despite the fact that it was now nine years since the war had ended, and the speed and engineering prowess of the manufacturers, especially the German NSU 125 and 250cc superbly built bikes that were dominating the World Championships that year. He flew home knowing he had a mountain to climb and with a suitcase full of chains, carburettors and tyres.

A year later, the Honda team started competing at the Mount Asama Volcano Race, located in a village at the foot of an active volcano on the island of Honshu, Japan. Just like at the TT, riders started in pairs to race around the 12-mile circuit track, although here the surface was of compressed volcanic ash. Their main challenge, especially in the smaller classes, came from Yamaha and Suzuki. Nothing had changed a decade later, the only difference being that they were now competing for a world title.

Twenty-four years before the issue would come to a head in a final explosion, the riders' discontent with just how badly they were treated by greedy, rich race organisers started to fizzle. This was not so much about safety on the road circuits, but the lack of prize and start money along with respect paid to the riders themselves. Matters came to a head at the 1955 Dutch TT in Assen, when 12 350cc riders completed just one lap in protest against the paltry start money being offered. The organisers panicked when the 500cc riders led by Duke threatened to do the same, but after some last-minute negotiations the race went ahead. The FIM were not happy with the rebels, led by the star Gilera riders Duke and Irishman Reg Armstrong. So much so, they suspended them at the end of the season from all competition for six months. After a tongue-in-cheek apology from Duke, the FIM relented, but only slightly, allowing them to race in domestic competitions but not the grands prix. In 1979, another 500cc World Champion, Kenny Roberts, led a similar campaign with much greater success.

Ironically, Duke had clinched the world title at the penultimate round in Ireland that year, when both he and his nearest challenger and fellow trade unionist Armstrong did not race because the Gilera factory could not reach a financial agreement with the organisers.

Once again, the title chase was marred by tragedy when the expected fight between Duke and Ray Amm never got off the ground. The Rhodesian had finished second in the championship the previous year riding the Norton before joining MV Agusta to take on Gilera and especially Duke in 1955, but was killed on his first outing for the Italian factory at an international race in Imola. Bill Lomas secured the 350cc title for Moto Guzzi and thought he'd done the double in the 250cc class after finishing fifth at the final round in Monza. The FIM had different ideas and eliminated him from the Dutch TT results, handing the title to 45-year-old German Hermann Paul Müller riding the over-the-counter NSU. He is and probably always will be the oldest rider to win a world title. Carlo Ubbiali took the 125cc title for MV Agusta.

A new challenger to Duke's crown and number one status in Britain burst onto the 500cc scene in 1956. John Surtees, brought up racing the Vincent and prepared by his father Jack around Brands Hatch, had already secured a grand prix win when MV Agusta recognised his potential and signed him to spearhead their attack on Gilera. The previous year, Surtees, in just his sixth grand prix, had won the 250cc Ulster Grand Prix and MV had seen enough. Their foresight was rewarded with their first premier class title in an amazing year for the factory better known for helicopter production. They also clinched the 125cc and 250cc world titles and at the Belgian Grand Prix at Spa won all four races. Surtees almost made it a clean sweep of World Championships for Count Agusta but crashed at Solitude in the 350cc race causing him to miss the rest of the season and leaving Lomas to retain the title for Moto Guzzi. The season had been a disaster for Duke after being banned from the first two rounds as a result of his protest in Assen – both won by Surtees – and his only win came in the final round at Monza.

It didn't get a lot better in 1957 for Duke, despite the fightback by Gilera. He damaged his shoulder in a pre-season crash at Imola and didn't win a race, although World Champion Surtees fared only a little better. He won only one race and finished third behind the all-conquering Gileras of Libero Liberati and Scotsman Bob McIntyre. Liberati took the title with victory at the final round in Monza, but it was Scotsman McIntyre who became the new darling of the TT.

Fourteen thousand fans sailed into harbour on the already packed island on the sunny morning of Friday 7 June to celebrate the golden jubilee of the TT races. To mark the occasion, the Senior race had been increased to eight laps, making the 302-mile race distance the longest ever in grand prix racing. The anticipation that somebody could lap the mountain circuit at over 100mph produced an electric atmosphere. Fifty years ago, when those pioneers had set off down that dusty track from Peel, nobody in their right mind would have thought it possible. But it was, and it was a Scotsman who did it. It was a Roger Bannister four-minute mile moment as the announcer's voice boomed out around the mountain circuit at the end of the second lap: 'Bob McIntyre leads the race on the Gilera after a second lap at an average of 101.'

The precise lap time of 101.03mph was drowned out by a roar of cheering and celebrations from the grandstand, Ballacraine, Ballaugh Bridge, Ramsey Hairpin, the Bungalow, Creg-ny-Baa and all the other iconic vantage points around the island. McIntyre completed three more 100mph plus laps en route to victory, which took him 3 hours, 2 minutes and 57 seconds. The modest Scotsman, who lost his life five years later in a crash at Oulton Park, had re-written the record books.

Keith Campbell became the first Australian World Champion when he clinched the 350cc crown for Moto Guzzi with Cecil Sandford the first British winner of the 250cc class. But changes were afoot. At the end of the 1957 season, the Italian factories withdrew from grand prix racing. The cost of supporting it, changes to the technical regulations and injuries to top riders brought about the decision – although MV Agusta did subsequently change their minds.

It was controversial, but the right decision because they won all four classes in 1958. Surtees and John Hartle dominated the 500cc and 350cc races. It was closer in the smaller classes with Tarquinio Provini fighting off the new two-stroke challenge from the East German MZ machine ridden by Horst Fügner, who brought the Walter Kaaden-inspired team their first grand prix win in Sweden. Also, an 18-year-old rider from Oxford by the name of Mike Hailwood made his World Championship debut, finishing third in the 250cc race at the TT on the NSU. Ubbiali clinched his fourth 125cc title to complete the clean sweep for Italy and MV Agusta.

Italy ruled for now, but all was about to change with the return of Soichiro Honda to the 1959 TT races, this time with his team. The Japanese had arrived.

In my defence, I was only 12 years old, but the pictures of those Japanese riders with strange-sounding names politely sitting in those uncomfortable, oh-so-British striped deckchairs on the lawn outside the Villa Marina as they waited for the prize giving for the 1959 TT races to start made me smile. But even if they felt out of place, no one could deny they were there for a very good reason. Engineers from the other teams smiled and shook their heads at the 125cc machines they had brought from Japan, while Honda just got on with the job of winning the Team Prize at their first World Championship race.

It was an amazing achievement that should have sent a shudder down the spine of the racing world, but it didn't. These were early days. Three Japanese riders who'd never competed in a race staged wholy on tarmac arrived on the Isle of Man to ride on the 10.79-mile Clypse course, which left out the mountain section of the TT circuit, riding the RC 142 Honda which featured a bevel-drive DOHC twin with four-valve heads. They were down on horsepower to the Italian and East German opposition and lack of practice on a road surface meant their handling was way behind the opposition, but typically they stuck to their task.

American Bill Hunt was the liaison officer, but also competed in the 107-mile race round the Clypse course alongside the Japanese riders Giichi Suzuki, Junzo Suzuki, Naomi Taniguchi and Teisuke Tanaka. The team was managed by Kiyoshi Kawashima, who later became the President of the Honda Motor Company. He collected the prize for the team with the most finishers in the ten-lap race at the Villa Marina that night and celebrated Honda's first World Championship point with Taniguchi finishing sixth. The race had been won by Tarquinio Provini who also won the 250cc race, both on MV Agusta machinery.

It was a much more familiar story elsewhere in 1959 with John Surtees and MV Agusta totally dominating the bigger classes. The combination was unbeatable, and Surtees won every 500 and 350cc grand prix of the season – a remarkable achievement, even when you take into account the superiority of his machinery. His main opposition came from MV team-mates – the Italian who never crashed, Remo Venturi, in the 500cc class and John Hartle in the 350s.

Hartle had been recommended to the team by Surtees after great success on the British short circuits. Ironically, nine years later in 1968 he was killed at one of those circuits, losing his life in a Scarborough accident. I always remember him because of his crew-cut hairstyle and the 'Caution With Hope' emblem on his crash helmet.

The remainder of the riders fought for points on the single-cylinder smooth-handling Nortons that just did not have the power to match the four-cylinder red Italian 'fire engines'. One of those chasers was Geoff Duke who had returned to Norton to bring that amazing grand prix career to a finish when he stood on the podium at the final round in Monza after finishing in third place.

The four-stroke superiority in the smaller classes was coming to an end. The two-strokes incorporated one power stroke for each revolution of the crankshaft, compared with two revolutions of the four-stroke. They were lighter and more powerful but were definitely harder to ride than the four-strokes. Keeping the revs high in the narrow power band through multiple gears was a rider's skill that became very much a part of their success.

The 1959 season may have produced the same MV domination, but both the 125 and 250cc classes showed glimpses of a two-stroke future. In true team-mate style, Provini and Carlo Ubbiali fought for superiority both on and off the track in these smaller classes. These two great Italian riders were very different characters. Ubbiali was the perfectionist who did not enjoy socialising with his rivals, whereas Provini was much more the extrovert. But it was Ubbiali who came out on top in both.

It was not only Honda who were preparing to challenge the mighty Italians. The East German MZ factory intended not just to challenge, but to take on and beat them. Welsh-born Rhodesian Gary Hocking, replacing the seriously injured Horst Fügner, brought the East German two-stroke machines success twice in the 250cc class. Hocking learnt his skills on the grass tracks of Rhodesia before switching to road racing. He arrived in Europe in 1958. Both MV Agusta and Honda were chasing his signature after those initial grands prix victories. It was a similar 125cc story where young, rookie East German Ernst Degner brought MZ success in Monza. His results as a rider and prowess as an engineer were making rival factories sit up and take notice.

The withdrawal of MV Agusta and the retirement of both Surtees and Ubbiali were the headlines that concluded the 1960 season. On reflection, there were even bigger pointers to where we were heading. In all four classes, MV Agusta lost just two grands prix and that is absolute domination. Honda and MZ were making inroads in the smaller classes but, in his final season, Surtees once again was unbeatable in both the 350 and 500cc classes. He lost just two 500cc grands – in Assen where he crashed and at the Ulster where he stopped to replace a broken gear pedal. Ubbiali repeated his double dose from the previous year in both 125 and 250cc classes.

Honda returned not only to the TT but for the complete 1960 World Championship, and with Australian Tom Phillis in the saddle. They took their first podium finish when Kenjiro Tanaka crossed the line third in the 250cc race at Solitude in Germany. The revolution had begun.

The MZ success story continued in the capable hands of Degner, with a 100mph plus victory in the 125cc race at Spa, while 20-year-old Mike Hailwood scored his first points and podium in the 500cc class. Times were a-changing!

The retirement of Surtees and Ubbiali at the end of the season probably tipped the balance in favour of Count Domenico Agusta's decision to withdraw his team that had totally dominated all classes for so long.

Domenico Agusta, together with his brother, had set up the motorcycle arm of their aviation business at the end of the Second World War to provide their employees with work. The extra expense that would be incurred with the inclusion of the Argentine Grand Prix in 1961, the first ever outside Europe, plus the questioning of just what else they could achieve made up his mind.

Surtees and Ubbiali were true giants of the history book. Surtees, with his seven world titles and 38 grands prix wins, developed the raw power of the 350 and 500cc MVs into beautiful racing motorcycles that were impossible to beat. He went on to stamp his biggest entry into the history books when he won the 1964 Formula One World Championship for Ferrari. A historic entry that will never be repeated. Fellow perfectionist Ubbiali won nine world titles and 39 grands prix in the smaller classes before retiring at the age of 30. They both left massive holes to fill, but as always, there were plenty queuing up to take over their mantle.

House of the Rising Sun
1961

WHERE DO YOU start in 1961? How about with a Cold War story and East/West defection that would do a John le Carré novel proud? Or perhaps with the first world title for Mike Hailwood; Gary Hocking's double on the 'Privat' MV's, or Honda's first grand prix win and world title …

Let's start with the racing. Count Agusta changed his mind about withdrawing just before the season got underway and gave a number of 500 and 350cc machines to various riders, including Hocking, who'd so impressed the previous two seasons with four 250cc grands prix wins. The word 'Privat' may have been displayed next to the MV Agusta motif, but the result was exactly the same. Hocking won both the 500 and 350cc titles with ease. Hailwood was on the charge and won three races at the TT – the 125 and 250cc – on Honda machinery supplied by the British importer and the Senior on a Norton.

Pathé News and Murray Walker kept my ferocious appetite for news on our local hero well filled. He then finished second at the next four grands prix on the Norton behind Hocking. Count Agusta had seen enough and gave Hailwood one of his 'fire engines' to ride in Monza. Unlike today, riders would compete in the different classes at each grand prix and on different makes of machinery. Hailwood won first time out and Hocking crashed chasing him, although the Rhodesian got revenge by winning the next race in Sweden.

What a year 1961 was for Honda. It started with their first grand prix win courtesy of Tom Phillis, in the 125cc race on the twisty, tree-lined circuit at Montjuïc Park, later the venue for the Olympic Games, overlooking the city of Barcelona. It was fitting that it was the Australian who brought Honda that first win. While others had sniggered at Honda in their 1959 TT debut, Phillis was impressed with their forward thinking and organisation. He made discreet enquiries to join them and was rewarded with his first factory contract.

Three weeks later, on the very different fast and flat Hockenheim arena in West Germany, Kunimitsu Takahashi became the first Japanese grand prix winner when he brought Honda victory in the 250cc race. The icing on the cake was Hailwood's victory at the penultimate round at Kristianstad in Sweden to bring both Honda and himself their first world title. Hailwood was the youngest ever World Champion and the first rider to win a title on Japanese machinery. However, in the 125cc class, it was a very different story for a very different reason.

This is a tale of totally contrasting factories who were locked in a fascinating championship fight. Walter Kaaden was a brilliant East German engineer who produced amazing results from his MZ two-stroke machines that were designed and built in a small factory way behind the Iron Curtain near the Sachsenring circuit, and were capable of taking on the new might of the Japanese and Honda with their unlimited resources. He was a superb forward-thinking engineer, who single-handedly built a grand prix winning two-stroke engine, despite the lack of materials and tools.

In the saddles of these competing machines sat, respectively, the East German Ernst Degner and Australian Tom Phillis. Two-stroke versus four-stroke; East versus West; David versus Goliath, in an ever-changing world. With two rounds remaining of the 125cc Championship, going in to that penultimate round at Kristianstad in Sweden, Degner led the way after wins in Hockenheim, Sachsenring and Monza.

Meanwhile, the Cold War was at its coldest. The Berlin Wall had just been built to divide a city and further divide a country. Degner was not only a brilliant rider but also engineer, and when the chance came to escape life and the restrictions inflicted on the East German people he took it with both hands. The Japanese Suzuki factory had joined rival Japanese factories in the grand prix fray, though lacking the resources of Honda. They were horrified by the sheer horsepower of the MZ engines and, try as they might, could not replicate the speed and revs. They turned to Degner to help them, providing him with the golden opportunity: to escape the communist regime for good. While Degner was en route to Sweden for the grand prix, accompanied by the usual East German Stasi policemen, a friend smuggled his wife and children in the boot of an American car through the Berlin Wall checkpoint to safety in West Berlin. Now it was time for the husband and father to escape the dreaded Stasi and join them in a new life, but first he had a grand prix to ride in.

He could have clinched the title at that penultimate round at Kristianstad in Sweden, but after two blistering laps in the lead the MZ engine cried 'enough!' and blew up. We will never know if Degner did it deliberately. I hope not, but he certainly had other things on his mind. He tricked the Stasi, got on a ferry to Denmark and defected, taking all the MZ two-stroke secrets, and some say engine parts, with him to Suzuki. Just what it meant to the Japanese factory was never better illustrated than when Degner brought them the very first 50cc title the next year on their two-stroke machine.

Rockers
1962–1964

PARK END STREET in Oxford was paradise for a sixties motorcyclist. Rows of parked machines, from those big black Vincents to the smaller Triumph Tiger Cubs, were lined up, all for sale. Not that I could ride, let alone buy one in the early sixties. In pride of place, near Oxford railway station, was the renowned Kings of Oxford with its motorcycle-themed stained glass windows, owned by a certain Stan Hailwood, millionaire father of new World Champion Mike.

En route to Magdalen College School, dreading the morning Latin and chemistry lessons, and thinking up another excuse for why my homework had not been completed, I passed Kings secondary showroom at the other end of the street when I spotted it in all its glory: Mike Hailwood's TT-winning 250cc four-stroke, four-cylinder Honda – here in Oxford! Forget Latin, chemistry and homework, this was the bike all the way from Japan that had been ridden to a TT win by somebody who lived three miles from my house. I had a new hero. When my elder sister Jill told me she'd met Mike at the Wednesday night Jazz Club at the Carfax Assembly Rooms in the centre of Oxford I told her she must ask him for a date, but she never did. My dream of having Mike Hailwood as my sister's boyfriend never happened.

Our idyllic village of Cumnor was no different from any other village in the early sixties, and it had its fair share of Teddy boys and motorcycles. They would roar up and down the High Street causing as much noise and chaos as possible on a variety of AJS, BSA, Triumph and Norton machinery. They were not popular with the older residents, but I loved the noise and always wanted one of the black leather jackets and those jeans with big turn ups. However, it was the good old Radio Rentals black and white television special deal that instigated my love affair with two wheels.

As improbable as it seems today, on a Saturday afternoon both major television channels BBC and ITV would show live motocross, or 'scrambling' as it was called in those days. BBC *Grandstand* and ITV's *World of Sport* would feature racing from all over the country come hell or high water. Suddenly the likes of Dave Bickers, Jeff Smith and Arthur Lampkin were household names on Saturday afternoons in parlours throughout the land. For the first time, we heard Murray Walker's dulcet tones on the BBC, eulogising the virtues of BSA, Greeves and Matchless machinery through the mud and over the jumps at venues such as Shrublands and Hawkstone Park. I became an instant armchair fan.

One Easter Monday, I decided it was time to forsake the television couch and find out for myself what scrambling was all about in the flesh. The Oxford Ixion Motorcycle Club was staging a meeting at the farm of Dave Curtis at Stoke Lyne near Bicester and I set out on my Gold Crest BSA bicycle to pedal the 15 miles on a voyage of discovery. To say I was not disappointed would be an understatement, especially with Dave Curtis himself flying through the air on the magnificent booming Matchless with the distinctive 'M' emblazoned on the tank. I just could not believe the speed, noise and smell – this was a completely new world, so very different to anything I'd experienced ever before, and I loved it.

I was at primary school with the Hickman twins Charlie and John, and their older brother Keith became our new sporting hero. He was a scrambler and that would have been enough, but he was a very good scrambler and always rode number 98, his house number in Oxford Road, Cumnor. We cycled hundreds of miles to watch Keith Hickman in action at Brill, Deddington and Stoke Lyne. I would shyly make my way into the paddock where the Hickman's Humber

Snipe was parked, with the 250cc two-stroke DOT and immaculate Cheney BSA prepared by his father Henry being unloaded from the trailer ready for action. Sometimes I would peer over the wall of number 98 to catch a glimpse of Henry preparing the bikes for the weekend.

It was all very well cycling to these local races, but we soon wanted to broaden our horizons and explore the world, or experience life at least 60 miles away from Cumnor. In stepped Cumnor's answer to National Express, B and C Coaches run by Harold Clack in the High Street. His two coaches would take our school class swimming on freezing cold Monday mornings to the outdoor Hinksey Pools, a round trip of a maximum of ten miles. However, any distance further and there was a reliability problem. We spent more than one Sunday night waiting for somebody's gallant dad to pick us up from Beenham Park or Glastonbury Tor after B and C's finest had struck problems far from home.

Harold's coaches also ran a regular Thursday night trip to Cowley Stadium to watch the Oxford Cheetahs Speedway team in action – although this presented fewer problems as it was only a journey of around 12 miles. These were the halcyon days for Speedway and especially for the Cheetahs. Those Thursday nights were a pure theatre of noise, excitement, danger and that smell of Castrol R oil.

The riders, led by the brilliant Dane Arne Pander, would march – or in many cases limp – into the arena like gladiators under the floodlights as the JAP engines roared their approval in the background cheered on by crowds of over 5,000 loud and loyal supporters. The announcer would bark out the riders' names as they prepared for the four-lap scrap in the shale at the starting gate. Throw in a hot dog, a programme that had to be filled in with every result, a stop at the Windsor Fish and Chip shop on the Botley Road and a bit of flirting with the girls from Dean Court estate in the back of the coach on the way home and it produced just about the perfect evening.

One day at school, my classmate Simon Jarvis asked if I wanted to go with him and his dad to Mallory Park to watch some road racing rather than scrambling. Getting out of the car at Mallory changed my allegiance in a couple of seconds. No church bells on this Sunday morning, but the piercing scream of sheer horsepower being tamed as Hailwood went down through the gearbox braking for the hairpin on the Honda. I could not even see him, but the sound was enough.

Hocking and Hailwood should have been a combination that dominated the world in 1962. They did in many ways, but the results really don't tell the true story. After winning the opening 500cc round at the TT on the Isle of Man, Hocking retired from racing, mortified by the death of his friend Tom Phillis. The Australian who had brought Honda that first grand prix victory was killed when he crashed on the second lap of the 350cc TT won by Hailwood. Hocking went back to what was then still known as Rhodesia, but was killed in a car race in South Africa before the end of the year. It was a shocking loss of two riders who simply epitomised the very spirit of grand prix riders in the sixties. They'd been riders who were prepared to risk everything to travel across continents and oceans to compete in Europe, but both Phillis and Hocking paid the ultimate price.

Hailwood on the MV had no real 500cc opposition, despite the brave efforts of the likes of Alan Shepherd and Phil Read on the aging British single-cylinder machines. It was a tough, morale-draining task for Shepherd and Read which stood them in good stead when they raced more competitive machinery to grands prix wins later in their careers. Hailwood clinched the title at Monza after five successive wins, but it was a different story with the 350s.

Another brilliant Rhodesian, Jim Redman, had arrived with Honda and won the championship on the bored out 250 to 285cc engine on their first attempt. He'd come to race in Britain and was recommended to Honda by Phillis after the Australian broke his collarbone at Assen in 1960. Redman made it a double in 1962 to soften the blow of Phillis's death, winning the 250cc title. Swiss rider Luigi Taveri made it an even better year for the Japanese factory, fighting off team-mates Redman and Tommy Robb to take the 125cc crown. In the new 50cc class, the two-strokes ruled with Degner bringing a revitalised Suzuki team their first world title.

What a contrast to the previous year for Degner, as his old MZ team was restricted to grands prix behind the Iron Curtain, namely the Sachsenring or Brno in then Czechoslovakia. Hailwood brought a rare smile to the face of Walter Kaaden and his beleaguered team when he rode their 250cc machine in a one-off ride at the East German Grand Prix. Urged on by a massive patriotic 300,000-strong crowd, Hailwood fought a breath-taking duel with Redman which he eventually lost by a fifth of a second.

Alongside the tragedies, it was also a year of records. Twenty-two-year-old Hailwood riding the MV Agusta became the youngest ever 500cc World Champion and Arthur Wheeler the oldest ever solo grand prix winner. At the tender age of 46 years and 70 days, Wheeler won the 250cc race at the Argentine Grand Prix, giving Moto Guzzi their last grand prix victory.

On into 1963 Hailwood once again dominated the 500cc class riding the MV Agusta, but he could not beat the Redman/Honda combination on the 350. Gilera returned briefly to the 500cc class under the Scuderia

Duke banner. Four years after his retirement, Duke had returned as team manager of Scuderia Duke providing John Hartle and Derek Minter with 1957 Gilera machines to ride. When Hailwood retired in Assen with mechanical problems, John Hartle brought them their last premier-class victory and eventually finished third in the championship behind Alan Shepherd. It was a different story in the other classes and especially the 250s.

The title was decided at the final round in the very first Japanese Grand Prix at Suzuka. Redman and Italian Tarquinio Provini arrived level on points. Hard-riding iconic Provini rode the single-cylinder Morini to the absolute limit and beyond, pushing the multi-cylinder Honda and Redman engine all the way, but he just lost out when Redman won on home territory for the Japanese factory. Hailwood went one better this year by bringing MZ success at the Sachsenring, and Yamaha took their first grand prix victory with Fumio Ito victorious at Spa on the two-stroke twin. A certain Giacomo Agostini made his grand prix debut on the 250cc Morini at Monza, leading the race before retiring with mechanical problems. That was just the start.

Redman comfortably retained the 350cc class with victory in Dundrod on the four-stroke Honda, but the two-strokes, Suzuki and New Zealander Hugh Anderson dominated the smaller classes. Anderson was another one of those pioneers who crossed the globe to race in Europe and Suzuki gave him the chance to return home as a double World Champion.

It was a special year for Suzuki, and their success was emphasised exactly where it had all started 14 years earlier: on the Isle of Man. Anderson was their first two-stroke 125cc race winner and Mitsuo Itoh the first Japanese winner on the island with victory in the 50cc race.

Hailwood and Redman continued their utter domination of the 500 and 350cc classes respectively in 1964. It all seemed so easy as Hailwood clinched the 500cc crown at Solitude after winning the first five grands prix. It was a similar story for Redman, who won all eight 350cc grands prix.

What a contrast with the 250s and the emergence of another Japanese factory and British rider. A totally focused Phil Read typically persuaded Yamaha to commit to a full season at the beginning of the year, and what a decision it turned out to be as Read brought them the 250cc title after winning in Monza on the RD56 two-stroke twin. Honda threw everything into retaining the title, bringing Redman a magnificent six-cylinder, four-stroke machine to Monza, but it was not enough to prevent Yamaha and Read taking their first world title with the first two-stroke machine to win the class.

In the 125s, Anderson made the perfect defence of his title by winning in Daytona at the first American Grand Prix but Honda, with a new four-cylinder, 125cc machine, fought back and Taveri regained the title he'd won two years previously with victory at Imatra in Finland. The new twin-cylinder Honda also pushed Anderson in the defence of his and Suzuki's 50cc crown, but he just held firm, successfully fighting off the challenge of Northern Ireland's Ralph Bryans with victory at the final round in Finland.

People waiting at the bus stop to catch the number 67 to work in Oxford were never given the choice between Bob Dylan or Murray Walker, but they always got one or the other. With speakers outside in the sunshine, my great mate Nicky Jennings would wind up the volume to maximum while he was building an extension to his parents' shop at the top of Chawley Lane.

Nicky's parents owned the newsagent at the top of the road. We were the same age and grew up together. We loved our motorcycles, and especially Mike Hailwood. Nicky wanted to become a scrambler and his dad bought him a 250cc DOT, but his racing debut in early 1964 ended in disaster when he broke his collarbone crashing at Stoke Lyne. He upset the nurses by jumping on the treatment table at the Radcliffe Infirmary still wearing his muddy boots.

Two weeks later we stood in the packed London Road terrace at the Manor Ground watching Oxford United beat First Division Blackburn Rovers in a massive FA Cup shock. Every time Nicky screamed I thought it was with delight at United's performance, but later over a number of celebratory pints he told me it was because of the pain from his strapped up shoulder as the packed crowd moved up and down the terrace.

Nicky and I would go to the Russell Acott record shop in Oxford High Street to buy those magnificent Stanley Schofield LPs that recorded all the sounds from the TT with Murray Walker providing the commentary. And so his voice would boom down Cumnor Hill – which we always pretended was Bray Hill on the island – accompanied by the throb of single-cylinder four-strokes, the piercing scream of two-strokes and that yowl of the multi-cylinder four-strokes as they fought for victory around the mountain circuit.

Those TT records brought Nicky and me the closest we'd been to a World Championship race, and we wore out the vinyl. We could almost smell the Castrol R oil and feel the chill of the mist drifting down the mountain while laughing at the startled look of the bus driver and his passengers about to be blasted away by Hailwood on the MV Agusta as they approached Hid's Copse Road past the police houses. Even Smithy, the much-feared

PC who often lay in wait behind the hedge there on his Triumph to book the locals, who also thought they were on Bray Hill, could not have caught the MV Agusta rider who lived just a couple of miles away over Cumnor Hurst at Boars Hill.

Glad's Tidings from the Island
1965–1968

WE LOVED BOB Dylan almost as much as we loved those race recordings and he told us, 'The Times They Are a-Changin'. They certainly were, and especially for me – forget Stanley Schofield, I was going to the island of my dreams to witness the 1965 TT in the flesh. Not the complete TT, mind, just a day trip on the Friday for the 50 and 500cc races, but that was enough to start.

I'd be a liar if I told you how much I enjoyed my very first trip round the 37.730-mile strip of hallowed tarmac, because I was fast asleep in the back of the coach at 6am on the Friday morning. The *Motorcycle Magazine* sponsored day trip really did mean day trip, but for around £10 who could grumble?

We caught a coach that took us to Liverpool in time to catch the ferry that arrived into Douglas just as the sun rose. And though I slept through the obligatory trip round the mountain circuit, I was wide awake as we arrived at the Keppel pub at Creg-ny-Baa and ready to witness my first World Championship event, the three-lap 50cc race.

You wait first for the sound, and then you catch sight of the bikes racing round Kate's Cottage a mile away, before they plunge down the foothills of the mountain, then down through the gears and braking hard for the right hander at the Creg, changing down five or six times and then up the same number on route to Brandish. And what a sight and sound it was. They were led by Taveri on the Honda twin, who was chased by the two-stroke Suzukis of Anderson and Degner. Taveri won the race, lapping at over 80mph.

The drizzle failed to dampen our enthusiasm as we waited for the start of the six-lap senior, featuring none other than Hailwood and his new team-mate Agostini – who'd already wooed all the ladies on the island. Earlier in the week, Ago had finished third in the 350cc race on his TT debut behind Redman and Read after Hailwood suffered with mechanical problems while leading.

At last I saw the bright red fairing of Mike Hailwood's MV. He'd announced its pending arrival five minutes earlier, screaming down the mountain towards Kate's Cottage, leading his team-mate by 25 seconds. A lap later it was only Hailwood who arrived and the tannoy announced that Ago had crashed without injury nine-and-a-half-miles out at Sarah's Cottage. One lap later the tannoy boomed out another announcement: the crowd, and especially I, went quiet and listened. Hailwood had crashed at exactly the same bend, re-started by pushing the MV back into life in the opposite direction of the circuit, and was back on his way. We waited apprehensively for him to arrive at the Creg and to a great roar from the crowd he raced into view with what appeared to be a bloody nose and a very second-hand looking motorcycle, featuring a broken screen and flattened exhaust megaphones. A long pit stop ensured he could complete the final three laps.

We were back on the ferry and to Liverpool by mid-night, Hailwood's status as our hero greatly enhanced.

In hindsight, surely 1965 was the pinnacle of an incredible era of technical innovation from both Japan and Italy that sadly left the once all-conquering British manufacturers among the also-rans. Yamaha produced a 125cc twin and then a four-cylinder 250cc two-stroke. Honda replied with their magnificent five-cylinder 125, Suzuki water-cooled their 125 and even MV realised that standing still would cost them dear and produced a 350 three-cylinder machine for Agostini to ride. The result: Hailwood comfortably retained the 500cc title, Redman won the final round of the 350cc title chase to clinch his fourth successive 350cc crown, Read retained the 250cc title with victory at the Ulster Grand Prix, and Anderson regained the 125cc title for Suzuki. Honda were so outpaced that they withdrew after Assen, but reversed the order with Ralph Bryans capturing the 50cc title on the four-stroke Honda twin. It is the only four-stroke machine to win the 50cc class and Bryans is the only rider from Northern Ireland to win a grand prix world title. There was a flashback to happier days in the 500cc race at the Ulster. Local man Dick Creith won on the Norton and the podium consisted for the very last time of three British machines. However, the MV team of Hailwood and Agostini had not entered.

Honda and Hailwood were on the move. The Japanese giant was ready to take on Agostini and MV Agusta and signed the World Champion to spearhead their challenge with the impressive Redman in the biggest test of them all at the 1966 World 500cc Championship. Hailwood celebrated his arrival by winning the final round of the 1965 250cc Championship at Suzuka on a 'Private' six-cylinder Honda. Redman celebrated by winning the opening two rounds of the 1966 500cc Championship in Hockenheim and Assen, only to crash and break his wrist at the next round in Spa, which wrecked his considerable championship chances.

MV were prepared for the Honda challenge and built Agostini a three-cylinder 500cc similar to their 350. It paid off, but only just. It came down to a last round decider at Monza where Agostini took his first world title, winning the race in front of the home crowd when Hailwood broke down.

Hailwood dominated both the 250 and 350cc Championships for Honda. Bill Ivy won his first 125cc grand prix for Yamaha, who produced a four-cylinder machine, but Taveri retained the title for Honda for the last time, while in the 50cc class German Hans Georg Anscheidt regained the title for Suzuki on their new twin-cylinder two-stroke.

It was June 1967, and I'd borrowed my parents' black Morris Minor with the split windscreen and pinched our Vidor portable radio, which you switched on by lifting the lid. I'd passed my car driving licence just a year earlier after a couple of attempts but was still using an old BSA 125cc former Post Office Bantam motorbike as my regular mode of transport – top speed 55mph down Cumnor Hill on a clear day. I don't think I would have ever bothered Hailwood.

I was on my way back from Wantage and I pulled over and parked in a lay-by in Grove. I tuned the Vidor to the BBC Light Programme and sat mesmerised as Murray Walker described what many thought was the greatest ever TT race. I'd been stopping every half an hour for the updates, but the finale of this amazing six-lap battle was coming to a climax and of course I was supporting Hailwood. The Oxford boy was riding the scarily fast but poor handling RC 181 Honda over the bumps, nooks and crannies of the mountain circuit at record speeds, in an attempt to fight off the challenge of the new golden boy of grand prix racing, Giacomo Agostini, who was celebrating his twenty-fifth birthday by riding the three-cylinder MV Agusta in a race to celebrate the Diamond Jubilee of the TT races.

It was an absolute classic between two of the greatest riders the world had ever witnessed – before or since. They constantly swapped the lead on time. Hailwood had a long pit stop to hammer a loose throttle back on the handlebars and it was close as they started their fifth lap. Suddenly the clock opposite the grandstand at the start and finish indicating where Ago was on the course stopped. Hailwood raced past the static clock to start his last of the 37.730 miles and the crowd groaned – the chain on Ago's MV had broken and he was coasting down the mountain with tears pouring down his face. Who knows what would have happened on that last lap, but as it was, Hailwood brought the Honda home in one of the greatest rides of his amazing career. That night Hailwood picked up his great rival and friend to take him to Agostini's birthday party, organised by Mike's father Stan.

Hailwood may have won that particular battle, but he lost the war for the second year running. And once again it went down to the last round. Mosport staged the only grand prix to be held in Canada and Ago arrived needing a single point to retain the 500cc title. Hailwood won the race, but Ago's second place was enough. We sat through the winter relishing the prospect of the battle continuing in 1968. But it never happened; Hailwood and Agostini never clashed again in a grand prix race.

In February 1968, Honda announced they were retiring from grand prix racing. That was that. The factory who had dominated grand prix racing since their arrival at the 1959 TT were quitting to plough their considerable resources and innovative engineering into four wheels and Formula One.

Hailwood certainly went out with a bang for Honda. In addition to finishing second in the 1967 500cc Championship, he retained both the 250 and 350cc world titles. At Assen that year, he brought Honda wins in the 500, 350 and 250cc races, covering over 273 miles in three hours of racing all on the same day. Honda gave Hailwood 350 and 500cc bikes to race in international non-championship meetings, but he soon turned to four wheels, winning the European Formula Two Championship before switching to Formula One. In 1973 he was awarded the George Cross Medal for pulling Clay Regazzoni out of a blazing car when he crashed at the South African Grand Prix at Kyalami.

Hailwood went to live in New Zealand, but bikes were always in his blood and he made a remarkable return to the TT in 1978. It was 11 years since he'd faced the mountain circuit, but he was not there to make up the numbers. Amid emotional scenes of celebration, he won the TT Formula One race on the Ducati and returned for his final TT appearance a year later to win the Senior on a Suzuki. In both races the 39-year-old set a new lap record. Tragically, 'Mike the Bike' was killed in a road traffic accident together with his daughter Michelle in March 1981. The grand prix family grieved for a long time.

While Hailwood was retaining those 250 and 350cc world titles in 1967, his great friend and often partner in crime Bill Ivy clinched the 125cc title for Yamaha with team-mate – as it turned out later, in name only – Phil Read coming in second.

This was the late sixties, and Hailwood and Ivy had fame by the bucketload and plenty of cash to spend. They enjoyed life off the track as much as they did racing on it.

Hans Georg Anscheidt retained the 50cc crown for Suzuki, but at the TT, Stuart Graham – the son of Les, the very first 500cc World Champion – won the 50cc race, making them the first ever father and son grand prix winners. In Assen, a young Spaniard by the name of Ángel Nieto stood on the podium for the first time; many more were to follow.

I was stuck at the back of the queue on a dark Liverpool dockside at 2am in the morning, drinking from a plastic cup full of scalding hot tea served by a lady in the kiosk who spoke with an accent I had no chance of understanding. I'd been dreaming of this moment for so many years.

Nicky Jennings and I had ridden up to Liverpool on the Friday night on my 250cc Honda Dream Sport to catch the ferry to the Isle of Man for the 1968 TT races. Your tank had to be pumped out before you were allowed on the ferry to eliminate any risk of fire. I never discovered where the petrol went, but fully understood the profit the garage on Douglas Promenade was making from the long queue of pushed motorcycles lined up to refill. It was all worth it if you could display your badge of honour for the rest of the season – the pumped out TT sticker on the tank of your bike.

There was of course no Mike Hailwood this time, who was off trying his hand in Formula Two, but at last I could spend a whole week at the TT. And the real icing on the cake – our friend Dave Lock was riding in the 50cc race. It just did not get any better than that. Even watching my much treasured Honda with the fairing painted in Hailwood's Honda colours being hoisted on and off the boat at either end of the comparatively smooth Irish Sea crossing did nothing to dampen our excitement.

In those days, everybody stayed in a guest house unless you were a works rider, industry boss or national newspaper journalist, and we certainly fitted into none of those particular categories. The Manx guest houses and their landladies were as legendary a part of TT history as kippers and the Laxey Wheel. Glad and her guest house overlooking the harbour on the road to Douglas Head were no exception. Six lads in one room with one sink in which Nicky insisted on washing his socks and underpants every night and a shared loo. Breakfast and evening meals, 'don't be late!' and the front door locked at midnight – although the loo window was always conveniently left open. No girls allowed, although I can't believe any girl in her right mind would have been tempted to venture into the delights of our smelly boudoir.

On the pavement opposite, racing and road bikes mingled side by side. In addition to Dave, who was riding his immaculate single-cylinder RC 110 50cc Honda, there were other TT riders staying at Glad's. You would hear alarm clocks going off at 4am followed by the hiss of the Primus stove being lit to provide a cup of tea before early morning practice. It was a great place to stay and Glad looked after us all brilliantly, well, unless we broke the rules too many times. Her husband, who she called 'the dog', was shouted at far more than the guests because he liked a drink or two. It was only when we waited to catch the ferry home, I realised he was the one in charge of hoisting the bikes on and off the boat. Good job I'd not known earlier.

Dave's three-lap 50cc race was on the Monday morning, and I spent the whole one-and-a-half hours praying he was not going to break down, and especially that he was not going to come into the pits, because he'd given me a special pit lane mechanic's pass. I honestly could not imagine anybody less qualified for the job. Changing a spark plug would have been a major feat. Here I was sitting in the same pit lane that 12 months earlier Hailwood had raced into to borrow a hammer to sort out his throttle in that epic battle with Ago.

I should not have worried because, despite a partial seizure on the last lap, Dave finished a brilliant fourth in the very last 50cc race at the TT, which was won by Australian Barry Smith. Now it was time to celebrate, and we all piled into the Thames van with the hand-change, three-speed gearbox – obligatory motorcycle racers' transport in the sixties – to drive on the back roads to the pub at Union Mills to watch the 250cc race in the afternoon. Bill Ivy won on the awesome four cylinder Yamaha and the celebrations continued that night when Dave received his silver replica at the prize giving in the Villa Marina. We were back at Glad's by midnight, though.

I'd only witnessed Ago in action on the TT course for that one single lap in 1965, but three years later I finally really understood what all the fuss was about.

On Wednesday afternoon we went to Greeba Castle to watch the 350cc junior race. Typically, a Manx lady let us sit on the wall of her garden, made us all a cup of tea and lent us her radio to follow the action. We didn't need the radio because we could hear him coming what seemed like ten miles away as the scream of the three cylinder cut through the air, first through Crosby and then flat out past the Highlander pub. He was getting closer and closer, and we were getting more excited. We all guessed what speed he would arrive at on the left-hand corner before roaring up the rise through the right-hander and out of sight.

He finally raced into view between the walls, trees and 30mph speed restriction signs at double the speed anybody had dared suggest. Momentarily it was a picture postcard of what the TT was all about before he'd disappeared and all that was left was the memory and a haze of exhaust smoke. Nobody spoke for at least 30 seconds. Our silence was shattered by the arrival of Renzo Pasolini on the four-cylinder Benelli in such a different way to the immaculate Agostini. He was all over the place, almost on the pavement as he chased his countryman across an island that had housed thousands of Italian prisoners of war a couple of decades earlier. We'd witnessed something very special and we knew it. That night, the loo window was useful back at Glad's after a night on the local Okell's ale.

We finished the week watching Read win the 125cc race, in which team-mate Bill Ivy set the first 125cc 100mph lap and, in the afternoon, Agostini dominate the Senior. Unfortunatey I'd got a bit carried away chasing a 500cc Velocette Venom on the cliff-top Marine Drive road. Agostini I may have thought I was, but the 250cc Honda with Nicky Jennings on the back was not the MV Agusta and rightly cried 'enough!' with a seized piston. We limped onto the ferry, but the bike finally expired on the way home and we were back in the Thames van.

That TT trip summed up the whole 1968 season, although watching from the outside there were things we didn't know. Agostini won every 500 and 350cc race he contested. Hans Georg Anscheidt clinched his third 50cc title with victory at Spa and then retired, but in the 125 and 250cc Championships it was a very different story, that only really came to light after the outcome.

With the departure of Honda, it was always going to be a straight all Yamaha fight between the two Brits, Read and Ivy, riding the four-cylinder two-strokes. It was nothing new for Yamaha to decide who they wanted to win which of the two championships. They went for current 125cc Champion Ivy to win the 250, and for Read to get his first 125, and everything was on track for their wishes to be delivered by the two riders. Little did we realise, innocently watching the 125cc TT, that

Ivy had let Read win who, as per the plan, clinched the title with victory in Brno.

It was time for Read to return the compliment in the 250cc race at Brno, but he didn't. He won the race and declared he was also chasing the 250cc title because he wanted Yamaha to commit to continuing in 1969, unlike Honda. Read also argued that he was the rider who'd done all the work to develop the 250 and had brought Yamaha their first world title. Ivy was totally gobsmacked and truly upset at the turn-around. He just could not understand why Read would renege on the agreement they made with Yamaha at the start of the season.

It came down to the very last round in a horrible weekend at Monza full of anger and accusations. Read beat Ivy in the 22-lap 250cc race and they ended up on equal points in the championship. Read took the title which was decided by combined times in races both had completed. It was a sad, cruel ending for the brilliant Ivy who retired to go car racing a very disillusioned man. His later return to two wheels ended in tragedy. Read continued to win world titles and upset team-mates.

After leaving school in 1964 with just one O level I hadn't known what I wanted to do. My parents were friends with Bunny Cole – who founded Cole & Cole solicitors and was well known in Oxford – and his wife Edith. Bunny fixed me up with a job as a legal executive trainee at his firm. I was grateful, but it was fairly clear that it wasn't the job for me. I'd arrived back from the 1968 TT to find that my boss had allocated me a tiny office of my own. The room, in an office in George Street, Oxford, just about housed a desk on which stood a pile of brown files and a dreaded Dictaphone. It was the moment of truth and, after that wonderful week on the island, I knew my heart was never going to be in it.

Three months later, though, and I was still there. It was the Friday afternoon at the end of another excruciatingly boring week. I was looking forward to the August Bank Holiday weekend, because on Monday we'd be back in the Thames van going to Oulton Park to watch Hailwood in action on his private Hondas. It would be rare appearance for Hailwood, who'd followed Honda's instructions of no grand prix races.

Next to a stack of virtually untouched files, the phone started ringing. It was a rare call from my amiable boss Bunny, telling me to go to his office. The last time I'd been summoned I was told that, with my long hair and scraggy beard, I looked a little too scruffy to represent the firm at a meeting in London. To be honest, I expected the same as I knocked on his door and stepped into his office. 'I could not let this gentleman leave before you met him,' he told me as Mike Hailwood stepped forward and shook my hand. He may never have been my sister's boyfriend, but at least I met him. For once in my life, I was speechless.

Spreading Our Wings

1969–1974

IN 1969, AGOSTINI and the all-conquering MV Agusta won every race they contested in the 500cc class, missing the last two rounds after clinching the title. The competition was a mish mash of machinery that tried unsuccessfully to stem the inevitable flow of success. The dedication to their MV-chasing cause and innovative mechanical genius was rewarded when Alberto Pagani brought the twin-cylinder Linto victory at Imola and Godfrey Nash brought Norton a historic final 500cc grand prix victory in Yugoslavia, which was also the final single-cylinder victory in the 500cc class.

Agostini had experienced a comparatively easy ride with little opposition when Honda brought the curtain down on the glorious era of multi-cylinder four-stroke motorcycles in 1969, that had started ten years earlier on the Isle of Man. That piercing scream of high revving multi-cylinder four-stroke engines clearing the very air that surrounded them which first pierced my receptive eardrums at Mallory Park had gone forever. Honda would return in the only way they knew how – by winning – but only after a hiccup.

By now, I'd left the solicitors' office to work in the local sports shop and I loved it. I was always up at Oxford United supplying boots, tracksuits and match balls to the renowned trainer Mr Fish. It was only after two years that he asked me to call him Ken. One Saturday afternoon, the radio was on in the shop. In between their coverage of Tony Jacklin winning the British Open golf the BBC radio news told me of the death of Bill Ivy at the Sachsenring on 12 July 1969. We grieved so much because we truly loved Bill Ivy. We were growing up in the sixties, the world was changing and Bill Ivy in so many ways, probably without realising it, was near the front in leading the revolution. His partner in crime had been Mike Hailwood and they turned up at Oulton Park to race dressed as flower-power hippies before putting on the leathers to entertain the crowd. There were plenty of fast cars and pretty girls, but most of all Ivy was a brilliant and brave motorcycle racer.

He'd had enough of the constant brain-draining mind games with former Yamaha team-mate Phil Read and had started what would have been a very successful career on four wheels, but he was short of the type of cash that was required to compete in the Formula Two class. To finance the proposed switch, he spearheaded the Jawa assault on the seemingly impregnable Agostini/ MV Agusta fortress in the 350cc class.

The Czech built V4 two-stroke machine was fast but unreliable and prone to seizing. Ivy pushed Ago hard at both Hockenheim and Assen and had huge support from the massive crowd at the East German Grand Prix at the legendary 5.352-mile, tree-lined Sachsenring road circuit as he took on the might of the Western world in the form of Ago and MV. But the Jawa seized once again in practice and Ivy was killed when his head hit a fence post. Observers suggested he was fiddling with his helmet strap at the time. A young Barry Sheene had been competing at Brands Hatch on the same afternoon and, on hearing of the death of his great mentor, suffered a huge asthma attack. He went on to honour the memory of Bill Ivy both on and off the track in a way he would have so appreciated.

Agostini was a comfortable winner of the 350cc Championship, although Jawa won the final round in Yugoslavia with Silvio Grassetti when Ago did not ride.

Of course, we returned to the TT that year because potential World Champions were still prepared to race on the island. I was nursing a king-sized hangover, lying on the grass at the Ramsey Hairpin after a night out in Douglas as Dave Simmonds screamed – and I mean screamed – the Kawasaki to victory in the 125cc race on route to the world title. He was the last British rider to win the 125cc Championship (although Danny Kent did bring British success in the new Moto3 class in 2015). Three years later, Simmonds was tragically killed when he dived into a burning caravan at the Rungis vegetable market which was staging the Grand Prix of Paris. He and fellow racer Billie Nelson thought Jack Findlay and his wife Nadia were trapped inside. It turned out nobody was in the caravan, but after they had doused the flames there was an explosion, probably caused by a gas container, and the former World Champion lost his life.

Earlier that week at the 1969 TT, we had watched Australian Kel Carruthers stem the two-stroke invasion, leaping over Ballaugh Bridge on the glorious sounding four-cylinder Benelli to win the 250cc race. He went on to win the world title in a contest that went right to the wire. At the final round at the Adriatica Grand Prix on the switch-back roads above the Adriatic coastal town of Opatija, just two points separated Carruthers, the Yamaha of Kent Andersson and the Ossa of Santiago Herrero, who earlier in the season had become the very first Spanish 250cc Grand Prix winner. Carruthers won the race and the title. The fact that he won a world title is often forgotten because Carruthers was the man who was the driving force to bring Kenny Roberts into grand prix racing followed by the likes of Eddie Lawson and Wayne Rainey in years to come. Ángel Nieto won the first of his 13 world titles fighting off the Kreidler challenge of Aalt Toersen by a single point riding the Derbi.

The usual problem – money – brought about the final demise of those exotic multi-cylinder machines. The glorious days of the five-cylinder 125cc Honda, the four-cylinder 125 and 250cc two-stroke Yamahas came to an end when the FIM changed the rules at the start of the 1970 season. To encourage more manufacturers to join the championship, they limited 50cc to a single cylinder, two for 125 and 250cc machines and four cylinders for 350 and 500s.

Ago once again dominated the 350 and 500cc classes. There was no real opposition in the 500cc class where he won his fifth successive title, but he was pushed harder by Pasolini and Carruthers on the Benellis in the 350cc races. In the smaller classes, the new rule changes worked, bringing more manufacturers on board and closer racing with it. Rod Gould won the 250cc title on the twin-cylinder Yamaha; German Dieter Braun brought Suzuki success in the 125cc class and Ángel Nieto once again fought off Aalt Toersen on the home-built 50cc Jamathi.

I've always been fascinated by the Sachsenring in Germany, because nowhere reflects the history of Europe quite like this old road circuit. Seven decades of conflict, divisions and ultimately unification played out on and around this tarmac, which snakes through the forest above the town of Hohenstein-Ernstthal, situated between Dresden and Leipzig. Two instances stand out in my mind, giving us a glimpse of what life was really like for millions of ordinary people caught up in the Cold War, trapped behind the Iron Curtain, and how motorcycle racing brought them joy.

In 1971, 125cc World Champion Dieter Braun was fighting for the 250cc Championship when the West German arrived for round six in East Germany at the Sachsenring. The dreaded Stasi secret police knew there was a chance of Braun winning, but try as they might could not stop him competing. They were determined to stop any celebrations too but failed. Braun won an emotional victory after a tremendous 15-lap battle with Gould and Read. The rules stated clearly that the circuit had to play the national anthem of the winner as they stood on the rostrum, but this was unthinkable to the Stasi. However, they had foreseen such a victory that would send the 280,000 crowd wild and switched off the public address system apart from on the main straight where the FIM officials were stood. As the 'Deutschlandlied' anthem boomed out to this part of the audience only, the local police with dogs patrolled the packed banks of fans, who still celebrated despite the threats and intimidation. Ironically, the demise of the old road circuit as a grand prix venue just a year later, long before many of the other dangerous road circuits were abandoned for good, was brought about not by safety concernes, but because the East German authorities were so distressed by West German Braun's win in front of their own people.

John Brown told me that he once drove to the Sachsenring with Phil Read in a Rolls-Royce, which you could imagine caused a right old commotion for the Stasi. And Iain Mackay told me about the fights that regularly took place with with the local police in the nearest town to the circuit, Karl-Marx-Stadt (now Chemnitz) on the Sunday night after the race, as the riders had to spend all their prize money, usually on alcohol, because they were not allowed to take the East German currency out of the country. Pictures of those incredibly precarious one-man grandstands on top of a 20-foot wobbly pole show the very size of the crowd – often over 300,000 – getting just a little taste of life on the other side of the Iron Curtain before the grand prix circus drove back over the border for another year.

I finally made it to the Sachsenring in 2000, to a very different 2.180-mile purpose-built circuit on a trading estate, described as a Go Kart track by World Champion Mick Doohan when racing finally returned in 1998. Go Kart track or not, certainly the extended circuit has some magnificent corners and drops, and I knew I was somewhere special where you could taste and smell the history of grand prix racing and what it meant to the East Germans. The story of Scotsman Jimmie Guthrie just epitomised that feeling.

On 8 August 1937, 40-year-old Scotsman Jimmie Guthrie was leading the German Grand Prix on the Sachsenring road circuit. Riding the Norton, he was chasing his third successive victory in Germany, where the rumble of war was looming fast. He'd already taken 19 grand prix victories and going into the last lap was leading comfortably. The 300,000-strong crowd packed around the road circuit prepared to celebrate. But he never arrived at the finish. Guthrie died in hospital after crashing into the woods on that fateful last lap.

Two years later, the Second World War was declared and the Hohenstein-Ernstthal area was never going to be the same again. When the war ended, the locals found themselves part of East Germany, a very different place to where they had lived before the war. However, the people had never forgotten a Scottish gentleman who won two grands prix at their circuit before the hostilities split the world wide apart. In 1949 a memorial placed at the location he crashed was their own special tribute to him. Nationality made no difference: he was a grand prix motorcycle racer.

According to folklore, every week for the last 70 years, a fresh bunch of flowers has been carefully laid on that simple stone memorial in the woods on the twisty undulating road near the entrance to the Sachsenring. Certainly, there was a fresh bunch of locally picked flowers there two years ago as we drove through the forest on the old road circuit en route to the first day of practice for the German Grand Prix.

Nine hundred and fifty miles away, across Europe and across both the North and Irish seas, another memorial to the same person glints in some rare Isle of Man sunshine. On the famous mountain climb out of Ramsey, looking back towards the Point of Ayre, a kiln of stones is lovingly preserved to commemorate the life of a great motorcycle racer and six times TT winner.

Ago won the 500cc race at the Sachsenring in 1971 to clinch his sixth successive premier class title, but the warning signs were flashing. The popular Jack Findlay won the Ulster Grand Prix on the Dundrod road circuit near Belfast to secure the first 500cc two-stroke victory for Suzuki. It was a historic race because not only were the two-strokes arriving but the road circuits were slowly disappearing with the 7.398-mile Dundrod circuit staging its last World Championship race. Agostini had given Ulster a miss, as he did the final round at Jarama in Spain where Dave Simmonds brought the two-stroke Kawasaki their first win. Ago won the 350cc race at the Imatra road circuit in Finland to capture his tenth world title, but a glimpse into both Agostini's and grand prix racing's two-stroke future was plain for all to see.

Jarno Saarinen finished second on the 350cc Yamaha twin and won his first Grand Prix on the old Brno road circuit in the Czech Republic, while Phil Read on a private Yamaha won his fourth 250cc title after a last round shoot-out with Gould, Saarinen, Braun and John Dodds. Nieto won his first 125cc crown with Barry Sheene second, but the Spaniard missed out to Dutchman Jan de Vries in the 50cc battle.

Ago held firm in 1972 but only just in the 350cc class. Saarinen was on the charge but Agostini, with a combination of the three-and four-cylinder Agusta, held him at bay to clinch the title at Saarinen's home circuit in Imatra. The Finnish rider more than made up for the disappointment however with victory in the 250cc race which brought him the world title. Agostini won 11 of the opening 12 500cc races to comfortably retain the 500cc crown. Nieto did the double in the 50 and 125cc Championships.

I'd left the sports shop by now, having been sort of head hunted to become distribution manager of a new free newspaper, the *Oxford Journal*. Our road-racing friends wanted to try us for treason when Nicky Jennings and I announced we were going to miss the 1973 TT. How could we swap our annual pilgrimage to the magical island for a trip across the channel to Holland to another TT, in Assen? We were not alone, though, in skipping the annual trip.

The man who'd won ten TT races on the hallowed Manx tarmac vowed he would never race there ever again, and Giacomo Agostini never broke his vow. He'd had breakfast with his great friend and championship contender Gilberto Parlotti. Two hours later, on a bleak, wet Friday morning, Parlotti was killed while leading the 1972 125cc race. We'd seen the Italian, who was chasing the 125cc world title, on the Morbidelli race past us in the spray for a couple of laps as we sheltered from the rain sipping a pint of Okell's at the Crosby Hotel. Parlotti never appeared for a third time after crashing on the mountain section at the Verandah.

Every time I'd been to the Isle of Man, I considered it well worth that choppy four-hour – if you were lucky – ferry trip just to see Ago in action on the evocative-sounding MV, but he was joining more and more grand prix stars in boycotting the British round of the World Championship because they thought the 37.73-mile circuit was just too dangerous.

The diehard British race fans called them cowards and told us that only real racers competed in the TT, but the riders were not wrong. It was too dangerous, and with a cockeyed point-scoring system in which you could pick your top seven results in the season to determine your final championship points tally, missing the Isle of Man was no great deal. The Spanish Federation had already banned its riders from competing after the death of the very talented Santiago Herrero two years earlier, and when the likes of World Champions Phil Read and Rodney Gould joined the boycott, Nicky and I decided it was time for a committee meeting at our local, the Bear and Ragged Staff, to announce to the rest of the group that we didn't think we should be going either.

All was not lost because, with no British Grand Prix on the mainland, the promoters at the likes of Silverstone, Brands Hatch, Mallory Park and even Cadwell Park dug deep into their pockets to entice the grand prix stars to compete in England in non-championship international races. The riders were prepared to put their reputations on the line for a brown paper envelope stuffed with fivers.

Sometimes, to our delight, the stars we'd dreamed of watching found the locals on their own home circuit a bit of a handful. None more so than the Derby garage proprietor with those moon eyes emblazoned on his helmet – a certain John Cooper – at the 1971 Race of the Year at Mallory Park. It felt more like being on a 1970s football terrace, jammed on the bank above Gerard's Bend waiting for Cooper, riding the British built BSA Rocket 3, to take on the mighty Agostini and the 500cc MV Agusta, a combination that had won eight

500cc grands prix that season. When Cooper beat Ago by three-tenths of one second in a duel that they both still remember today, the noise generated by the 50,000 plus crowd was on the scale of that of a revved up football crowd celebrating a goal. The garage proprietor from Derby beating probably the most handsome, charismatic sportsman in the world – it didn't get a lot better than that.

And then there was the added bonus of our first glimpse of a rider whose name we could not pronounce and whose nationality we had to check in the programme. We first witnessed the knee-out style of Jarno Saarinen riding the 350cc Yamaha that day at Mallory. How the purists hated the new style from a rider brought up in the tough world of ice racing with those big spikey tyres back in Finland. We loved it, and especially watching him take on the bigger bikes on his 250 and 350cc Yamahas and win, but it was a trip to the John Player International at nearby Silverstone that convinced us he was our man.

As usual, after the racing we trawled the paddock hoping to catch a glimpse our heroes and their mighty steeds. We found the humble Saarinen hitching an enclosed two-bike trailer housing the Yamahas to his VW Camper van, ready to set off with his gorgeous wife, Soili, for the next grand prix. He could have been just a clubman's racer en route to Cadwell, but he was not. Saarinen was something special. I could not find the courage to speak to him, but met his brothers and wife Soili when he was inducted as a MotoGP Legend many years later.

After winning the 1972 250cc World Championship and pushing Ago to the limit in the 350cc class, Yamaha asked Saarinen to spearhead their much-publicised assault on the prestigious 500cc class on the two-stroke four cylinders across the frame machine. Four-stroke versus two-stroke; Saarinen versus Agostini and Read. That's what did it, and we were on our way to Assen after a vote passed unanimously in the Bear and Ragged Staff. Of course, we would be sad to miss the 'real' TT, but we would still travel to the island in September for the amateur Manx Grand Prix which made us feel a little less guilty and would also ensure that my mum and dad got their usual package of Manx kippers posted from the Kipper shop in Peel. It would just be three months later than usual. They would still taste, and certainly smell, the same.

It had been a long, hot afternoon in the field, especially after a rather heavy previous evening, for Cumnor's Sunday cricket side on 20 May 1973. I'd bowled a good number of rather wayward overs and was looking forward to a cuppa and some of Mrs Parker's glorious egg sandwiches as we trooped across the road to the back room of the Bear. The radio was on in the background as we sat down, and the big tea pot arrived.

Through the babble of conversation concerning missed catches, LBWs and the night before I heard the words Monza and Saarinen mentioned in the background on BBC radio news. I jumped up to be closer to the radio as the newsreader returned to their top story. I was horrified when he announced the death of motorcycle racers Jarno Saarinen and Renzo Pasolini after a multi-rider crash on the first lap of the 250cc race in the Gran Premio at Monza in Italy. Our hero Saarinen and the bespectacled Pasolini, our TT hero all those years ago, both dead. I just could not believe it.

With no internet in those distant days I had to wait an agonising couple of hours before tuning into the BBC sports news at 7pm to hear the dulcet tones of Chris Carter explain what had happened in more detail. After oil had been dropped on the tarmac in the previous race, Saarinen and Pasolini had been involved in a 15-rider multiple accident on the first lap of the 250cc race at the Armco-surrounded Grand Curve. Many years later, my old *Motor Cycle Weekly News* editor Mick Woollett told me it was one of the worst moments of his distinguished career when the riders did not arrive at the end of the first lap. There was total silence with a pall of smoke rising from above the Grand Curve the only indication that something dreadful had occurred before distraught riders appeared, riding slowly and mournfully back to the pits the wrong way around the circuit.

The impact of the crash and especially the death of Saarinen was massive. He had been leading the 500cc World Championship on the two-stroke Yamaha after winning in France and Austria. Only a broken chain had prevented him making it a hat-trick in Germany before the Monza race. He'd also started the defence of his 250cc World Championship with three straight wins. The world mourned the death of a brilliant rider who epitomised the spirit of the early seventies, a fantastic engineer who drove around Europe in a Camper van with the bikes hitched behind on a trailer. The official inquiry into the accident found that the cause was the seizure of the engine in Renzo Pasolini's motorcycle but many thought otherwise given the lax safety measures prevalent at the time. Whatever the cause, safety clearly was an issue and something had to change. But it took another seven years and more riders' deaths and horrendous injuries for it to happen. Yamaha immediately withdrew from the 500cc World Championship and, ironically, the challenge to MV came from a most unlikely source – and resulted in the same tragic outcome.

Another brilliant engineer, Kim Newcombe produced a two-stroke 500cc engine from a West German flat-four König outboard boat engine. The New Zealander won in Yugoslavia, where both Read and Agostini refused to compete on the frighteningly dangerous Opatija road circuit. Newcombe lay second in the championship to

Read when he arrived at Silverstone to compete in one of the big British international meetings that no doubt helped finance his considerable efforts on the König against the mighty MV factory.

I loved those international meetings at Silverstone. Not only was it a rare chance to watch the world's stars in action, but I could play football in the morning and rush to Silverstone with my jeans covering muddy knees and dirty socks. After practice, Newcombe told the organisers he would like some more straw bales at the iconic Stowe Corner, but they were reported to have said that there were enough already and did nothing. Newcombe crashed at Stowe during the race, hitting his head on an unprotected concrete post, and died in hospital three days later. Another great talent, and a father, killed for greed and laziness with a total lack of respect.

Following the death of our hero Saarinen we ummed and ahhed about going to Holland but decided we would make the journey to the Cathedral of Motorcycle Racing out of respect for both the Finn and Pasolini. On a glorious weekend at the end of June, four of us took time off work and drove to Dover to find our seats on one of the 25 Tee Mill tour coaches that would first transport us to the ferry and then drive us to the most famous grand prix motorcycle racing circuit of them all. For race fans, Tee Mill was the gateway to Europe and even beyond. Coach trips were the easiest, cheapest and most accessible way to watch grand prix racing. The company identified and captured a market, later expanding across the Atlantic to Daytona in Florida.

They started racing motorcycles around the streets of this city in north Holland in 1925, and gradually the track was altered to a 4.787-mile purpose-built flat track which included some glorious fast sweeping corners with iconic sounding Dutch names. The Veenslang, Ruskenhoek and Ramshoek corners were going to replace our usual Bray Hill, Ramsey Hairpin and the Bungalow. The Dutch TT was, and still is, the biggest sporting event of the year in the Netherlands, with crowds of over 100,000 packing the grass banks on the Saturday race day. Up until the last couple of years, the races were always held on a Saturday because in those early pioneering days they did not want to prevent the locals from going to church. In later years, I loved the Saturday arrangement, because I could get home for Sunday lunch which was a rare treat during the eight months of constant travel.

It might have had the same TT title, but it felt like that was about the only thing that connected it to our experiences on the Isle of Man. Perhaps the ferry trip to get there and the fans, too. To us parochial Brits embarking on a new adventure abroad, it opened up a completely new world. We loved every minute of it, and not only the racing.

The windmills, the canals, the cows, the bicycles – we were wide-eyed as we arrived at Assen at 6am on a beautiful midsummer's morning. We had a great courier on board our coach with Brands Hatch star Pat Mahoney keeping us amused all the way there – and especially on the way back, via Amsterdam. We'd never seen so many people and bicycles. And you could buy beer and chips covered in mayonnaise at that time in the morning. Six World Championship races, including sidecars, around the most famous circuit in the World and the sun never stopped shining. The icing on the cake? Phil Read winning the 500cc race on the MV Agusta.

Four-strokes still ruled the roost, but not for much longer. Ago made it an MV double with victory in the 350cc race, while we loved the sight and sound of the 50cc race won by the Kreidler of Bruno Kneubühler, the 125s with the Maico of Eugenio Lazzarini and our first ever look at the West German Dieter Braun, who went on to win the 250cc World Championship.

Then all back on the coach and a night in Amsterdam where we thought the barman liked us so much that he didn't charge us for each round of drinks. It was only when we were leaving that the bill appeared. Very different to the old Saddle pub near the harbour in Douglas, Isle of Man. We realised, rather like the riders, that the revolution was gaining momentum. We had already missed so much, and we would start making up for lost time. Travel plans in the future would be changed.

Read went on to win his first 500cc title to go with his 125 and 250cc crowns. Ago had to settle for his thirteenth world title, but in the 350cc class. Perhaps he had his mind on other things.

And so it proved – when Yamaha returned to the 500cc class in 1974, Agostini was at the helm. He definitely despaired at team-mate Read's mind games, but after dominating for so long on the MV it was time to show just why he was regarded by so many, and especially in Italy, as the greatest rider of all time. To crown such an amazing career, he set about becoming the first two-stroke rider to win the premier class.

Ago took to the two-stroke like a duck to water, winning the two big pre-season internationals in Daytona and Imola. The grand prix season turned into a war. MV Agusta versus Yamaha. Four-stroke versus two-stroke. The main bout on the card: Read versus Agostini. Read was at his best on and off the track, sniping at the great man at every opportunity in the media and then facing him head on when the flag dropped.

After our Assen adventures we once again gave the Isle of Man TT a miss but still sent the kippers home from the Manx in September. We broadened our European travel experience by Tee Mill Touring it to the magnificent Spa-Francorchamps circuit for the 1974 Belgian Grand Prix.

Read did not let us down. The massive crowd were at fever pitch as the riders raced down the hill through the so, so fast Eau Rouge; left and right at the bottom and in a blink disappeared into the woods amid a symphony of sound and smoke at the top of the hill. We waited for them to return after their 8.761-mile journey through the wooded hillsides of the Ardennes. We first heard, and then saw, just one thing: Read and the majestic MV Agusta. The four-stroke spine-chilling wail just bounced off the trees before Read's red leathers and familiar Premier helmet flashed into view with not another rider within sight or sound. The four-stroke era was coming to an end, but what a finale for us to witness with Read, surely the most underestimated rider of all time, beating Agostini by an incredible 72 seconds, averaging 131.98mph in 106 miles of pure, musical poetry.

The championship was virtually decided at the next round at somewhere as polar opposite to Spa as you could ever imagine: the aerodrome at Anderstorp in Sweden. Ago crashed and broke his shoulder. He would have to wait another year to challenge but would have to be quick about it because a new name and new hero was on the block.

We loved Barry Sheene right from the start – long hair, fancy leathers, plenty to say about everything, a bit of a rebel. We'd already watched him in those British international races and followed his progress in the 1971

125cc World Championship. He won his first grand prix that year at Spa and finished second in the championship to Ángel Nieto, but it was when he stepped onto the RG 500 Suzuki in 1974 that everything changed. British motorcycle racing would never be the same again. He grabbed his first podium finish, coming in second to Read at Clermont-Ferrand in France in the opening round and eventually finished sixth in the championship. Nineteen seventy-five was going to be his year and his fans were going to be there. It was time to spread our wings and cross the Atlantic to Daytona in Florida. It was a week in the sunshine that signalled the turning point in Sheene's career for both good and bad reasons. But as it turned out, as Norrie Whyte used to say, all news is good news.

It was our trip of a lifetime. Fly to New York with Freddie Laker, spend a couple of days with my great Cumnor mate Mick Roden, a very talented lead guitarist who was carving a career in America, and then Greyhound bus down the east coast to Daytona to cheer on our new hero.

The first part went brilliantly, but on arrival at the bikers' paradise we were gobsmacked to hear that Barry had crashed in practice on the famous Daytona banking and was in hospital with multiple fractures. It may have been bad news for us, although we soon got into the Daytona spirit, but it was a crash that became the opening chapter in the Sheene legacy.

Thames Television had sent Frank Cvitanovich to Daytona to produce a documentary about the new emerging star, but ended up with a programme that turned Barry Sheene into a household name. As he raced onto the banking at 175mph, his 750cc Suzuki wrenched sideways, throwing the stricken rider into the air and culminating in a 300-yard slide along the unforgiving tarmac. All captured on camera, but two shots made Barry an instant hero: crumpled in a heap, he tried to undo his helmet strap with a broken right arm, and then, while lying in the hospital casualty department, he described his injuries to the camera. A broken right femur, a broken right arm, compression fractures to several vertebrae and the loss of much of the skin from his back, he told the camera before, of course, asking for the customary cigarette. Back home the viewers just could not believe it and Barry was on the road to stardom which reached way beyond the limited world of grand prix motorcycle racing.

Typically, he returned to race at Cadwell Park just seven weeks later, denying the doctors and the pain to milk every opportunity, and of course it worked. His new-found popularity and fame simply shattered the ceiling. He was already a national hero and had not even won a premier class race, but Barry soon put that right and we, the royal We because there were around 20 of us, witnessed, celebrated and drank an enormous quantity of Dutch beer to celebrate.

After our adventures in Assen and Spa the previous years, the numbers of our touring party had swelled considerably by converted Isle of Man fans. We were on a high long before we arrived for the 1975 Dutch TT in Assen on Saturday 28 June, upsetting the Dover Harbour Master by swimming in his precious harbour and leaving one member of the group's underpants hanging in the bar of the local pub before we caught the ferry.

We'd come to support Barry with a big Union Jack flag 'borrowed' from the flagstaff above the Oxford Town Hall. We sat in the sunshine in the open grandstand on the start and finish line, cheered *Motor Cycle News* grand prix reporter John Brown when he crossed the grid, enjoyed the battles in the smaller classes, ate plenty of chips covered in mayonnaise and drank a lot more beer – but it was the 16-lap 500cc we'd come to watch.

It was an all two-stroke fight between Agostini and Sheene, with Read a mere spectator in third on the aging MV. Ago had made a brilliant start to his season winning three of the opening four races while Sheene, still recovering from his Daytona injuries, had yet to open his account. We stood the whole time as Barry shadowed the master lap after lap; each time as they came into the start and finish straight he went to pass him on the left-hand side but stayed in his slipstream. It was going to be decided at that final corner, with the 135,000-crowd going crazy, but none more so than us.

We first heard and then saw them arrive at that final corner for the very last time. This was it: Barry feigned to go left again, Ago moved to block and our man was through. They crossed the line side by side, the time keepers could not separate them, but we let the start line judges know, as did Barry's father Franco in pit lane, just who the winner was with some crazy, beer-fuelled, loud and probably excessive celebrations. They duly obliged. It was the only time before or since that two riders in the premier class could not be separated on time. We also could not be separated, still hugging each other as we boarded the coach en route to Amsterdam for a long night. We never did return the Union Jack to its rightful owner and it could still be adorning the wall of the Banana Bar in downtown Amsterdam.

Just eight days later, Sheene continued on his record-breaking way, although he did not win the Belgian Grand at the fast, so very fast Spa circuit. Before breaking down after an epic battle with Read, he set the fastest ever lap in a premier class race when he averaged 135.8mph around the tree-lined 8.761-mile circuit.

Read and the MV won again in the Ardennes, but it was Agostini who clinched the title for Yamaha and two-stroke engineering. Once again, the cockeyed scoring system in which you counted your best six finishes in the ten-round season confused the issue, but Ago's four wins to Read's two were the key. Ago had to settle for second place behind 19-year-old Venezuelan Johnny Cecotto in the 350cc class, Walter Villa retained the 250cc title, Italian Paolo Pileri brought Morbidelli their first 125cc title while the prolific Ángel Nieto continued his domination of the 50s.

The Jacket
1975

I SO WANTED to become a full-time journalist. Even at primary school I was having football match reports pinned on the notice board, but that one O level, which was not even in English, did not give me a great start to achieving that early ambition. Nonetheless, I started compiling a sports column in the *Oxford Journal* when I became distribution manager and I finally got my wish in the August of 1975, but at a cost.

I must be the only person who had to sell his motorbike to join *Motor Cycle News*. I'd also had to sell my recently purchased first home after getting caught by the dreaded Capital Gains Tax for renting it out, but nothing was going to stop me from buying a car to travel the 60-odd miles up the A43 to Kettering to join a newspaper that had been my bible for 15 years.

The advert on page three of *MCN* was for a general reporter. I was embarrassed to apply but was persuaded and to my amazement was summoned for an interview. I arrived in the *Oxford Journal* company's Ford Capri armed with a folder of my recent features, including one on some laps of Silverstone on my beloved GT 550 Suzuki and a special supplement on the recent British round of the World Motocross Sidecar Championship at the Fox and Hounds circuit near Newbury.

Having arrived at the EMAP reception desk, I was duly taken to the *MCN* offices. They were definitely not what I expected. Up the back stairs in an alley above the Burton's men's clothing shop, 'suits a speciality', off Kettering High Street. Editor Peter Strong's office was just portioned off by some flimsy chip board in the corner of an empty, untidy open-plan room opposite Woolworths and overlooking the pretty dismal High Street. The giveaway had been the array of the world's latest motorcycles haphazardly parked outside and the posters on the walls from grands prix and events all over the world.

The interview seemed to be going well, and Peter liked my features, and then the shouting started. The legendary John Brown was bringing the lads back from some lunchtime refreshment at the *MCN* local stronghold, the Three Cocks pub. It was like the Pied Piper leading the children out of Hamelin as they noisily climbed the back stairs, and the office came alive in an instant. To my amazement and delight I got the job.

It was less money than the *Oxford Journal*, there was no company car and I had to promise to live in

Kettering. Who cared, I was joining *Motor Cycle News* and was ready to follow John Brown (JB) wherever he led me, which turned out over the years to be to some pretty dodgy places.

So I took the Suzuki on a last nostalgic trip together to the island for the Manx Grand Prix. My local car dealer was a former motorcycle racer Andrew French, who always reminded me that he once beat World Champion Luigi Taveri at Mallory Park. Through his brother Jim I part exchanged the love of my life for a Volkswagen Beetle. I went to pick it up the day before I started at *MCN*, but he'd sold it and I got a decrepit old Vauxhall Viva instead.

When I started in Kettering, I was put up in the George Hotel in the Market Square, together with another new recruit Ron Pearson, while we sorted out our accommodation. It was the perfect arrangement and we did little to find somewhere to live while free breakfast and the hotel bar made life very pleasant. After two weeks we returned back to the hotel one night to find our bags in the lobby – *MCN* were paying no more bills.

Oxford born, Oxford bred, thick in the arm, thick in the head as they used to say and for me it was about right. I may have been 27 years old, but I'd always lived at home and worked in Oxford. Even when I was a teenager, I used to get so homesick on holiday with my mates I would send a postcard to my mum and dad every day. I found the perfect solution, although it proved hard work for the decaying Viva. I stayed back at Mum and Dad's, choosing to travel the 60 miles and back to Kettering every day unless I was away on a job. My travelling benchmark was to be passing the entrance to Silverstone when *The Archers* started with that familiar theme tune on the BBC Radio 4 at 6.45pm. I became an avid fan of the 'story of country folk' and the goings on in Ambridge. The journey was so worth the effort.

The sight of a Welsh prop forward's Y-fronts, well used and extra-large, leading the charge around the luggage carousel at Milan's Linate Airport should have been the warning. I was nervous enough already having to fly to Milan, collect a hire car and then drive on the 'wrong' side of the autostrada the 135 miles to Misano on the Adriatic coast. Ever since the imposing – both in stature and treatment of junior staff – news editor Norrie Whyte had called me over to his desk with a crook of the finger to tell me I was going to Misano to report on the pre-season March 1976 international at the new circuit, I'd thought of little else. John Brown was going to Daytona that weekend and so they were sending 'the boy' – in his words – he informed me in that Scottish way which suggested that questions were not an option. When Norrie added that both Giacomo Agostini and Phil Read would be competing and that he wanted at least two pages of Paddock Gossip, plus the race report, I realised the moment of truth had arrived. After four and a half months of the British Sidecar Trials Championship, advertising features and the road test of a 125cc Honda, the new boy at *Motor Cycle News* was finally on the road.

The Y-fronts had been liberated from their suitcase by a touring Welsh rugby team who had somehow managed to get hold of the prop forward with the biggest cauliflower ears' luggage first, had opened his case and displayed the contents to the other passengers waiting for their luggage to arrive. At first I thought it was funny, but then that dreaded realisation which we have all experienced dawned: I was the only person waiting at the carousel which had ceased carouselling and was both silent and stationary. No luggage for the weekend. I could have done with those Y-fronts, whatever the size.

I'd gone over the route a hundred times in my newly acquired AA road book of Europe before leaving for Italy and, without a hiccup, found my way to Misano in a Fiat car, the first time I'd ever driven a hire car and on the right-hand side of the road. I passed the city of Bologna on the way. Almost three years earlier to the day I'd travelled to Italy to report on my first football match since my Cumnor Primary School versus Dunmore Abingdon handwritten report had been pinned on the classroom notice board by headmaster

Eric Brodie 15 years earlier. However, on that visit I'd
been travelling with the team. This time I was on my
own, with just my new blue and white *MCN* anorak
for company. It was a very different trip. I was sent to
Bologna when I was still the distribution manager for
the new Oxford free newspaper run by the aspiring
chairman of Oxford United. It was a pretty routine
Monday morning scooping up wet dumped newspapers
from under Donnington Bridge among the dog shit and
used syringes, when I was summoned back to the office.
Apparently, my early attempts as a journalist via a column
on the back page had been acknowledged. Tony Rosser
told me to find my passport (which took three hours) and
get on the Milan-bound plane tomorrow to report on the
Bologna/Oxford United Anglo-Italian Cup tie.

I travelled with the team, which was great. On the
plane I sat next to Scottish international Hughie Curran
who told me not to worry after I naively told the team
I'd never been on a plane before. 'Count up to 15
and if we're not up by then we are in big trouble,' he
advised me and the listening audience as the old, very
old Caravelle jet lurched along the Heathrow runway
bound for Milan.

No lurching this time but also no clothes as I sought
out the Hotel Abner's on the Riccione seafront. The pre-
season international races had been held on the legendary
streets and seafronts of these Adriatic resorts for many

years and the reception at Abner's was adorned with photographs of Italian legends Agostini, Bergamonti and Pagani to name but a few. However, like so many of the road circuits, the Riccione seafront was a dangerous place to race grand prix motorcycles, and a tragic accident in 1971 involving one of Italy's rising stars set the wheels in motion to start building a purpose-built circuit on the outskirts of Misano.

MV Agusta factory rider Angelo Bergamonti had won the final rounds of both the 350 and 500cc World Championships at Montjuïc Park in Spain the previous year. His preparation for the new season included the national races on the Riccione seafront. The original meeting had to be called off because of heavy rain, but a week later in early April the races went ahead despite the threat of more rain. It started to fall during the 350cc race while Bergamonti was chasing MV team-mate Agostini into a roundabout leading onto the seafront. The 32-year-old Italian, who had such a bright future in front of him, crashed and was killed when his helmet split open.

Norrie, who despite all his gruffness did care for his flock, had booked me into the Abner's which turned out to be a master stroke because I soon found out that it was the BEST place to stay in town. The manager took pity on me after a rather breathless arrival in reception with no luggage apart from a portable typewriter that belonged to an old girlfriend, a notebook and of course my *MCN* jacket. He told me there was another Englishman staying at the hotel and pointed him out sitting below those racing portraits in reception reading a well-thumbed paperback.

To Iain Mackay being called an Englishman could have only been worsened by being accused of supporting Rangers. After sorting out his nationality, and later on his love of Celtic Football Club, we hit it off. Mac, in that soft Highland tone of his, told me he was working as a two-stroke mechanic. Typically, Mac asked me if I'd like to join him and his team for dinner in the first-floor restaurant of the hotel that evening. I wasn't quite sure what racing team he meant, but eagerly accepted, happy for some company on my first night as an international grand prix reporter.

I arrived on the first floor to meet the team and enjoy the meal. Sitting at the head of the table as I entered the room was the leader of the team, a certain Giacomo Agostini. Yes, Agostini, the 15-time World Champion and all the rest of it. The Italian who was then and still is now the most successful motorcycle racer in the 70-year history of the World Championship stood up to shake hands with *MCN*'s latest raw recruit, wearing what was, by now, although it got a great deal worse, a smelly shirt and pair of jeans – the jacket had been left in my room for the night. Shell shocked was not strong enough, but I managed to mumble a sort of 'thank you' and sat down next to Mac. He explained he was working for Agostini looking after the 500cc two-stroke Suzuki with which Ago was campaigning in his very last season, the legendary four-stroke MV Agusta finding life tough in its lone battle with the two-stroke invaders. I said little but nodded when spoken to and just ate what was put in front of me. Ago was soon off to bed with practice in the morning. I loosened up just a little over a beer with Mac, whose knowledge and opinions on motorcycle racing, football and the world in general would become a part of my life for the next 40 years on the road.

Practice day dawned with a rather weak and watery sun rising above a grey and uninviting Adriatic Sea. The Misano circuit is situated a couple of miles inland and, although it was not quite an out-of-season Blackpool, the closed-up campsites and ice-cream parlours, and the rare sight of an Italian beach devoid of sun loungers, made the prospect of an international motorcycle race feel rather surreal. The atmosphere at track was a lot livelier and certainly nosier, however, not least because of the screaming and smoke from highly tuned two-stroke engines, endorsing the fact that something was actually happening on this March weekend.

I was nervous, very nervous. I somehow parked the Fiat in a jam-packed car park and walked into the tiny chaotic paddock with a pass round my neck, wearing that standout *MCN* blue jacket. Any top rider who had not gone to Daytona was here before the World Championship got underway a month later at Le Mans in France. I just stood there wondering what to do. Riders were zipping up leathers and putting on helmets ready for the first practice session, their mechanics were busy and so who could I talk to? Look busy, look professional and look like you know what you are doing was the plan as I walked around with notebook and pen in hand.

The last time I had walked around a paddock was the previous year after the Race of the Year at Mallory Park with programme and pen in hand seeking autographs. For 30 long minutes I stopped and looked at bikes, smiled at riders and panicked. I pretended to write a few notes as I stumbled around but I could have been filling in my pools coupon back home for all the good it was doing. At least I can write the race report tomorrow I thought, but two pages of the treasured Paddock Gossip seemed a million miles away and Norrie would not be happy. As I was wallowing in a bout of self-pity and doubt, telling myself that they should have sent somebody else, a Kiwi voice butted in. The *MCN* jacket was coming into its own and had proved a life saver. The door had opened.

New Zealander Stu Avant was a long way from home and about to make his European debut on an RG 500 Suzuki. Together with mechanic and best friend Mike

Sinclair they were embarking on a life-changing World Championship adventure and needed all the help they could get, especially in the press and definitely from *MCN*. All three of us were on new territory it seemed. Stu told me he'd taken a mighty big plunge by selling up in New Zealand, where he was a top motorcycle racer as well as decent rugby player, to go racing in Europe.

In very similar style to Mac, we became good friends, especially when he based himself in Reading. Once again football was our great common interest, although as an Oxford boy, sanctioning him supporting Reading was never going to happen. I gratefully scribbled down Stu's story – at last something for Norrie back in Kettering. In that instant the self-doubt disappeared. I was up and running.

Legendary journalists Austrian Gunther Wiesinger and Italian Paolo Scalera introduced themselves and Paolo took me to meet 250cc World Champion Walter Villa who went on to win both the 250 and 350cc world titles for Harley-Davidson that year. Villa didn't speak any English, but the smile and handshake were enough to push up the confidence level. They found me some lunch and made me feel very much part of the international paddock. What had all the fuss been about? I even got a nod from last night's dinner host Mr Agostini as he walked by.

Phil Read and Agostini were never friends, and their fractious relationship while so-called MV teammates just made the situation even worse. The Misano promoters loved it though. This was the first time the pair with 22 world titles between them had clashed this season and both riding the same machinery, the RG 500 Suzuki. The previous year, Ago had brought Yamaha the first ever 500cc two-stroke world title after a season-long battle with Read on the four-stroke MV. Now they were on equal machinery to prove who was the best at Misano.

Typically, the never shy Phil turned up wearing a massive fur coat over his leathers in the paddock. I don't think it was that cold, but the fun and games were already starting and that good old *MCN* jacket once again came into its own when Phil spotted me. You must be the new man from *Motor Cycle News*, he said, and promptly invited me to dinner that night. 'I'm staying at the Abner's, if you know it,' he told me, 'and the restaurant is on the first floor.' Know it, oh my God I'm a regular and was there with your great mate Mr Agostini just last night!

At least I knew where to go, and once again followed my host's advice on food selection. We got on well, although I left most of the talking to Phil, and he even gave me a couple of t-shirts when learning about, and not smelling I hope, the lost luggage. Phil was certainly confident about his own ability which he had every right to be. It was a great shame he upset so many people because success-wise, he was right up there with the Hailwoods and Dukes. I lay on the bed in my room wanting to phone my mates back home and tell them that this was a doddle. I'd had dinner with Ago and Phil, met Walter Villa and really didn't understand what all the fuss was about this job. (No need to mention the doubts at the start of the morning, of course.)

A few flurries of sleet falling into the uninviting sea greeted the breakfast guests at the start of my big day. Perhaps Phil Read had been right to wear that big fur coat after all, I thought as I drove past those desolate empty campsites en route to the circuit. On arrival, groups of officials, chain-smoking members of the local Carabinieri, riders, mechanics and journalists stood around – something was wrong. The usual bustle, noise, nerves and anticipation of a race-morning paddock were missing, and I soon found out why. Ago, on looking out of his Abner's bedroom window, had decided the sleet was actually snow and had told the Misano organisers that he would not race. They made a quick calculation and decided no Ago, no meeting and called it off. That was that.

I was stunned but at least I had some precious Paddock Gossip. All I could do was make my way back to Milan because there would be no racing to report. Norrie had told me to book into the motel next to the airport ready for my flight back to London the next morning. I sat in my room disappointed with the day's events but relieved I'd circumnavigated all the traffic to find the hotel. I started to type up my notes about the likes of Avant and Villa, better to hand straight to the subs when I got back to Kettering, when I realised the one person I'd not spoken to about the sudden cancellation was Phil Read. Despite the shock and disappointment, I should have sought out his opinions about Ago's decision. I had one slim chance and phoned the Abner's from my bedside phone. Thank God my friendly manager answered and told me that Phil was still in the hotel. He put me through to his room, Phil answered, and my day suddenly got a great deal brighter.

I knew it was a reporter's dream, even as inexperienced as I was, as Phil launched into a scathing attack on the 15-times World Champion, calling his decision not to race 'pathetic'. I was ecstatic when I put the phone down and pictured the front-page story with my by-line when 150,000 *MCNs* hit the newsstands on Wednesday morning. I bashed out the story on the old portable before a couple of hours' sleep, dreaming of snowmen and headlines. My luggage was waiting to be picked up at the airport and I flew home. Norrie almost smiled when I handed him my precious copy, although he told me there was not enough Paddock Gossip and mentioned something about a couple more pages the next time. Sure enough, the 'Pathetic' headline made it to the front page with my precious by-line on Wednesday morning. Despite a tummy bug after drinking the tap water at the motel in all the excitement, I was happy. I'd come home when a race meeting had been cancelled with a front-page story involving two riders with 22 world titles between them.

Putting it bluntly, I was a pain in the arse. I thought I was Jack the Lad strutting around the office. I wore my *MCN* jacket down to the Bear and Ragged Staff, where my mates soon got bored of hearing what the menu was when I'd been invited to dinner by Giacomo Agostini and Phil Read – 22 world titles between them you know. Despite that glazed look of boredom in their eyes I kept telling them and I continued to wear that bright blue anorak wherever I went, including to the old Manor Ground to report on the exploits of Oxford United for BBC Radio Oxford. I really thought that now I'd made it as an international grand prix reporter, covering Oxford United for a local radio station was kids' stuff.

Things got even better when the crook of Norrie's finger once again signalled me to his desk a week later. He told the new international grand prix reporter, not 'the boy' this time, that the Misano meeting had been re-scheduled to run at the Autodromo di Modena that coming weekend and their new top reporter – my words not his – was being duly dispatched to come back with the goods.

Out came the AA road book of Europe, which informed me that Modena was some 25 miles north-east of Bologna. The flight to Milan was booked and the new John Brown was on the road again, *MCN* anorak and all. As I left the office, Norrie gently reminded me that he wanted six pages of Paddock Gossip this time and not the paltry two I'd produced from Misano. Six pages would have filled half the paper, but I cared little.

I had no worries this time as I strutted into the makeshift paddock – no Misano nerves for the new reporter with his finger on the pulse, and of course wearing *that* jacket. I looked across the paddock for some familiar faces and there was my old dinner partner Ago standing on a mound of earth that was used as a viewing area for the riders. I set off to converse with my new friend, probably get a story out of him and make the front page once again.

As I got closer to the legend, I saw he was engrossed, reading a newspaper, or more precisely *Motor Cycle News*, and seemed particularly interested in a certain headline that highlighted the word 'pathetic'. The blue anorak let me down badly this time. As I started to back pedal he looked up, spotted the jacket with my signature proudly emblazoned on the breast pocket and summoned me onto his mound of earth for a little chat.

A small crowd gathered because he was mad, really mad. He enquired whether I really thought a 15-time World Champion with over 100 grand prix victories was pathetic and was not capable of deciding if it was in fact safe to race. Did I seek his reasons for not riding at Misano, or were Phil Read's opinions enough? Surely a proper reporter seeks both sides of the story! The crowd got bigger and I got smaller and just wanted to dig a hole in that mound of earth. Our little chat ended with a burst of furious Italian from Ago which I was reliably informed did not include another invitation to dinner. He stomped off to start practice and I slid off to hide at the back of the press centre, which was an old army tent situated on the edge of the aerodrome, with my tail firmly between my legs. Not quite the Jack the Lad I'd thought I was, and I still had a lot to learn. It was a shock that my bubble had to be burst by the greatest motorcycle racer of all time, but always aim for the top.

I returned back to the office on Monday with two pages of Paddock Gossip plus the race report. It was back to the British Sidecar Trials Championship for the time being, but not for long.

Barry
1976

WE MAY NOT have yet got the Silverstone Grand Prix, but *Motor Cycle News* sponsored the 1976 British Superbike Championship that was the envy of the world. All the British grand prix riders returned home to race in the championship that drew in massive crowds, plus provided lucrative and welcome earnings for the top riders, and especially Barry Sheene. Norrie's instructions to not forget to see Barry Sheene and then write his column for the paper stopped me in my tracks.

Just four weeks after my Agostini experience I had been summoned by the customary finger signal to be dispatched to report on the second round of the championship at Cadwell Park in Lincolnshire. I thought I could manage that, but the Sheene mission was a bombshell.

I walked past Barry's motorhome in the packed confines of the Cadwell paddock at least ten times before finding the courage to knock on the door. His mum, Iris, opened the door. I introduced myself and two minutes later I was sitting in the warm drinking tea with

Iris and Barry's girlfriend Stephanie. In walked the man himself who could not have been friendlier. Barry, who on hearing my name immediately nicknamed me Nickel Arse – which stood for ever – told me to come back after the race to write the column and also to witness how everything, namely the cash pay-out, worked.

Barry duly won the race around the tight narrow circuit after a tremendous battle with his great rival Mick Grant and I followed Barry's instructions, arriving back at the motorhome and knocking on the door first time round. The column was easy after such a great battle with Grant, witnessed by 25,000 racing mad fans, but then we were off to Cadwell boss Charlie Wilkinson's office for a little bit of Sheene-style negotiation.

The queue of riders stretched well outside the door in a snake-like line. Mr Wilkinson sat like a headmaster with a giant cash ledger on his desk and summoned the bidders in one by one to discuss their results for the day, to remember and even change the start money he'd agreed to pay them. Barry never queued in his life for anything and so it was straight to the front. No need to check the results or check the ledger because the fee had already been agreed. A paper bag emerged from the draw of Mr Wilkinson's desk and, rather like a modern-day drug dealer, Barry checked the wad of notes was the correct amount and that was that. I honestly never discovered how much it was, but when your appearance can put 10,000 extra spectators through the gate it was not peanuts.

Barry told me many years later that on a visit to the HMRC Inspectors' office they produced newspaper cuttings of his races from the previous ten years. They had worked out the winnings and estimated the start money, which in all our experiences was never going to be an underestimate. It was at that moment Barry decided to emigrate to Australia. He told the world it was to keep those broken bones and all the metal plates holding them together nice and warm, but the thought of paying the bill demanded by HMRC was the real reason. Of course, he did a video for Pickfords to ensure all his furniture and belongings were shipped free of charge to the Gold Coast of Australia.

As I left Cadwell on route to the office in Kettering with the films ready for processing and a notebook with the precious Sheene column, a large queue, rather like the riders waiting for their start and prize money, was forming outside the Sheene motorhome. Two hours after racing had finished, the man himself sat outside and signed everything that was put in front of him, which included various bodyparts in addition to the usual programmes and autograph books. Everybody was greeted by Barry as if he'd known them all his life. Of course, he did not know their names and so he resorted to his usual tactic of calling everybody Ace, which made you feel so special. He sat there for at least an hour and the contents of that brown paper bag were well earned both on and off the track. The circuit owners and promotors knew it, but probably not quite as much as Barry. Winning that precious World 500cc title later in the year just doubled the price.

I may have watched Barry capture that first 1976 world title from afar and through the eyes of John Brown when he returned from the grands prix to the offices above Burton's in Kettering High Street with tales from the races and lots more, but I was happy. The *MCN* Superbike Championship went right down to the last bend at the last race of the year at Brands Hatch when I reported on Sheene pipping Grant for the title.

I was sent to the Isle of Man for the TT – flying there this time, for the first time. I was put up in the legendary Castle Mona Hotel, which was the *MCN* headquarters on the island for so many years. On arrival, I was met by JB at Ronaldsway airport to be informed that the start of the production race had been delayed because of the infamous mist on the mountain and so the standard journalistic procedures would be put in place, namely stopping at every pub from the airport to the grandstand. The mist may have cleared from the mountain to let the racing start by the time we finally arrived, but it did not clear from my head until the next morning.

My assignment, apart from drinking as much Okell's ale as my more experienced colleagues – more experienced in both in writing and drinking – was to write the day-to-day diary of last year's TT Senior winner Mick Grant. I loved calling him 'the gritty Yorkshireman' because that's what he was – a top-class rider both on the roads and circuits. He was a racing legend to the British fans and the previous year had won the Senior TT riding the three-cylinder Kawasaki. Mick was a double 250cc grand prix winner and had many a mighty battle with Barry Sheene in the British Superbike Championship and on the tight twisty Scarborough road circuit Oliver's Mount in his native Yorkshire. I was in heaven following Mick around the island, including breakfast at the Castletown Golf Links Hotel, in the paddock and on the legendary Glencrutchery Road start line. Unfortunately for the diary, his Kawasaki broke down on the mountain and so Mick did not repeat his success of the previous year.

Little did I realise at the time, when Tom Herron crossed the finishing line to win the six-lap Senior race riding the 350cc Yamaha and the four-lap 250cc race on the Yamaha, that I'd witnessed the last World Championship races to be held on the 37.73-mile mountain circuit. The page finally turned after 28 years of the British round of the World Championship and Silverstone beckoned. Once again, these really were the times of change.

*

Remember that summer of 1976, the hottest ever recorded at the time? In the sunshine I travelled around in the old Viva reporting on the sport I loved, and what I thought was mixing it with the stars of the sport. I went to Cadwell Park with Phil Read after he'd persuaded MV Agusta to give him a couple of machines to celebrate the end of the four-stroke era for both the factory and the rider. I was flown again to the Isle of Man to report on the Manx Grand Prix, sandwiched between some feisty old Superbike battles between Sheene, the Kawasakis of Grant and Barry Ditchburn, Dave Potter and John Williams.

I think it was fitting that Ago secured his last ever Grand Prix win in 1976 at the legendary 14.189-mile Nürburgring circuit on the aging MV Agusta. It was the end of an era for the most successful rider in the history of the sport; the end of an era for the 500cc four-stroke and the beginning of the end for those road circuits that had formed the very foundations of the championship for its opening three decades. Ago had seen it all. Fifteen world titles, 122 grands prix wins, two-strokes and four-strokes, tragedy and so much more.

My ideal life could not last and it didn't. A reverse up the hard shoulder of the M4 motorway brought my idyllic existence to an abrupt, muddy, dusty but a very important halt. *MCN*'s motocross correspondent Brian (Badger) Creighton had missed the turning for

Donington Park, the venue for the British Motocross Grand Prix. Being Badger, he decided that reversing back up the hard shoulder would be quicker than finding the next turning and coming back. Unfortunately, he was spotted by the police and the resulting court case was good news for neither him nor me. He was banned from driving and I was summoned at the end of September 1976 to Peter Strong's office to be told I was the new *Motor Cycle News* motocross correspondent and would have a company car, a Morris Marina.

On reflection it was a great career move, but at the time I was really pissed off. After all, I was Jack the Lad, mixing with the stars, and I'd even ordered a brand new Ford Capri with a black roof to go with the image. Next stop was the road racing World Championship for the lad who, just three years ago, was picking up wet newspapers under Donnington Bridge. Instead it was off to Tweseldown on a freezing cold November afternoon in the pale green Marina, the only nourishment a Cherryson's hot dog filled with a sausage that had been boiled in hot water and a tepid cup of weak tea. How the mighty had fallen I thought initially, but I soon changed my mind.

From Russia with Love
1977–1979

WHILE BARRY WAS retaining that world title and Kenny Roberts arrived from the States to completely change the face of grand prix racing, I was learning my trade travelling, often alone, through Europe to the motocross grand prix venues. That AA book of Europe became my bible and I learnt to write copy quickly on that same old portable typewriter that had made its debut in Misano earlier in the year. Often just a tent served as the media centre, with no phones and no facilities. I discovered how to fill pages of Motocross Talk rather than Paddock Gossip, collect the films or even take my own, not very good, photographs.

The 1977 World Championship was an amazing one in which to learn my trade, and I was lucky to be involved when the greats of the sport, such as Roger De Coster, Heikki Mikkola and our very own Graham Noyce, were racing. Although in Noyce's case, motocross paddock parties made road-racing parties look like a vicar's afternoon tea gathering. They rode hard and played hard and the main thing I learnt was to keep out of trouble when the real fun and games started.

The riders' favourite trip of the year was the double-headed grand prix in Finland and Sweden, which I thought would make a great feature: 'On the Road with Honda'. It was ten days of hell with Noyce and his team-mate Brad Lackey, with a couple of grands prix thrown in. I remember on the very first night finding myself on the top of a redundant ski jump after a party at Öhlins in Sweden.

I thought I was jinxed after the Misano sleet – sorry snow – cancellation when my first international motocross event in 1977 at Lommel in Belgium was called off because of heavy rain but, rather like Ago and Read in Misano, I met and interviewed De Coster and his Suzuki team-mate Gerrit Wolsink to set me on my way. De Coster was a motocross legend and multi World Champion, while Wolsink combined racing with being a dentist. There was no Ago/Read split this time. They provided me with some great copy, but not about each other.

There was no harder way to learn but the death of a great friend in April 1977 had a profound effect on how I managed to deal with and then report fatal accidents. The advice from Colin Fenton on a Sunday evening when all I wanted to do was grieve stayed with me for the rest of my career. I'd first followed and supported, and then the previous year reported on the impressive career of Oxford rider Mick Patrick, which was definitely going places. He'd finished runner-up in the British Championship and was now competing in the prestigious *MCN* British Superbike Championship.

On a rare weekend off from my motocross duties, Mick asked me to go to Cadwell with him for the Superbike round, but with such a busy schedule ahead I elected to stay at home. I was playing darts in the Bear and Ragged Staff when the phone rang on the Sunday evening and I was called to take the call. Colin Fenton told me he had bad news from Cadwell, and that Mick had been killed. I was devastated but Colin insisted that I met him at Radio Oxford and together we would prepare and voice over an obituary for our great friend. I protested vehemently but Colin was adamant.

Every town had a Colin Fenton. The archetypical newsman who knew everybody and was on top of every story, usually sourced from the city pubs. Colin was a legend and it was rumoured he had got to the headquarters of the Great Train Robbers at Leatherslade Farm in 1963 before the police arrived after a tip off over a pint in the Oxford Conservative Club. After persuading the police that he'd not actually been robbing the train, he spent most of that afternoon in the call box on the local village green phoning his story to the national newspapers. He always had a pocket full of change for the phone box.

Colin was also a decent motorcycle racer, especially on the Isle of Man in the Manx Grand Prix. Colin told me on that dreadful Sunday evening that I had a duty to my great friend to report his death both correctly and professionally. To honour his life I had to forget my grief and do things in the proper way. It was wonderful advice which I've tried to follow ever since. Before I got my first mobile phone, I also always had plenty of loose change.

Nothing prepared me better for the grand prix adventures that lay ahead in the next 40 years than an unaccompanied journey at the end of the 1978 motocross season to the heart of communist Russia to report on the final round of the 250cc World Championship. The Russian Grand Prix was taking place near then Leningrad, now St Petersburg. British rider Neil Hudson was in with a chance of capturing the world title from the Russian KTM star Guennady Moisseev, and so I suggested I should go, thinking the new editor Bob Berry would say no, but he said yes. I was on my way after a few hiccups. I waited for two days at the Russian Embassy in London to get my visa. I had to go straight to the airport, and they told me I would be met by an Intourist representative at Leningrad airport who would then accompany me throughout the trip.

The plane was packed until we stopped in Copenhagen. Just three of us remained for the flight to Leningrad.

Nobody was there to meet me, and then the real fun and games started. Two Americans were the only other passengers on the flight, and I joined them in a taxi to a hotel in central Leningrad. In the morning I queued at the reception desk of the hotel for over half an hour to enquire about how to find and then travel to the motocross. I was greeted with a blank stare and shake of the head – it seemed my impression of riding a motocross bike to illustrate my dilemma was not really appreciated.

Stuck behind the Iron Curtain in a hotel where nobody spoke English or had the slightest interest in motocross, I went outside for a think but was soon back. This time it was not the infamous *MCN* jacket with my name still emblazoned on the pocket but my jeans that caused a great commotion, and many offers of cash gifts and certain favours in exchange. Feeling defeated, I sat down in the hotel reception and was saved by a picture of Moisseev on the front page of the local newspaper. Another half-hour wait at reception and pointing at the picture resulted in a taxi being ordered. I don't really think the taxi driver had the faintest idea where we were really going as he circumnavigated the large holes in the wide streets of Leningrad, surrounded by statues of Stalin and large queues outside food shops.

After about an hour and a half, we finally arrived at the circuit which was constructed around an out-of-season ski jump on the outskirts of this vast city. I'd never been so relieved to talk my way into the paddock and a little piece of normality. The paddock was our home for the next couple of days and was guarded day and night by some very impressively dressed, important-looking military gentlemen. Not only did they stop anybody getting into and us getting out of the paddock where the Western riders were parked, but also soon made it clear they were up for swapping anything they thought was Western. Soon cap badges, bottles of vodka and even a fur hat were exchanged for copies of *Motor Cycle News*, pens and Camel-sponsored caps.

After practice, the Western riders and myself assembled in a convoy of vans in the paddock, surrounded by a cordon of police cars ready to drive back to the spartan Sputnik Hotel on a trading estate about five miles from the track. Despite the police guard, the trip took about half an hour, with cars dodging in and out of the convoy, and people leaning out of the windows banging on the side of the riders' vans. Apparently, they wanted to exchange money, but we never stopped to find out.

A massive crowd celebrated Moisseev clinching the title on the Sunday after and the KTM World Champion was presented with a brand new BMW car for his achievement. We certainly never saw another such luxury that weekend. Now it was time to get home, which proved even more difficult than arriving.

On the Monday afternoon after the race I found myself on the top floor of a Moscow hotel, the home of the British Embassy. I'd missed the London flight after my flight from Leningrad had apparently been delayed and I could not understand the airport signs in Russian. We were on board and about to take off for Moscow when suddenly an announcement was made, and everybody got off. I just followed the group of passengers, and then sat with them in the lounge without exchanging a word. When they stood up to board another plane, I followed. Thank God it was going to Moscow, although we landed at a different Moscow airport to where I should have been to catch the already departed London flight.

I'd been out of contact with the Western world for four days. I should have been back by now, and people at home, and especially the office who wanted my copy, were starting to worry. I got in the nearest taxi and asked to be taken to the British Embassy. My knight in shining armour, well a Savile Row suit, was the only person on duty at the embassy on this Bank Holiday afternoon. He first made me a cup of tea and then telexed the office in Kettering. The reply was instant; they said they were relieved I was safe, before typically asking where my copy was. My new friend then sent my whole report by telex, re-booked my flight and gave me directions for a visit to Red Square before I flew home.

On arrival in London, I drove straight to Kettering with the films which were developed just in time for the pictures to appear alongside the report in the paper the next day. The vodka given to me by the military gentleman in exchange for a copy of *Motor Cycle News* took both the varnish and polishes off the bar in the Bear and Ragged Staff. We decided not to drink it. The fur hat had fleas.

For two glorious years, Barry Sheene dominated the 500cc World Championship and the headlines on both the back and front of the national newspapers. Riding the RG 500 Suzuki he won the 1976 title at Anderstorp in Sweden with three rounds remaining, which he decided not to contest.

To be honest, Barry could earn so much more money not racing motorcycles. Advertising campaigns with the likes of boxing legend Henry Cooper and a front-page revelation in the *Daily Mirror* on the eve of the Austrian Grand Prix about his romance with Stephanie, plus his antics with Formula One World Champion James Hunt brought him celebrity status and put the sport in a spotlight it had never experienced previously.

It was a comfortable championship victory and despite all the distractions he typically put on a repeat performance the next season. He won six of the nine races he competed in, fighting off the challenge from

American Stevie Baker on the new reed valve Yamaha. To really put the icing on the already well-iced cake, Barry desperately wanted to win that very first British Grand Prix in 1977. But it was his team-mate and great friend Steve Parrish who came within a whisker – or perhaps a raindrop – of re-writing so many new pages in the history books.

Barry hung over pit wall holding the signal board that was going to herald a new chapter in the history of British motorcycle racing. The GAS IT WANKER message brought a smile to the face of his great mate Steve as he raced towards Copse Corner, leading the first British Grand Prix with just a few laps remaining.

It was an August afternoon in 1977 in these incredible times and now the prospect of a British winner – it did not get any better than this, although perhaps a Sheene victory would have been the ultimate ending to the most perfect day. After 28 years, the British round of the World Championship was being held on the mainland and the timing was perfect. Barry had already retained the 500cc World Championship, and to make it the perfect season he was starting the race in pole position. To say Silverstone was buzzing would be a vast understatement.

The so-wanted Sheene victory did not materialise though, as the World Champion was forced to retire with mechanical problems. But, led by Barry, the patriotic crowd switched their allegiance to his partner in crime,

Steve Parrish. Even after that there was a backup, with John Williams riding another RG 500 Suzuki in second place in front of Sheene's team-mate and not-great friend American Pat Hennen. Everybody was on their feet as Parrish raced between those towering grandstands at Woodcote with just a few laps of the 28 remaining – but don't forget this was England in August. A few spots of rain spattered on Parrish's visor as he turned his head to read Sheene's typical message. Less than ten miles of the flat Northamptonshire countryside to negotiate and Parrish would win his first grand prix and would be crowned the very first winner of the British Grand Prix.

The national anthem and the Union Jack were being prepared at the podium, but it was the stars and stripes that would be required. Going into the first corner at Copse to commence the most important few laps of his life, Parrish lost the front end of his Suzuki and went down. Before the crowd could even utter a moan, Williams crashed three bends later leaving the way clear for Hennen to win his second 500cc grand prix.

That was that. No British rider has won the premier class race at the British Grand Prix in the 41 years since; the unfortunate Steve Parrish never won a grand prix and American riders dominated the championship for the next ten years. It could all have been so different.

So many talented British riders have tried to emulate Sheene, but the fact that he was the last British rider to win the premier class title in 1977 and that we had to wait 35 years for another British rider to win a premier class grand prix after Barry is the perfect illustration of what he was all about. Forget all the off-track distractions, when it mattered, he was ruthless in every way and came up with the goods on the track. He would try every trick in the book to unsettle opponents and take full advantage of any situation. Mr Casual on the start line, he had a hole drilled in the front of his helmet so he could puff on a last-minute cigarette. He'd have a look at everybody's machines, sometimes shaking his head to suggest something was wrong. Forty years on and a certain Valentino Rossi has certainly taken a leaf out of Barry's book.

There may have been warning signs, but nobody could have foreseen the unbelievable effect Kenny Roberts was going to have over the next 30 years of World Championship racing. Barry Sheene in particular had not thought for one single second that Kenny was going to steal that coveted world crown for the next three years, but he did so with a style that turned the world upside down. Not only did he win grands prix and world titles, but he also played a major role in changing track safety and getting the riders the respect and prize money they deserved, before producing a son who won the 500cc world title too. Not bad for a dirt tracker from Modesto in California who'd plied his trade in the rough, tough world of the AMA Grand National Championship and mile and half-mile dirt ovals. Kenny took on the all-conquering Harley and the AMA title on two occasions and then managed to adapt that sliding style when he switched to road racing with such a devastating effect.

The Europeans had been warned after watching Roberts in action on both the 250 and 750cc Yamahas in Daytona, the Imola 200 and in Britain at the Transatlantic Trophy races, but nothing prepared them for his 500cc grand prix arrival on the OW35 Yamaha, fitted with Goodyear tyres in 1978. He simply blew them apart on the track, laughing at Sheene's attempts to unsettle him in the equally startled European media. The floodgates for the American invasion on the bastion of European sport had opened. Their sarcastic sense of humour, fun and confidence just added more fuel to the Europeans' at first sceptical annoyance, but very soon it turned to admiration. Kenny clinched the 500cc title with a third place at the final round at the Nürburgring just a couple of weeks after 'winning' the British Grand Prix in torrential rain with the timekeepers really unable to cope in the spray still using a simple stop watch.

It was just the start, and Roberts repeated the dose a year later despite missing the first round in Venezuela after a big testing crash in Japan which resulted in a serious back injury and the removal of his spleen. Sheene did not go down without a great fight and no more so than at the penultimate round of the championship at Silverstone. If you were there on that August afternoon in 1979 you are still boring the grandchildren recounting every single lap of the 28-lap encounter. That probably accounts for around 60,000 fans, but millions of television viewers tuned in when the BBC took the rare chance of upsetting their Formula One car-racing orientated bosses by showing some overtaking. With the iconic Murray Walker at the microphone, they produced a live broadcast that is still talked about today and no wonder why. Sheene, so determined to defeat the dreaded Roberts in front of the home crowd and to keep his championship chances alive; two contrasting riding styles around the flat, fast Silverstone circuit and Yamaha versus Suzuki in a mighty showdown. Lap after lap they swapped the lead and even Murray realised Barry was not waving when he showed two fingers to Roberts as they raced down the Hangar Straight at over 180mph towards Stowe Corner.

It all pointed to a last lap showdown until fate took over. They could hardly be separated as they raced through the fearsome Woodcote Corner to start the last lap. Ironically, in front of them was backmarker George Fogarty, father of Carl who won four World Superbike titles to become the Sheene of the nineties for the success-starved British fans. Roberts went up the inside of Fogarty and Barry round the outside which dropped him back over 100 yards as they started lap 28. Inch by inch, foot by foot, yard by yard Barry closed the gap, urged on by the crazy crowd, while millions of television viewers were fired up by some classic Murray commentary.

As they raced into Woodcote, Sheene continued to close, Roberts drifted slightly wide at over 120mph forcing Sheene even wider. He just clipped the grass and that was enough for the American to claim victory by three-hundredths of one second. It was the pair at the very pinnacle of their chosen profession and many people felt it was Sheene's greatest ever grand prix ride. Roberts duly retained his title at the next and final round by finishing third at Le Mans in the race won by Sheene.

Amid all the Roberts/Sheene shenanigans at the Silverstone Grand Prix, Honda returned to grand prix racing with a truly extraordinary motorcycle. To start with, it was a four-stroke, which had been long left behind in the two-stroke revolution. Oval pistons with two connecting rods and each of the four cylinders with eight valves and two spark plugs was just the start. An aluminium monocoque frame and 16-inch wheels made the bike look small. It was an amazing motorcycle but despite the innovation and brilliant engineering, it just could not match the all-conquering two-strokes. Mick Grant and Takazumi Katayama failed to score a World Championship point, but Honda's return with a two-stroke 500 just two and a half years later was a very different story.

South African Kork Ballington totally dominated the 250 and 350cc Championships on the Kawasakis, winning both titles in 1978/79, while Eugenio Lazzarini captured the 125cc crown in 1978, but could not stop Nieto regaining the title a year later. Another Spaniard, Ricardo Tormo, won the first of his 50cc titles in 1978. The Valencia circuit in Spain which stages the final round of the MotoGP World Championship is named after their local hero who later died of leukaemia. Lazzarini followed up his 125cc success with the 50cc title in 1979.

For some strange reason, after two years' travelling around Europe, I naively decided that I'd had enough of life on the road. I don't think I was getting homesick and Oxford United were not setting the world alight, but when Bob Berry asked me to become news editor at MCN, my stupid pride took over, and I accepted. It was a step up, and perhaps one day they wanted me to be editor? At least it made me realise what I really wanted to do. The day I asked the new grand prix reporter Andrew McKinnon to go to Daytona, I realised I'd made a dreadful, stupid mistake. I wanted to go to Daytona and not send somebody else and those two years on the road had actually only whetted my appetite. What was I playing at, stuck behind a desk above Burton's in Kettering High Street sending my colleagues to places I wanted to be?

After six months of regret, and despite trips to the TT, a couple of motocross grands prix and a front-page interview with Barry Sheene, I hatched my escape plan in a swimming pool at Namur in Belgium. I was there to write a personal feature on Graham Noyce, who was poised to be the first British rider to win the World 500cc Motocross Championship since Jeff Smith back in 1965. It turned into a double celebration. I was in the pool with Chris Myers from *Motor Cycle Weekly* who told me sports editor and grand prix reporter Chris Carter was leaving and would I be interested in joining them to cover the grands prix? Would I be interested!

Noyce won the championship the next day, although his attempts to celebrate by swimming across the swirling River Meuse in the early hours of Monday morning nearly made much bigger headlines. Noyce winning that world title was a great way to finish at *Motor Cycle News*. We had become good friends and he had tipped me off at the end of the previous season that he would be joining Honda from Maico for the biggest signing-on fee ever paid at the time to any motorcycle racer. It was a great scoop and I duly prepared the front-page story, only to be pipped by my boyhood hero Mike Hailwood, who announced he was returning to ride at the TT.

I duly took *Motor Cycle News* editor Bob Berry into the Alpine lounge (our name and not landlord Doug's) at the Three Cocks to tell him I was leaving to join *Motor Cycle Weekly*. His final assignment for me was a really kind thank you and leaving present – would I like to go down to Devon to interview Kenny Roberts? What a chance to meet the mighty man of grand prix racing before I started reporting with the opposition, although the meeting did not go quite as well as expected.

Kenny would be riding the legendary Harley-gobbling Yamaha TZ 750cc on which he'd won those two AMA titles at a special long-track event at Exeter Racecourse. He was staying at a Holiday Inn type hotel on the A38 nearby and kept delaying the interview until finally, at around 10pm on the Saturday night, I found myself in his compact hotel bedroom with the television on in the corner by the bed. As I started to go through my pre-written questions for the World Champion, *Match of the Day* was just starting on the television. No great problem I thought, as Kenny described what it was like riding on the dirt once again. It will be the usual *Match of the Day* diet of Manchester United, Spurs and Liverpool on the screen but – hang on a minute – those yellow shirts and blue shorts have a familiar look. Oh my God! It was the rarest of rare appearances on *Match of the Day* for my beloved Oxford United and I was in the middle of an interview with the man who'd turned grand prix motorcycle racing on its head. I silently cheered a United goal and we got through the 15-minute interview. Kenny had no idea about the football and anyway was ready for his bed.

My next interview with Kenny less than six months later was not such a friendly affair. It was goodbye to Kettering and welcome to IPC's Surrey House in Sutton, Surrey. The building housed nine floors of journalists, with our office next to *Nursing Mirror* and *Rugby World*. There was a a wine bar on the High Street and a London culture that was so different to the Three Cocks and Kettering. It was great. At last I was a grand prix reporter.

What Falkland Islands?

1980–1982

TALK ABOUT LIGHTNING striking twice. When I'd started my motocross reporting career at *Motor Cycle News* three years previously, I'd missed the opening couple of grands prix because of a strike and here it was happening again. The much-anticipated start to my career as a grand prix reporter in 1980 suffered exactly the same fate. *Motor Cycle Weekly* stopped publication for over a month because of a dispute between IPC (International Publishing Corporation) and the National Union of Journalists. No newspaper, no copy, no grands prix and no pay. I'd had a taste of what to expect before the picket lines formed on my second meeting with Kenny Roberts.

I was summonsed on a Sunday morning to Brussels Zaventem airport to a so-called press conference at the Holiday Inn. The World Series revolution against the establishment was well underway and there was big news. At Silverstone the previous year, Roberts and former *Guardian* journalist Barry Coleman had been rushed into the announcement of the launch of the

Freddie Frith rounds Governors Bridge in the Isle of Man riding the 350cc Velocette to that historic first ever World Championship win in 1949.

Geoff Duke on route to the podium to celebrate that first 500cc World Championship win at the 1950 TT races.

Assen in all its glory – the cathedral of grand prix racing in 1952.

What a honeymoon – Dick Madsen Mygdal leads the 1953 Clubmans TT on the mighty Vincent before the crash.

John Surtees prepares for action in 1955. The only man to win premier class World titles on two and four wheels.

Greetings from the Isle of Man – the Honda team line up before the start of their World Championship debut at the 1959 TT races.

The man behind the empire. Soichiro Honda fulfilled his dream by racing and winning at the TT races.

Sound of the glorious sixties – Giacomo Agostini leads MV Agusta team-mate Mike Hailwood at Assen in 1965.

Ernst Degner defected to Japan and brought Suzuki their first world title.

Yamaha team-mates in name only – Phil Read leads Billy Ivy in 1968.

Thank goodness he didn't call into the pits – Dave Lock on his way to fourth place in 1968 TT 50cc race.

The classic TT Shot –Giacomo Agostini powers the MV Agusta out from the bottom of Bray Hill on one wheel in 1970.

22 – MOTOR CYCLE WEEKLY 13 June 1981

SPORTS EDITOR Nick Harris achieved a life-long ambition last week when he passengered three-times TT winner Trevor Ireson in the first official practice session for the Sidecar TT around the most famous circuit in the world. Covered in bruises, Nick gives a blow-by-blow account of the quickest 37¾-miles in his life. At the end he's covered the Mountain course in 24 minutes 41.2 seconds – an average speed of just under 92 mph.

My chario

On the way to Quarter Bridge, Trevor and Nick ease the super-quick Yamaha round one of the bends.

ALL I could do was scream and shut my eyes as I arrived in my own personal hell. My whole body, apart from my seemingly inadequate hands, had long lost contact with the sidecar platform and was situated at various heights in the thin Manx air.

Suddenly at 130mph the outfit pancaked over yet another venomous bump and leaving the ground rushed up to smash into my feeble frame which was on its way down.

The scene of my own personal torture chamber was Trevor Ireson's 750 Yamaha outfit and the all-to-keen torturer was the infamous Sulby straight, half way round the TT course. It was 37¾ miles of pure undiluted agony for the over zealous reporter, who, despite some magnificent bruises, will never forget the most incredible 24 minutes 41.2 seconds of his life.

Trevor and passenger Clive Pollington's instructions of "Just lay back and enjoy it" might have sounded more suited to some erotic novel, as we completed one of our many laps by car, but nothing could have been less erotic that the pounding my body was about to receive as I tried to sneak my way into the warming-up area on a sun-blessed Tuesday evening.

However, for somebody who spends his life chasing

Bruised but unbowed, Sports Editor Nick Harris shows off his painful trophies after his ride of a lifetime with Trevor Ireson.

and haranging riders for quotes and stories sneaking into anywhere wearing a set of leathers is not an easy thing and soon the story got around.

Graeme Crosby just shook my hand and asked if I owed him any money because he'd like to sort it out before I went. Mick Grant's wife, Carol, stood in the corner and could not stop laughing while Roger Marshall, who I'd just watched through the start and finish at around 130mph, said I was a braver man than he.

Hardly the stuff to inspire confidence but once in the warming-up area and under the fatherly care of passenger Clive, who looked after me all day, keeping me busy with little jobs and errands and making me eat, I felt better and I knew there was no going back.

Trevor, as always, was a picture of composure and just reminded me what we'd gone over a hundred times before – "Just lay in the chair the whole way round, if in trouble shake your head and for God's sake just hang on."

Others came up and wis[h] me luck and advice; D[…] Greasley told me to re[…] when possible to ease the t[…] sion on my wrists; Chas B[…] taped-up the laces of my c[…] spicuously new white bask[…] ball boots, while Benga […] hansson wished me luck.

Then suddenly, a yea[r's] planning bore fruitition a[…] we were on the Glen Crut[…] ery Road the light flashed a[…] my agony and ecstacy had […] gun.

I knew when I opened […] eyes for the first time with […] outfit airborne coming out […] the dip at the bottom of B[…] Hill, that all the tough adv[…] I'd had drilled into me abo[…] hanging on was so true.

Handholds

The position I'd practic[…] with Clive – laying in t[…] chair holding the front a[…] side handholds with my le[…] trailing out the back […] seemed fine in the garage th[…] afternoon, but that was a […] cry from the bumping a[…] boring racing towards Quart[…] Bridge. My first real test ca[…] as Trevor braked hard for t[…] right-hander and already ju[…] 1½ miles out, my wrists ach[…] as I took the strain.

It's funny, despite the pa[…] and concentration how yo[…] think of little things. I r[…] member looking at the sea […] faces at Quarter Bridge an[…] stupidly thinking all tho[…] people had come to see me.

Such fantasies were soo[…] forgotten after Bradda[…] Bridge and through Unio[…] Mills and on the flat-out se[…]

Take-off

THIS has been an almost totally disastrous season so far, with meeting after meeting cancelled because of the weather. But hopefully it will come to life in a big way as the British championships get under way in Lincolnshire and Kent on Sunday.

The events are the two championship qualifiers and they are certain to provide the hottest racing of the season so far and probably as close as anything to come.

The reason for this confident forecast is that only a handful of riders go through from the formidable list at each qualifier.

Take a look for example, at the entry of the 1,000cc sidecars at Holbeach: Alan Artus, Colin Banks, Alan Blewitt, Ray Chapman, Mick Dawkins, Steve Dewison, Trevor Jones, Paul Pinfold, Ted Scott, Dennis Teasdale and Ted Tucker are 11 of the 16 who will be fighting for just six places in the final. Fireworks are assured.

The 500 solos at Maidstone inclue Terry Birkumshaw, Tony Briggs, Andy Campbell, Neil Farnish, Alan Gardiner, Mike Garrad, Don Godden, Martin Goodwin, Martin Hagon, Chris Hendrickson, Graham Hurry, Bernie Lee, Steve Schofield and Clayton Williams in the 36 from who just nine will qualify!

The ACU selectors tried very hard to make sure the two events were evenly balanced in terms of entry. Looking down the list I have to say that perhaps chairs have a marginal easier passage at Maidstone than 500 solos in the same position at Holbeach. But only time will tell whether there is any justification for that comment.

But what is certain is that these are not meetings to miss. More details in "What's On" page 47.

Navenby debut for Cox Yamaha

BRUCE Cox, the Anglo-American promoter who has a tie-up with Yamaha, is aiming to make a Yamaha-engined grass track 500.

The prototype machine made its appearance at the Navenby meeting on May 31, ridden by Richard "Chippy" Moore, in one of his Chipmoore frames and won the second race.

The plan is to develop the bike over the rest of this season with the idea of marketing it as a clubman's racer at a very competitive price. But we could see a top name rider on it for at least some meetings later in the year.

The engine is an XT500 two-valver, as fitted in the well-known flat track racers in the States but although on methanol still only has a 12:1 compression ratio. Development envisaged includes fitting a hotter piston and converting the five-speed gearbox with its left side foot change to either a semi-automatic two-speeder or an ordinary three-speeder with pedal on the right.

At Navenby, Moore, who has in fact retired from full competitive racing, only intended to give the bike a trial run. In his first heat the motor started missing, under-jetting was diagnosed and he won his next heat, but the misfires returned in the final. Cox thinks a bigger carb is called for.

Chippy found a rather wider spread of power than he had expected. The engine had been prepared by an American tuner who reckons it is turning out just 50bhp at the rear wheel.

They're right

THE ACU grass track and speedway committee has given themselves a modest pat on the back over their once-controversial selection of riders for the world long track and European grass track championships.

"We were well pleased with the results of the qualifiers", said spokesman Gerry Wheeler after nine out of 12 made the semis in the grass series – plus one reserve – and eight out of ten in the long track. Just one wee niggling note – it might be remembered that Mike Beaumont, only named as grass track reserve, and not too pleased about it, was equal first in his qualifying event.

Suggestions

ANY ideas on better presentation, in every sense of the world, for grass meetings?

If you have, the ACU would be pleased to hear from you as the grass track and speedway committee tries to do anything it can to uplift the sport in the eyes of the general public. Write to Brian Coombs, ACU Millbrook House, Corporation Street, Rugby, Warks, CV21 2DN.

Grassless

PHIL Collins, a British semi-finalist in the World 1,000 metre long track, was recently placed third in a grass meeting in Sweden – only there wasn't any grass.

The circuit has been bulldozed out of a field so in effect it was more like beach sand racing. Winner was a Norwegian of whom Phil had never heard.

No backlog

ACU officials claim the backlog of competition license applications has now been cleared and new applicants should get their documents within ten days.

One up for Wigg

SIMON Wigg was again in form at the recent German meetings. He was second to Wilhelm Duden in the solo class at the Ludinghausen, European championship sidecar qualifier and followed it up with a win at Rastede three days later.

Peter Collins scored one of his best results so far this season, when he was third at Hechthausen, the biggest European event at the weekend. Winner was Egon Muller.

Gerald Short's wrist is at last beginning to mend. He won a race at Hereford and is now reported as wishing he hadn't withdrawn from the world long track!

Try again

THE courageous Frittenden club, although several hundred pounds out of pocket by two abortive attempts at running their Grand Slam, both flooded off, are planning to have yet another go.

Encouraged by pledges of support from riders, they are now seeking a date for a re-run later in the season, said club official Ron Hopkins. We all wish them well.

500 CHAIRS WIN SPONSOR

SUFFOLK passenger and outfit owner Dave Brown, through the recently-formed 500cc Sidecar Drivers' Association, has set up a Sponsored Riders Support Championship scheme which, it is hoped, will encourage more top organisers to include 500 chairs in their programme.

He has found a mystery sponsor – who doesn't want to be named at present – to put up £250 in cash. To this will be added £25 from each driver taking part – which at ten would be another £250.

This would be split between four meetings and each club would match the resulting £125, giving prize money of £250 per event – and although that doesn't sound a lot, it is far more than is given to 500cc outfits at most meetings, said Dave.

He has written to four organisers asking if they are interested. To date he has had two replies – one a verbal "yes" from Wimborne, for the Wimborne Whoppa, and a no from Auto 66 at the York Stadium long track. He has not heard so far from Whitchurch, regarding the Sandford Super, or Lydden promoter Bill Chesson.

Dave would be very interested to hear from other big organisers, who do not at present cater for 500s. I hope he gets some response. Whatever your views on 500 chairs, this scheme shows initiative and deserves to succeed. Dave's phone number – Stowmarket (04492) 75184.

Is he through?

AS REPORTED in *Grass Roo[ts]* last week, former Britis[h] 500cc champion Clyde Car[…] won through to the final […] the European sidecars in f[…] style.

But ACU representativ[e] Harry Louis is taking up th[e] case of veteran Dick Barto[n] who, it now appears migh[t] have earned reserve spot wi[th] seventh place at the qualifie[r] at Ludinghausen.

At the meeting, a Dutc[h] driver who finished 11th claims he would go throug[h] as sixth and final qualifier because he was the best from his country, which automatically has one from each qualifier because Holland host[s] the final, at Assen, on July 13.

Barton and his supporter[s] think that only the best of the four Dutchmen from the two qualifiers get their place and this is currently being looked into. The other qualifier is a[t] Bad Waldsee on July 5. British drivers are Geoff Eyears and Malcolm Chinnery, both of whom have an excellent chance of qualifying.

Fencing rules

THE ACU's grass track and speedway committee are recommending to the General Council later this month that the new safety fencing regulations should come into force from August 1.

This follows the printing of a booklet setting out these and other regulations. Up to now they have been virtually unenforceable because they have not been officially published. The booklet will now be available shortly to centre secretaries.

Main features of the new regulations are that there must be four ropes everywhere where the public is allowed – three wrecking fences and a crowd control fence, all 2.3 metres apart. Distance from spectators to the edge of track is only slightly increased.

Just to prove I did it – The 1981 *Motor Cycle Weekly* TT feature.

to hell!

...from Glen Vine to Greeba Side. Suddenly, as we hit yet another bump and my neck stiffened to wrench itself from the rest of my body, I realised just what I'd taken on in changing this lap.

...Crosby I could hardly breathe, I felt sick, I ached head to foot as we seemed to hit bump after bump at 140mph. Only later did I realise there was far more to come, and we had pulled exactly five miles.

...with a mere 32¾ miles left I was seriously thinking of giving my head and crying enough" when we leapt over a big dip down past the Highlander and started braking for Greeba Castle.

One of my earliest and greatest TT memories is watching Giacomo Agostini, riding the MV Agusta, and the great Renzo Pasolini, on the four-cylinder Benelli, sweep through this particular section which inspired me to know it was lucky. That is not the word I would have used at the time, for we racing on the very same piece of tarmac. I knew I had least at least to the pub at Ballacraine.

...before I had time to think about a wonderful pint, we'd arrived and any thoughts of picking up or a drink was soon forgotten as I used every ounce of strength on my body, every part, to stop joining the bailor at the front of the car and the Glen Helen section, and more bumps, were under the wheels.

Suddenly, out of the blue, the outfit appeared in front of us and to my amazement we overtook it in the Doran's Bend section and I knew from then that I was going to have to grin and bear it right to the finish, whatever the cost. Out of Sarah's Cottage we flew onto the Cronk-y-Voddee and Trevor's words during the car journey the day before came back to me. "It's no problem along here since they really smoothed it out," he explained, "years ago when I went home after racing and practice I used to urinate blood for a couple of weeks following the bashing my kidneys had along here."

Smoothed out, my brain pounded as my thigh pummelled into the sidecar wheelarch. "If this is smooth," I thought, "what was that Sulby Straight going to be like?"

Before then we had the small matter of seven miles to negotiate including the famous Baaregarney Hill. Again Trevor's words drifted into my buzzing ear: "This is a real beauty and you'll love going down here."

More a love-hate relationship flashed through my mind as we screamed through the bottom, almost touching the kerb, and after a few seconds of trying to keep right down on the platform to give my neck a rest, we were

Flashed

Without a doubt, my lowest point of resistance was approaching and when the 16 mile board flashed past I just could not believe it. I thought we must be somewhere near Ramsey and well over half way home but realising I still had 20 miles to go came as a real shocker, not that there was much time for reflection as we hopped over Ballaugh Bridge, nothing like as painful as the thousand other bumps my thigh bone was finding and just Quarry Bend to negotiate and Sulby was approaching.

"Just suck up your ... and hang on. You will feel like you've done ten rounds with Muhammed Ali by the time we reach the smooth bit," said Trevor the day before.

Now I know what Joe Frazer must have felt like when he was pounded by Ali's fists, although some of my bruises would have been classed a little under the belt but when you reach this smooth bit just before the bridge it's pure heaven before the brakes go on once again and the battle continues.

Trevor's early description of the run into Ramsey "Like a ride through the Berkshire lanes on a summer's evening," was brought to an abrupt airborne halt as we hit the infamous bump going into Schoolhouse Corner which seemed to throw up so high in the air I thought we would never come down to get round the bend.

Coming out of Parliament Square, Trevor gave me another of his long glances and indicated to look behind where Mick Boddice and Chas Birks, unbeknown to me, had been following us since four miles out at Glen Vine. They gave me an encouraging smile and I felt that we were nearly home and dry with only

the Mountain climb and descent between me and the grandstand I was so looking forward to seeing.

Nothing could have been further from the truth, I found my much-abused hand aching badly once again as we screamed out of Ramsey hairpin with my body trying to prise itself from my wrists under the fierce acceleration uphill towards the Gooseneck ... and they promised this would be one of the easiest sections!

The whole Mountain was now becoming a blur as I fought a totally personal battle just to stand the pounding for a few more minutes and I actually prayed for the Glencrutchry road to come into sight. We passed another outfit and the so smooth Verandah section arrived like a prayer from above and the descent and the bumps that tried to throw you out of the front instead the back made certain my last few minutes

were not to be forgotten. As we rounded Keppel Gate the shortest glimpse of Douglas Bay way below bathed in the evening sunshine and I knew then that whatever the spiteful piece of 37¾ miles of tarmac was going to throw my way I was going to stick it out.

Any wind I had left in me was completely knocked out by the drop down to Craig-Ny-Baa where we slowed to avoid the oil warning flags and I actually caught sight of some lads drinking a pint ... oh the very thought, but my biggest thrill was still to come.

Coming out of the Creg, Trevor looked down, grinned and indicated to hang on because he was going to give it the works and he did just that. For the first time he burst the 750 motor to over the 11,000 rpm mark, a speed of about 150mph in top gear and we rocketed down to Brandish where the braking for the corner caused me more pain and problems than the speed down the straight.

We continued through Hillberry and Signpost and even the bumps at Bedstead could not ruin the promise of a hot bath and a pint of lager. Through the dip at Governor's Bridge and I could not believe, we were on the Glencrutchry road. My prayers had been answered. I wanted to pat Trevor on the back as we went past the Grandstand, I wanted to wave to our photographer but I just didn't have the energy to do either.

I just fell out into the arms of Clive when we stopped. He took off my helmet and all I could do was sit on the wall and gasp. To be honest I thanked God the pounding, buzzing and pain had stopped.

Thanks Trevor, Clive and Suzanne, Trevor's girlfriend, mechanic Buggy and sponsor Joe Henderson for allowing and encouraging me to achieve a life-long ambition.

Would I do it again? ... I'll let you know when the bruises have disappeared.

Past TT winner Trevor Ireson and his new crewman, MCW's Sports Editor Nick Harris.

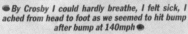

● By Crosby I could hardly breathe, I felt sick, I ached from head to foot as we seemed to hit bump after bump at 140mph ●

Trevor Ireson powers his 750 Yamaha round Quarter Bridge. Harris cowers as low as possible, grits his teeth and hangs on. There's many more bruising miles ahead.

Wearing THE JACKET in 1978 as I interview Roger De Coster with Guenther Wiesinger.

Barry and Stephanie – The Beckhams of the seventies.

World Series in direct competition with the FIM World Championship. Fed up with banging their heads against a brick wall, or in most cases Armco barriers, about safety, prize money and respect from the FIM and the grand prix promoters, they brought together all the top riders to compete in the rival series that would be for 250 and 500cc classes only. Coleman and Roberts wanted to wait a year, but the riders were so disillusioned that they insisted on immediate action. Mick Woollett, my editor at *Motor Cycle Weekly*, was old school and a former grand prix sidecar passenger. He'd written a number of features condemning the new series and to say Coleman and Roberts in particular were not happy would be a vast understatement.

On arrival at the Holiday Inn, I was escorted to Kenny's room for a mafia-style meeting by his henchman Randy Mamola. Before I had a chance to explain that I had not written the features, Kenny launched into a very one-sided barrage of expletives about the British media, the FIM, promoters, safety and money. I left after about an hour, hardly able to slip in a word but with no doubt where his allegiance lay. I'd expected those *Godfather*-style wire cheese cutters to arrive at any minute.

The history books show that the World Series never got off the ground, but you only have to read between the lines to discover what an enormous influence it had on the very future of the sport. The FIM's reaction was predictable, damning the new championship either to run alongside their existing World Championship or as the total alternative – there would be no combining the two. However, they immediately increased the grand prix prize money by a staggering 500 per cent, and scrapped the controversial start-money fiasco. Before this point, organisers would agree a start fee for riders to compete and paid paltry prize money. Riders would have to queue up after the end of racing to collect their agreed money. Now, the FIM had been forced to change the status quo for the better.

In the end, though, the series failed, possibly because of the lack of circuits brave enough to risk taking on the FIM, who warned they would not provide permits for venues to stage World Series races. The riders returned to their familiar haunts the next season but attitudes to safety, respect and definitely liveable prize money had changed for good. The revolution had started thanks to Coleman and Roberts, although it still had a long way to go.

The beginning of the season could not have been worse for a strike-stricken journalist who'd returned to the wheel of a big white Transit van delivering *Oxford Journal* newspapers to pay the mortgage. In my absence, the opening two grands prix were cancelled – Venezuela for monetary reasons and Austria because of thick snow. Fresh from his battles with the FIM, it appeared actually winning grands prix was a lot easier for Roberts, who won the opening three rounds in Italy, Spain and France.

I borrowed a 750cc Suzuki to get to the TT, and I slept in the loft of a house hired by Southern Television at the bottom of Bray Hill. Then it was announced that the IPC dispute was settled. We were back in business. I'd be reporting on my first grand prix at last, at my old haunt the Dutch TT in Assen. Dutchman Jack Middelburg sent the patriotic and boisterous home crowd crazy winning the 500cc race. Randy Mamola won the next round in the one and only grand prix at Zolder in Belgium where 18-year-old Freddie Spencer made his grand prix debut.

Barry Sheene was struggling after an acrimonious departure from Suzuki to form his own private and heavily sponsored Yamaha team. His standard TZ 500 machine could not match the factory bikes, much to his frustration, as we arrived in Imatra for the Finnish Grand Prix.

Barry had warned me about Imatra, and particularly how he'd famously burned down the toilets in the paddock because he did not think they were fit for human use. The dangerous tree-lined road circuit on the edge of a lake featured an infamous bend that actually crossed the railway lines. Barry said the only surprise was that they actually stopped the trains when they were racing. What he didn't tell me about was how close we were to the Russian border, the constant smell of wood pulp, 24-hour daylight and the Valtionhotelli.

With an enormous hangover banging away in my head, I was convinced I'd strayed into Russia when the large uniformed policeman raised his hand for me to stop early on the Saturday morning. We'd flown into the tiny airport at Lappeenranta in the south-east corner of Finland from Helsinki the previous lunchtime. The airport was so small that the gentleman who checked boarding passes and organised luggage also handed out the hire cars and served the coffee in the café. It was a 25-mile drive through forests and past lakes before we arrived at the magnificent Valtionhotelli, the headquarters of the grand prix in the middle of Imatra. The vodka drinking started almost immediately, followed by dancing in the good old-fashioned discotheque downstairs, where it was rumoured the girls from Helsinki would queue for six hours to gain admission. Around midnight and with no sign of darkness outside, Vince French from Champion Spark Plugs offered me an invitation to a party and off we drove, following the car in front through the forests in the direction of Russia, some four miles away.

I remember very little about the actual party but woke up on the couch in the lounge of a flat in the middle of a forest the next morning. At least my hire car was parked outside, but there was no sign of Vince. I had no idea where I was, I certainly would have failed a breathalyser test, even in Finland, and grand prix practice was starting in two hours' time. I just followed the road hoping for some sign of Imatra when I rounded the corner to be confronted by a line of policemen across the road.

I explained my predicament to the uniformed officer who'd stopped me, but his lack of English and my alcohol fumed breath was not making a great impression. I feared the worst when out of the gaggle stepped a gentleman wearing a pair of jeans and casual jacket who, most importantly for me, spoke English. He laughed when I told him my story. He rang it in and told me to take my passport, which was back in the hotel, to the police station in Imatra, before pointing me in the right direction and wishing me well. I did as I was told, and they laughed even more in the police station.

I was on time, although very second hand, for the start of practice. I don't think I'd strayed into Russia, but never enquired why the police road block was in place. I didn't stray as far the next night and instead watched Seb Coe win the 1,500 metres at the Moscow Olympics on a giant screen in the square outside the Valtionhotelli. I was so relieved I was not in Russia to celebrate with him.

Dutchman Will Hartog won the 500cc race riding the Suzuki, but Roberts, who finished second at the circuit he disliked so much, was closing in on his third successive title. Ironically, he clinched the title at another circuit he'd campaigned so hard to be erased from the grand prix calendar. The famous 14.189 miles Nürburgring road circuit staged its last ever motorcycle grand prix at the end of 1980. Kenny's fourth place in the six-lap race won by Italian Marco Lucchinelli was enough to see off the challenge of Mamola. It had been quite a year for King Kenny.

Toni Mang beat Kawasaki team-mate Kork Ballington to claim his first World 250cc title. Pier Paolo Bianchi clinched his third title on the 125cc MBA while fellow Italian Eugenio Lazzarini retained his 50cc crown. The real fight came in the 350cc class that brought a fitting end to grand prix racing at the Nürburgring. It culminated in a winner takes all showdown at the 'Ring' between the privateer of all privateers, South African Jon Ekerold, and German Toni Mang, who was chasing his second world title of the season. Ekerold came with a fearsome reputation, brought up in a racing world of hard knocks, start-money negotiations and risk-taking just to pay for the next can of petrol. This was his big chance to win a world title riding the Bimota-framed Yamaha and nothing was going to stop him. Especially not a cocky newcomer journalist asking stupid questions at the wrong time.

The penultimate round of the championship saw my return to travelling behind the Iron Curtain after my motocross adventures a couple of years previously. You would fly into Vienna before making the 70-mile drive to the Brno road circuit in Czechoslovakia. It was important to learn the rules quickly. Don't moan at the surly guards on the border lined with scary machine-gun posts every quarter of a mile, even if you have to wait a minimum of two hours to get across from Austria. Don't change your money at the border, you get a better black market rate in the paddock, and don't bring any back because nowhere else in the world would accept it. Don't expect any milk in your tea, stay away from the girls that flocked to the hotel bar because they were after your cash and sidecar driver George O'Dell was your man when you wanted to order some famous Brno crystal glasses for the right price.

I'd got all that sorted out, but I still had lessons to learn about questioning the right people at the right time – and one came courtesy of Jon Ekerold. Just getting to Brno was a tough enough task for the rider chasing the 350cc Championship. His two mechanics, Gregg Irvine and Keith Petersen, had been refused Czech visas because they had South African passports. Jon himself had only been allowed a precious visa because he'd inherited a Norwegian passport from his father.

Race day was scorching hot and the crowd enormous as Mang and Ekerold raced from the start line towards the first village in the vital 13-lap race that could decide the outcome of the championship. Mang led the way with Ekerold looking happy in second place. The South African had a 14-point lead in the championship and so he was comfortably on track for that title. Suddenly he began to slow with what we later discovered was a broken piston ring. Mang disappeared at the front and Ekerold's Yamaha just got slower and slower. Through sheer guts and determination, he started the last lap in third place, but the chasing pack were preparing for the kill and there was nothing Ekerold could do. He limped across the line in tenth place. Mang's victory and 15 precious points meant they would arrive at the Nürburgring equal on points, winner take all.

Nobody spoke when Ekerold pulled into pit lane. The team and the experienced journalists knew this was not the time for questions, something that was lost on the grand prix newcomer from *Motor Cycle Weekly* who dived straight in almost before Jon's helmet was off. His reply when I enquired as to what had happened would never have been printed anyway. I was learning all the time, but sometimes the hard way.

The Nürburgring was on its last legs. The surface at the legendary circuit nestling in the Eifel Mountains was deteriorating and the trees and Armco barriers could never be moved. The riders did not want to be there, but world titles were still to be decided. I'd never been there before and was excited as I drove into the paddock before this vital championship-deciding weekend. Standing at the paddock gate was Jon Ekerold and my heart sank as he signalled me over. Before I could utter a word of apology, he stuck out his hand to shake mine. He apologised for his outburst in Brno saying I was only doing my job and he was out of order. I didn't necessarily agree with him, but this was no time to argue as he disappeared into the paddock to win that world title. Win it he did and in brilliant style.

What a way for the Nürburgring to bow out, with a magnificent duel that did the old circuit proud. This was a race Ekerold was not going to lose at any cost. His last lap of the six summed him up both as a man and a rider. With Mang almost touching his back wheel as they disappeared into the German countryside to start the most important 14.189 miles of his life, Ekerold moved into a zone that only a few great sportsmen have ever experienced. He took the chequered flag and 350cc world title after a lap that would have qualified him in second on the 500cc grid. His race time was fast enough to put him at fourth place in the 500cc race in front of World Champion Kenny Roberts. Never in the history of the sport has there been a more deserved rider to win the ultimate prize, the World Championship.

Roberts's and Yamaha's domination of the 500cc class came to an end in 1981. They both realised they had to change to fight off the Suzukis and introduced a new square two-stroke engine with disc-valves housed in an aluminium frame. It was to no avail though, and Marco Lucchinelli won the title for the Roberto Gallina Nava Suzuki team on the XR 35 square-four machine after finishing ninth in the Swedish Grand Prix. The race was won by Barry Sheene, now on the square-four Yamaha. Once again Mamola finished runner-up with Roberts in third place. Mang gained revenge on Ekerold in the 350cc class with victory at Silverstone which the injured South African missed. The German won ten 250cc grands prix to comfortably retain his title for Kawasaki. At Hockenheim, American Eddie Lawson made his 250cc grand prix debut, Ángel Nieto took his fourth 125cc title and Ricardo Tormo regained his 50cc crown.

In 1981, grand prix racing returned to Monza for the first time since the death of Saarinen and Pasolini in 1973. Roberts won the 500cc race, but it was the 250cc race that still pricks my conscience. Before the race started it began to drizzle and the riders queued at Dunlop and Michelin to have their tyres changed to wets. Three riders were still waiting to have their tyres fitted when the warm-up lap was about to start. Young Frenchman Éric Saul's girlfriend Aline went to the starting grid to ask the officials to delay the start, but her protests fell on deaf ears and she was removed from the grid by the police. A furious Saul then went to the grid and sat on his starting position, delaying the start until his bike was ready. It was a right old babble of chaos and confusion but eventually, with a full grid, proceedings got underway. Of course, in the circumstances Saul won his first grand prix and everybody appeared happy but the FIM jury. After a meeting late into that night they disqualified Saul. Now on to my confession.

Andrew McKinnon, who was the grand prix correspondent for *Motor Cycle News* and a good friend, left the circuit and went back to our hotel. I stayed for the news – following a long jury meeting – that Saul had been disqualified. On my return to the hotel, Andrew was just tucking into his ice-cream sweet after a typical big Italian dinner and I was starving. He asked me if there was any news and I told him no news. Our two stories from the 250cc race at the Gran Premio delle Nazioni had a different winner – sorry Andrew. Saul was later reinstated as the race winner.

I don't know how we did it but somehow Peter Clifford and I persuaded our editor Mick Woollett that it would make a great feature. We wanted to ride two Honda road bikes from Buenos Aires to the border of Chile high in the Andes on a Che Guevara style journey before reporting on the opening round of the 1982 World Championship back in Buenos Aires. He eventually agreed rather reluctantly. It was not Mick we should have worried about but a certain war with Argentina over the Falkland Islands. We honestly knew nothing about the impending hostilities as we flew into Buenos Aires and neither, it appeared, did the citizens of Argentina who made us very welcome.

The trip could not have started better for *MCW*'s technical editor Peter Clifford. We found our way to Honda's headquarters in the sprawling capital to be told everybody was at lunch and our bikes were in the workshop having their batteries charged. The workshop was deserted apart from our two bikes, two battery chargers and three brand new NS 500 Hondas in various stages of preparation for their grand prix debut in ten days' time. The secret three-cylinder two-stroke reed valve machines were being prepared for Freddie Spencer, World Champion Lucchinelli and Takazumi Katayama to spearhead the Japanese giant's return to grand prix racing. For ten minutes Peter wrote and photographed without uttering a word before a surprised Team Manager Erv Kanemoto and his grand prix team returned. We bade them a quick farewell and disappeared into the sprawling traffic to begin the trip of a lifetime.

What a ride across the edge of the Pampas with the snow-clad Andes getting close as we approached Mendoza, the city of the Condor, before riding to the Chilean border. No mention of the Falklands and the only problem was constantly being stopped for so-called speeding by the police from various provinces. They would delay us for around half an hour, receive their payment after a bit of bartering and wave us on our way. Once we got escorted to the local police station where a rifle hanging on the wall was a reminder not to argue.

We returned from the memorable 1,000-mile road trip to Buenos Aires and the expected grand prix battle between the new Hondas and the Yamahas of Roberts and Sheene. We'd seen a newspaper headline in Mendoza about the Falkland Islands, but thought nothing more. Even when Barry Sheene lent me his hire car to take some colour films to the airport in order to have pictures on the front page next Wednesday, I didn't much notice the presence of military transport aircraft on the runway.

We were having such a great time in an amazing city, although there were glimpses of worrying aspects. One evening, when seeking a shop that sold cheap leather jackets, we found ourselves in the middle of a demonstration. Thousands of women with placards were demanding to find out what had happened to their lost sons, and the large contingent of riot police armed with water cannons was a grim sight. It was only years later that I learned of these mothers' anguish, as thousands of their sons – '*los desaparecidos*' (the disappeared) – had been abducted and slaughtered by the military junta.

Away from demonstration, Buenos Aires was buzzing. Great restaurants, nightlife and still not a mention of the Falklands. There were always queues outside the cinemas to watch that quintessentially British film, *Chariots of Fire*. We rode our Honda road bikes to the circuit on the morning of the race. New Zealander Graeme Crosby, who had just signed a massive deal to ride for Giacomo Agostini's factory Yamaha team, insisted on a lift with Peter before his much publicised debut. A pair of flip flops and shorts were not the ideal clothes for the occasion, but this was Croz. We had no money for the toll booth leading to the motorway, but a front-page *Motor Cycle Weekly* picture of Croz winning at Daytona a couple of weeks earlier did the trick.

Of course, what with Croz being being the TT and Daytona winner, it was not going to be an easy ride and on the approach roads to the parkland circuit he started standing on the rear footrests and generally playing around. It was obvious to me riding behind what was going to happen and of course it did: Croz lying in the middle of the road with a Honda road bike on top of him a couple of hours before his factory Yamaha debut with blood pouring from his knee.

A little bit of instant first aid and a grazed Croz arrived on time for his debut. Yamaha and Ago were none the wiser. The 32-lap 500cc race around the 2.476-mile Autodromo was a classic. At the finish, Roberts beat Sheene by just 0.67 seconds with Spencer an impressive third. Racing over, we rushed to the airport to catch the British Caledonian Sunday night flight to Gatwick. Good job because it was one of the last flights to fly out of Argentina to England for many a long year but, still, we were oblivious to what was happening. *Motor Cycle News* photographer John Noble was so enamoured with Argentina that he declared to the whole plane he was going to bring his wife back on holiday as soon as possible! Arrival at Gatwick changed all that, with the morning newspaper headlines screaming about Argentina's invasion of the Falkland Islands. We had escaped by the skin of our teeth and war was declared two days later.

Safety was improving all the time with better medical facilities and track run-off areas, but still the riders were prepared to stand firm if they were not happy. They assembled in Sheene's motorhome at Nogaro in France and got me to draft the letter which all the leading riders signed to state they would not ride because the circuit was not safe for grand prix racing. That would not have happened a few years earlier.

Roberts gave the V-4 Yamaha its first win at Jarama and Spencer became the youngest ever 500cc grand prix winner with victory in Spa on the new Honda. Sheene was in the form of his life with second places in Argentina, Austria, Spain and Belgium still riding the old square-four machine. The new V-4 was quick but did not handle well. But Barry wanted one and had been nagging Yamaha as only he could. At last they relented on the Monday before the British Grand Prix at Silverstone. With four rounds of the championship remaining, Roberts and Sheene shared second place 20 points adrift of Franco Uncini on the Gallina Suzuki. Silverstone would not only decide the outcome of the championship but increase the legendary status of Sheene. It really was a race one of them had to win to stay in the hunt. For both it was probably their last chance of becoming a World Champion once again.

The Wednesday before official practice got underway on the Friday of the Grand Prix was declared an open practice day for all classes. It was a recipe for disaster with bikes that had such a massive speed difference plus riders with such a vast talent gap all out together. Barry had already sampled the delights of the Yamaha's erratic handling on the Monday and returned on Wednesday after several modifications to the front end by the Midland-based Spondon Engineering Company, which seemed to be working. There were not that many people there and John Brown and I were the only journalists present. People were packing up at 4.30pm when Barry decided to just sneak in one more lap around the flat 2.97-mile Northamptonshire circuit before the chequered flag was due. The Yamaha was working, and Barry wound on the power with last year's Silverstone winner Jack Middelburg on his tail. They raced through Abbey Curve up towards the legendary *Daily Express* Bridge at 160mph.

A minute earlier, Frenchman Patrick Igoa had crashed after clipping the 125cc MBA of Alfred Waibel and was lying unseen with his Yamaha in the middle of the track. The impact was explosive as Barry's front wheel smashed into the engine of Igoa's stricken machine, creating an enormous ball of flame. Middelburg could not avoid the debris and ploughed into it all. We were convinced that neither Barry nor Jack could have survived, but they did. Both were in the medical centre and then en route to Northampton General by the time I'd arrived at the scene that resembled an aircraft crash with hundreds of pieces of smouldering debris scattered over a vast area.

There was nothing John Brown and I could do but tell the story properly. We gathered up all our loose change and occupied the two phone boxes in the paddock for a couple of hours, phoning every national newspaper, news outlet plus radio and television station with the news that was bad but could have been worse. Barry was truly battered, suffering a snapped left wrist and broken knuckles after they were trapped between his knees and the handlebars, but it was his legs that took the full impact. Both had smashed into the handlebars and hung broken and loose beneath his shattered knees. Also, his eyebrows were burnt off as he emerged from the fireball.

Surely this was the end of his amazing career. Of course not. This was Barry. But he was a mess.

Four days later, when Roberts crashed on the first lap of the race, the championship was all over. Little did Uncini know at the time he crossed the line to win the race that Roberts would not ride again that season and that he was the World Champion.

It had been one hell of a five days since the Sheene crash and I was sleeping it off on the Monday morning at home when the phone rang. 'Where is the Sheene column?' barked news editor John Bowles down the line. I didn't stand a chance and was on the road to Northampton General within 15 minutes with not a hope in hell of seeing Barry to compile his regular weekly column. I arrived in the reception of the hospital to be greeted by the sight of many of Fleet Street's finest, bored and fed up, either outside having a fag or consuming yet another coffee out of those dreadful plastic cups.

They smiled – or in some cases sniggered – when I told reception I'd come to see Barry Sheene. One phone call to Stephanie and I was in the lift on my way to see Barry. He lay there surrounded by flowers and get-well cards with both his shattered legs enclosed in a metal framed trellis with the scars of the seven and a half hour operations to pin them together with 28 screws and two plates very evident. He just about managed a painful smile as he pulled himself – courtesy of a trapeze-type contraption – up, but as always he was thinking ahead.

Despite some massive offers, the only column he was doing was his usual weekly one with little old *Motor Cycle Weekly*, a mere tiny pinprick in the bigger media picture, but no photographs because he'd done a deal with the *Daily Mail*. His loyalty, along with the front-page headline 'Sheene: I'm sickened! Someone could have got killed out there, but little did I realise it was so nearly going to be me', is something I will never forget. I was never tempted to take the offers from the frustrated journalists that came my way when I reappeared in the hospital reception.

That same year, the 350cc Championship came to an end. The 250 and 350cc races had become almost identical and there was no great mourning. Mang clinched that last title with a second place in the final round in front of his home crowd in Hockenheim. It was a happy ending on a tough day for the German. Despite winning the 250cc race he lost the championship to Frenchman Jean-Louis Tournadre whose fourth place brought him the title by a single point. Ángel Nieto clinched the 125cc title for the fifth time riding the Garelli while Stefan Dörflinger won the 50cc crown.

Double Time
1983–1986

THE TIDE STARTED to turn dramatically in 1983. In a reverse direction to the pilgrim fathers, the Americans were arriving in Europe by the boat load and they were very, very good. New World Champions were replacing the old, Yamaha and Honda were fighting back against the all-conquering Suzukis in the 500cc class and the 50s signed off to be replaced by 80cc machines. Grand prix racing made its debut in apartheid-ridden South Africa and I was made redundant. It all started at the Kyalami circuit on the outskirts of Johannesburg in the middle of March.

I remember coming through the arrival gate at Jan Smuts airport in Johannesburg recalling the television pictures of the controversial arrival of Graham Gooch and the rebel England cricket team the previous year and wondering if I had done the right thing. I left five days later proud in the knowledge that the grand prix paddock had done the right thing by not adhering to the segregation laws that had been imposed on the black population. Sometimes it was not easy, and you could have turned a blind eye, but we didn't. I received some pretty scary letters on my return after magazine pictures appeared of me sitting on the Honda road bike I'd borrowed for the weekend, surrounded by a group of black workers at the Kyalami circuit.

Even before I'd arrived, Barry Sheene had made the front page of the national newspapers after being refused entry into a restaurant because he was wearing jeans. He was big news because this was his comeback race six months after the Silverstone crash and everybody including the BBC wanted to speak to him.

The night before the race, BBC Radio Sport rang me saying they had been trying to get an interview with Barry but, with their usual reporter Chris Carter switching to ITV for live television coverage of the historic come back, had failed – could I help? It was not that late, but Barry and Stephanie were already in bed when I knocked on their hotel room door. I asked Barry about doing the interview and he simply picked up the bedside phone, dialled the number and said, 'Good evening, this is Barry Sheene, I believe you want to interview me.' My career with BBC radio was guaranteed.

Barry, who'd returned to Suzuki, finished a brave tenth in the 30-lap race to make all the headlines back home, though it was Spencer's victory that was the talking point worldwide. He embarked on his title chase and a civil war with his old hero Kenny Roberts, riding the new OW70 Yamaha with the disc-valve engine housed in an aluminium frame that was the trail blazer for Yamaha's success for almost the next two decades. Kenny, riding for Giacomo Agostini's Marlboro Yamaha team, had won the last three grands prix in Silverstone, Spa and Assen, closing the gap at the top of the championship to a paltry two points. The real crunch came at the penultimate round at Anderstorp in Sweden where my Jon Ekerold experience in Brno three years earlier stood me in good stead – meaning this time I kept my mouth shut.

For 29 laps Freddie was happy to prepare for a mighty last lap confrontation, showing Kenny that he was ready for the finale by shoving the front wheel of his NS 500 Honda alongside the Yamaha. The tension was mounting and mounting every lap and even the usually rather staid Swedish crowd stirred, sensing the moment that would decide the outcome of the championship had arrived. It had, catching Kenny by surprise. He pulled a massive 160mph wheelie on the back straight, which also doubled up as the runway for the local airport, before braking for the crucial right hander, but Freddie left his braking even later and there was nowhere for the Yamaha to go as Kenny turned onto the corner. Both bikes careered onto the grass at 80mph but Freddie on the inside was first back on the tarmac to take the chequered flag and 15 precious points.

This time I kept quiet, as did everybody in Parc Fermé, apart from the loser in this all American showdown who was never afraid of expressing his opinions. Kenny was not happy but shook hands with his victor on the podium and later admitted that he'd underestimated Freddie when it came to the ultimate crunch. There was an agonising four-week break before the final round at Imola in Italy and they both flew home to wait. Freddie to Shreveport, Louisiana, and Kenny to his Californian ranch in Modesto. Little did we realise, but this would be the last grand prix in Kenny's amazing career, a career that had totally revolutionised racing on and off the track for ever.

He tried every trick in the book around the 3.132-mile Imola circuit, where he'd made his European debut nine years earlier, to bow out with a fourth world title, but to do so Kenny needed to win outright, while Freddie knew second place was enough. They swapped the lead, Kenny constantly upped and then slowed the pace hoping that his team-mate Eddie Lawson would relegate Freddie to third. The Honda rider stayed calm to become the youngest ever 500cc World Champion. It was total chaos after the race when thousands of Italian fans besieged the paddock where Freddie seemed to have more problems producing a urine sample than finishing second to win the title.

In the nicest possible way, Freddie was an odd-ball among the rest of them in the adrenaline-fuelled, party-loving, law-breaking grand prix paddock. Religious and teetotal was not something you would associate with grand prix racing in the eighties. Freddie was rarely seen in the paddock when not riding and spent most of the time with his fiancée Sarie, a former Miss Louisiana, in his motorhome drinking his favourite tipple, Dr Pepper. His ties to home were strong and he would often fly in and out of Europe on Concorde. I was once summonsed to the penthouse suite of the Park Lane Hilton overlooking Hyde Park in London to meet the 'Shreveport Mafia' to discuss writing a weekly column for Freddie, which I did. He was a really easy guy to deal with, once you actually managed to get to see him. A more different person to his predecessor Kenny Roberts you could not imagine.

The 1982 World Champion Franco Uncini had been critically injured on the second lap in Assen in an appalling crash witnessed by millions of television viewers worldwide. The Italian fell from his Suzuki and was hit by the Honda of Australian grand prix debutant Wayne Gardner who could not avoid the stricken Uncini as he tried to run from the track. Such was the force of the impact his helmet split. Franco survived and raced again, and the distraught Gardner did not retire after just one grand prix – something which he'd suggested after visiting Uncini in hospital.

Safety was improving but 1983 illustrated just how much there was still to be done as tragically four 500cc riders lost their lives. Swiss rider Michel Frutschi, who a year earlier had won that boycotted race in Nogaro, was killed in Le Mans. Another Le Mans fatality was Japanese rider Iwao Ishikawa who lost his life in a practice accident. Worst was to follow on a truly appalling afternoon at the British Grand Prix at Silverstone. Former TT winner Northern Irishman Norman Brown was touring on his Suzuki with mechanical problems coming out of Stowe Corner on the fifth lap. Unsighted Swiss rider Peter Huber, tucked behind the screen of his machine and racing at full speed coming out of Stowe, crashed into the back of him and both riders were killed in a terrible accident.

The red flag at the start and finish to stop the race was not shown for two and a half laps as the critically injured riders were being treated, fighting for their lives on the side of the track. For months and even years the accusations were thrown around about why there was such a delay. Some – never proved – scandalously suggested the red flag was in the boot of somebody's car, while others accused the riders of not slowing down when the oil flags were displayed at the scene. That two riders lost their lives in appalling circumstances showed there was still so much to do to make the sport as safe as it could be.

Venezuelan Carlos Lavado won his first 250cc title for Yamaha, and on a cold Easter Sunday afternoon 18-year-old Alan Carter won the French Grand Prix at Le Mans. We had to wait another 18 years before a British rider won again in the 250cc class and at the time Carter, brother of Speedway star Kenny, was the youngest ever grand prix winner. Ángel Nieto continued his domination of the 125cc class while the 50cc class bowed out with Stefan Dörflinger winning the championship. The following year the 50s were replaced by the 80cc class.

In October 1983 IPC announced the closure of *Motor Cycle Weekly* – sales hadn't recovered from that strike three years ago. Now I was on my own, although I had a lot of help from my friends and especially Paul Fowler and John Brown plus photographer Ray Daniels and his wife Olwyn. Ray was a top class photographer but his claim to fame was that he only realised a certain Bob Dylan was living on the farm next door in his North Wales village when he spotted his face on the back of an album cover in an Aberystwyth record shop, and wondered just what farm-hand Tom was doing on the back of a record sleeve. The whole world was searching for Bob – he'd famously gone to ground – and all the time he was working on the farm next to Ray.

Without IPC's cash to fund my hotel stays, a camp bed in Ray's awning became my new home for a grand prix weekend. Paul and John helped with the hire cars and cheap flights – or in the case of Assen and Spa, ferries – to get us where we wanted to go. The newly formed Nick Harris Media Communications Company and the IPC redundancy money somehow funded the flight to Johannesburg for the opening round of the 1984 season. World Champion Freddie Spencer was on the new V-4 NSR Honda but missed the wet race after crashing when his rear wheel collapsed in practice. He helped me fly my pictures of the race back to England by hiding the films under the seat of his wheelchair at the airport customs check. The South African authorities were not so keen on films being flown out of their country before they'd seen what was on them. I wonder why?

Lawson won his first grand prix on the Yamaha to commence a serious championship challenge and Barry Sheene took his very last podium finish with a brilliant third place and fastest lap in the rain. Spencer bounced back with victory on the V-4 at Misano but injuries and Lawson's consistency blighted his chances of retaining the title. First, he missed Jarama in Spain and then the remainder of the season after winning at Spa when he was injured at a non-championship race at home in Laguna Seca. Lawson clinched the first of his four premier class titles with victory at Anderstorp with the impressive Randy Mamola second after wins at Assen, Silverstone and Mugello on the Honda despite missing the first couple of races. Barry Sheene announced his retirement and moved to Australia to start a new and equally impressive career in television. Frenchman Christian Sarron won the 250cc title with second place in Anderstorp. Nieto continued his total domination of the smaller classes with his thirteenth world title, winning the 125cc class and Dörflinger was crowned the very first 80cc World Champion.

One big announcement in the summer of that year did so much to help grand prix motorcycle racing come out of the dark ages. Whatever other harm their products were doing, Rothmans' title sponsorship of the Honda grand prix and Honda Britain race teams in 1985 did my prospects no harm whatsoever, as they invited me to become their media manager.

Their first major contribution was massive, when they and Honda persuaded Spencer to chase both the 250 and 500cc titles in same 1985 season, a feat that had never been achieved even by legends Hailwood, Agostini, Redman or Surtees. It was a massive ask but a fully fit Spencer was up for it. In scorching conditions at the opening round in Kyalami he won the 250cc race, just had time to gulp down a few litres of water, change his leathers and return to the track to finish second to Lawson in the punishing 30-lap 500cc race around the 2.5-mile circuit.

In Mugello he stood on the top step of the podium after winning the 500cc race just as the 250cc machines were being wheeled to the grid. Second placed Lawson turned to him after 'The Star-Spangled Banner' anthem and said, 'Rather you than me.' Freddie won the 250cc race to become the first 250 and 500 winner since Jarno Saarinen 12 years earlier. The doubles continued and there was nothing Lawson or Yamaha could do to stop him. He finished fourth in appalling conditions at Silverstone to complete the first part of the deal: win the 250cc title. One week later the deal was completed when he won the 500cc Swedish Grand Prix at Anderstorp in much more pleasant conditions. Little did we, Honda, Rothmans and especially Freddie realise that this would be the very last time he stood on a grand prix podium.

It was an amazing feat in a 12-round championship. It was a feat that never has and probably never will be repeated. The 250cc World Champion Christian Sarron finished a brilliant third behind Lawson in the 500cc class which included victory at Hockenheim. Fausto Gresini took his first 125cc title with Dörflinger retaining the 80cc crown.

In addition to covering the grands prix for BBC radio and various magazines, I was having a ball running the Rothmans media service for the Honda Britain team. What a great crowd of talented riders. At the TT I worked with the legendary Joey Dunlop, at the British and Formula One Championships with the likes of Roger Marshall and Roger Burnett, and I covered the World

Trials Championship with the so very talented Steve Saunders. This was also the year I first met quite the scariest man I've ever worked with: Brian Kreisky, the boss of Video Vision, who tragically was killed in an air crash in 2000. Five people died when his plane crashed just after taking off from Blackbushe aerodrome. Four of those killed were from his family, including his brother.

His company, which was then based in Bedfordshire but later in the Isle of Man for obvious reasons, produced all the videos and films for Rothmans. Brian could and probably did pick more than one fight in a phone box and he scared me and a good few others. Going to his studios to voice over the videos was a nightmare as he would shout, swear and then argue all day over a £5 request for petrol money.

Then Rothmans asked me to go to the Belgian round of the World Trials Championship near Liège to help Brian with his filming. It was my very first job actually in front of the cameras and I was nervous tramping through the mud from section to section. Brian gave me a hard time and asked to retake a piece to camera 12 times before he was satisfied, but we got through it. He then insisted I flew back to Luton from Liège with him and his team although my car was parked at Heathrow. I didn't think it was the time to argue. He employed a pilot to fly his twin-engine plane and all was going well until the landing lights appeared on the Luton runway.

Brian then insisted on taking over the controls to land the plane at this busy airport and I don't think he had a pilot's licence. But – with eyes shut – again, I didn't think it was the appropriate moment to ask.

Brian was a legend in the grand prix paddock and employed some very talented people who produced superb videos. He really was the pioneer of the television and video coverage which began what we see today. He certainly didn't mind making enemies getting what he wanted though. I was walking through San Francisco airport one morning after the grand prix at Laguna Seca with Brian and his team when this guy raced over, shouting 'Brian Kreisky! I've found you at last! And I've been waiting for this moment for years!' He then started to attack Brian before being pulled off by some of the burlier cameramen. When Brian was knocked over in the Salzburgring paddock by a police motorcycle he did not get, and surely did not expect, too much sympathy. In fact, a cheer went up when the news spread.

I sat in the commentary box opposite pit lane at the back of the Jarama grandstand for the opening grand prix of 1986 and nothing seemed to have changed. Spencer was leading around the twisty two-mile circuit on the outskirts of Madrid. Out of the blue on lap 15 he pulled into pit lane and retired and that was almost that in his career as a grand prix rider and three times World Champion. His new team-mate on the V-4 Honda

Wayne Gardner won his first grand prix and we were told Freddie had retired suffering from tendonitis in his wrist and would return soon. He re-appeared at the fourth race of the season in Austria but finished a lowly sixteenth and then flew back home to America never to re-appear for the remainder of the year. Not even Honda really understood what had happened and would prepare his machines ready for him to arrive in the paddock, but he never did. This prompted the brilliant Paul Fowler 'Wish you were here' caption to the postcard-style picture in *Motor Cycle News* of the team and bikes ready for Freddie's arrival. I've spoken to Freddie many times about his disappearance and he insists it was the injured wrist that kept him away, but I wonder if the mental and physical strain of that double-winning year finally took its toll. At least Ray Daniels didn't find him working on the farm next door.

Gardner did a sterling job in the absence of his celebrated team-mate but, despite further wins in Assen and Silverstone, had to settle for second place in the championship. The immaculate Lawson clinched his second 500cc crown with victory in Sweden, his sixth win of the season which he made seven at the final round. The party to celebrate the title in a rather smart eco-style hotel in the forest next to a lake near the Anderstorp circuit resulted in letters of apology and compensation payments. All of the furniture and a good number of the staff ended up in the swimming pool, which left no room for swimming.

Kenny Roberts could not stay away and managed a new Lucky Strike Yamaha team spearheaded by Randy Mamola who finished third in the championship, including a victory in Spa. With Spencer out of the way, Carlos Lavado regained his 250cc title. Luca Cadalora clinched the 125cc crown with Jorge Martínez's second place on the Derbi in the final round bringing him the 80cc title. Cheered on by his so very enthusiastic heart surgeon father, Ian McConnachie won the 80cc race at Silverstone to become the only British solo winner at his home grand prix until its departure to Donington the next year.

After 21 years of grand prix racing which brought him a staggering 13 world titles, Spaniard Ángel Nieto retired. A legend back home in Spain, he'd dominated the smaller classes for two decades and was second only to Agostini in World Championship titles. He was tough and uncompromising on the track and lived the life of a grand prix rider off it. Also, being very superstitious he would never refer to his 13 world titles but always say '12 plus 1'. Tragically his luck ran out when he was killed in a road traffic accident a couple of years ago. Spain and the grand prix paddock mourned the loss of a truly great champion.

Have I Got News for You
1987–1989

FOR 38 YEARS, riders had had to push start their machines to fire up the engines to begin a grand prix race. Some sat side-saddle, rather like royalty riding a horse, cocking the leg onto the footrest once the engine fired into life. Others just pushed and pushed, jumping on while hoping they had enough speed to interest the engine. Whatever the method, it was a pretty haphazard way to start a grand prix and in 1987, at last, clutch starts were introduced in all classes.

Clutch starts were one of many changes in 1987. Grand prix racing returned to Japan after a 20-year absence, Jerez in Spain staged its first grand prix, the British Grand Prix switched from Silverstone to Donington Park, the new Brno purpose-built track replacing the old road circuit was ready for action and Brazil staged its first ever grand prix in the party city of Goiânia. Grand prix racing was in a healthy state – there were now 15 grands prix compared with just 11 in 1986.

I went with John Brown on my first ever trip to Japan for the opening round at Suzuka. We were treated like royalty from the moment we arrived. The coach that picked us up from Nagoya airport to take us to our hotel in Yokkaichi City had pretty lace curtains. The back seat packed with McDonald's meals. I think that was the only food the Japanese thought Westerners would eat. We'd never met a coach driver wearing a smart peaked cap. The hotel was tiny, and nobody spoke a word of English, but the staff smiled and bowed as they organised a phone for Mr Harris and beer for Mr Brown. The media centre at the circuit was in a giant sports hall in the massive theme park that surrounded the track. When we departed in a fleet of coaches on Monday afternoon after the grand prix, everybody from the circuit plus a magnificent brass band came out to wish us *bon voyage*.

The icing on the cake for JB and me would have been a British winner and it so nearly came about. Niall Mackenzie qualified in pole position on his Honda factory debut. Niall was a very talented rider who, after a distinguished grand prix career, returned home to win three British Championships. I'd first met him when he rode for the Silverstone Armstrong team in 1985. It was my first PR contract after redundancy to promote Niall and fellow Scotsman Donnie McLeod in the British team run by Chas Mortimer and financed by the Silverstone circuit. One of my first tasks was to inform the legendary and imposing boss of Silverstone Jimmy Brown that both Niall and Donnie may have to miss the long-planned and lavish launch because they'd been arrested for fighting. What I didn't tell him was that it was for actually fighting each other at an awards dinner, but they made it in the end despite heavy snow. Unfortunately, Niall crashed out of third place on the last lap of a damp Japanese race. Mamola won from Gardner with World Champion Lawson retiring after pulling in to change tyres.

Back in that dusty Jarama commentary box on the outskirts of Madrid reporting on the thirteenth round of the 1987 championship, the words I wanted to hear rattled through my earphones all the way from the BBC studio in London. The instructions from producer Derek Mitchell as usual were plain, simple and to the point – 'Book your tickets for Brazil.' I needed no second invitation. Gardner had just finished fourth in the Portuguese Grand Prix and with his nearest championship rival Mamola finishing second, the title could be decided at the penultimate round in Goiânia. My 'all expenses paid' trip was so much down to the efforts of Gardner out on track and the now disgraced radio presenter Stuart Hall back in the studio.

I'd first met Wayne in 1981 at Daytona where he was riding the four-stroke Moriwaki Kawasaki before he decided to come to England from Australia with girlfriend Donna to seek fame, fortune and ultimately the World Championship. In those early days they would often have to sleep in the back of their old Austin 1800 and eat plenty of fish and chips. Wayne was not only very quick but hard as nails. Perhaps not the style and immaculate smooth lines of Lawson but a frightening determination to succeed at any cost, usually involving pain and his own personal safety. He needed all that speed and determination as he wrestled and fought his way on the re-vamped NSR Honda to head the championship after wins in Jerez, Monza, Salzburg, Rijeka, Anderstorp and Brno.

Thanks to the considerable efforts of Motorsport Producer Pat Thornton, BBC radio gave grand prix racing on two wheels the airtime it deserved. Stuart Hall and Wayne hit it off immediately after their first post-grand prix chat when Wayne described how he'd injured his wrist arm wrestling on the ferry to Assen. Lost in translation, the circuit doctor prescribed two suppositories to ease the pain, which caused far more problems in the race than the original injury. Every week there would be a different story. Hall just loved it and soon was telling listeners about 'my boy Wayne'.

I had no idea where Goiânia was, but two weeks before the grand prix it made the world headlines when a radiation leak caused four deaths. All that seemed forgotten when I flew in via Rio and Brasilia. Nearly one and a half million people lived in the sprawling city in western central Brazil. The majority of them enjoyed a good party and we were ready to accept their hospitality.

The Miss Brazilian Grand Prix competition was going down a storm with the paddock *funcionários* sat around the swimming pool. It was the night before practice got underway around the 2.383-mile circuit and the caipirinhas were flowing as the contestants took to the cat walk. The announcer was perplexed as he introduced each contestant by name because last up was somebody who was not on his list. Blonde hair and plenty of red lipstick was the only clue. The cat walk was completed with a little bow and then a customary grin. He may have been fighting for the most prestigious prize in the sport over the next three days, but Randy Mamola could never resist a challenge. Off came the wig, the place went crazy and the next morning Randy went about the business of trying to win the world title after finishing second on three previous occasions.

I was determined to get Wayne live on air immediately after the race whatever the result. I'd waited two days for anybody from the national broadcaster to arrive at the circuit. They finally turned up on the Saturday morning and assured me there was a line in the grandstand opposite the pits and podium and that it would be linked to London the next day. My enquiry about a microphone brought a blank stare. Apparently, a microphone had not been requested but at a price they might be able to hire me one. After the cash had duly been handed over, a microphone miraculously appeared, and I had to take their word on the line to London the next day.

The next problem was getting Wayne from the podium – if he finished on it – and up to the commentary point opposite. Speaking to the right person in these situations and especially in South America was crucial. I got lucky and picked the chief of police who assured me Wayne would be escorted to my commentary position immediately after the podium ceremony. I certainly believed him because he had the air of somebody who liked to be obeyed when he issued instructions. The chief was true to his word, as was Wayne.

The boy from Wollongong won the race to become the first Australian 500cc World Champion. With his part of the deal complete, Wayne duly arrived at my commentary position with the World Championship winning t-shirt over his leathers and stinking of champagne, escorted by a large contingent of heavily armed police. Part two completed and I finished my part of the deal when an exuberant Stuart Hall was the first person in the world to interview the new World Champion. Then the celebrations began before the mightily hung over paddock flew off to Argentina for the final round and I flew back to London with the job done.

Lawson won the race in Buenos Aires but Randy Mamola's second place in front of Gardner brought him the runner-up spot in the championship for the fourth time. Toni Mang won his third 250cc title and Gresini almost made it a full house of 125cc grands prix victories, winning the first ten but crashing in the final round at Jarama. Jorge Martínez retained his 80cc title with victory at Donington after winning six of the opening seven races.

Times were constantly changing on the track, but off it the sport was still very much in the dark ages, especially in terms of the media. The time for change had arrived and, rather like the riders and the threat of World Series, it was down to us to do something about it. New big sponsors such as Rothmans, Marlboro and Lucky Strike demanded such a change. We simply could not continue in the same way.

Two years previously, I'd stood in an old army tent on the outskirts of a Swedish aerodrome phoning over the story proclaiming Freddie Spencer as the only rider to ever win both the 250 and 500cc Championships in the same season. It was one of those regular very long nights. That very first sentence of your carefully constructed copy, dictated down the phone, was a true indication how long the night was going to be. If asked 'how do you spell that?' by the copytaker, when starting the opening paragraph with the words 'Freddie Spencer', you knew any thought of food or a beer that night had to be put to bed.

In many ways, that historic Swedish Grand Prix at Anderstorp in 1985 was the start of the media revolution. It had little to do with technology but much more to do with a growing understanding of just how important the media was for the sport. Big sponsors, mostly from the tobacco industry, arrived to pour millions into grand prix motorcycle racing and, rightly, they demanded some reward for their massive investment.

Up until then, a lack of facilities and in many cases care about the media made grand prix reporting and photography a constant battle. Around 50 permanent journalists and photographers would travel to each round in various place in Europe, until Argentina and South Africa joined in the early eighties. Passes had to be applied for at each individual grand prix and there were always problems. The media centre was usually the smallest and darkest building in the grand prix paddock while in places like Anderstorp an old flapping army tent was our home for the weekend.

You could put up with all these inconveniences though, as long as you got access to a phone that worked. Without a working phone you were struggling, completely stymied in getting your reports, gossip and features into the hands of the totally unsympathetic chief sub editor back in London. He just wanted the copy to pull apart and criticise and was never the tiniest bit interested in issues with phone lines – just file the copy. Sending BBC radio reports without a phone was a virtually impossible task.

Getting that copy back to the beloved chief sub was done in two ways. Early copy from practice, qualifying plus features and gossip were dispatched by telex. An operator would sit in the media centre and duly type your copy into a machine that would produce a tape with holes in. The contents from this unreadable tape were sent down the line to London where it was miraculously turned back to copy. The only way to get the results back to the office was also by telex, but only after you had painstakingly typed out every single result from grands prix that sometimes had six classes.

After the races you had to find, beg, steal or borrow a precious phone with a connected international line plus an operator at the end of it who understood what reverse the charges meant. You then had to make the big decision either to stay at the circuit and risk the phone line or go back to your hotel, where they could never understand why you were on the phone for around three hours on a Sunday night. At least in some hostelries they would provide a sandwich or even a beer to gulp down while explaining the complexities of the 50cc race to a bored copytaker at the other end. What a thankless task it must have been for those copytakers, spending their precious hours on a Sunday night listening to our drivel. The regulars were great and could type almost as fast as you spoke the 2,000-odd words. The newcomers could make the difference of a couple of hours. It was pot luck.

Finding that precious phone was my number one priority of the weekend. At Rijeka in what was then Yugoslavia, the only way to get phone lines into the circuit was to divert them from local houses. The whole operation and most importantly allocation of the lines was down to a local lady who spent a great deal of the grand prix weekend sampling the delights of a particular local brew. The result? Total chaos. Even when you managed to get a phone, the lines were often blocked by somebody, usually a relative, phoning the number to speak to somebody at their house where the original line came from.

There were no press conferences during the weekend at any circuit. The only way to talk to riders was to find them in the paddock or grab a word with the successful ones before and after they jumped on the podium. It turned into a game which both parties enjoyed. Eddie Lawson was the master and you had to be smart to catch him. One journalist actually lay down on the steps of his motorhome making it impossible not to stop and speak between the laughter.

Matters were reaching breaking point, and when the riders formed the International Road Racing Teams

Association, the media followed suit with the International Road Racing Press Association. Led by two doyens of the sport, Dennis Noyes and Hans van Loozenoord, there was even talk of delaying the start of a race by putting a line of desks across the start line to highlight our unhappiness. Revolution was in the air, but this time it was the tobacco companies that led the charge.

At that first Japanese Grand Prix a gentleman turned up at the media centre with something called a fax machine. Mr Fax, as we quickly called him, could not convince us that if we put in a piece of typed paper in his box of tricks it would appear at the other end in London. We tried it and then rang the office – phones were no problem in Japan – and Mr Fax had been telling the truth all along. No more typing out the results and no more tape with holes in it. We were on our way.

At the same Japanese Grand Prix, I remember there was no hot water available, which meant the photographers could not develop their films into prints. One enterprising snapper used scalding hot cans of tea from the many hot drinks machines. The prints appeared fine although smelt a bit strange. Either you developed your films at the circuit or gave the journalist returning to London a bag of films which he got developed back in the office. The journalist then chose the pictures needed for the newspaper from a contact sheet. Getting that bag of films from the photographer before the end of the last race in time to catch the ferry or plane home could be a problem. I remember having a bag of films thrown at me across the track from the inside of La Source hairpin at Spa-Francorchamps, dodging the sidecars competing in the last race of the day.

After that final European Grand Prix of the season in Jarama, I sat down with Iain Mackay – 11 years after that first meeting in Misano – and his business partner Debbie Van Zom to plan the media revolution (and also make a few extra quid). We approached David Beck at Rothmans with our plans and he agreed.

The first European race of the 1988 season was again at Jarama. It could not have been a greater contrast with the previous year. We set up our own press centre fitted with phones and fax machines. As the newly instated 'media manager' for the team, I hosted pre-event and post-qualifying and race press conferences with the Rothmans Honda riders from 500 and 250cc classes. We produced press releases in English, French and the mother tongue of the venue and of course provided proper hospitality. We organised one-to-one interviews with the riders and flew important media personnel to the circuit to help spread the word. After each race we dispatched – by post on Monday afternoon – race reports and previews of the next event plus colour slides and black and white prints to hundreds of major media outlets throughout the world.

It was like a bomb had dropped. Of course, the media loved it, being treated like human beings and having facilities to help them do their job. Other big sponsors soon followed suit and the official media centres at the circuits became sad, empty places. The organisers and the FIM knew the game was up and to their credit instigated and paid for changes. Rather like those safety changes for the riders, it didn't happen overnight, but I smiled and thought back to those dark, taxing days when hosting Marc Márquez's title-winning press conference in Valencia 30 years down the road.

Six hundred journalists, photographers and cameramen had descended on the Spanish circuit from all over the world to witness and report the race. For well over an hour, still dressed in his leathers, Marc told the story of the race and then the championship, first in English and then Spanish. His words and pictures were beamed around the world in seconds with millions of people worldwide watching, listening and reading how he'd won his fifth MotoGP world title. Not one journalist asked him how he spelt his name.

Today, instant access to all information wherever you are in the world is just part of everyday life. Whether it's pictures, video or just old-fashioned copy, it's available to the world's hungry media 24 hours a day. Dorna have embraced all this modern technology to provide a great media service, but have still managed to personalise it by providing opportunities for all journalists with access. There are at least five press conferences every grand prix weekend, exciting pre-event activities and a permanent pass system that cuts out so much hassle for the MotoGP regulars. The teams have followed suit with media briefings at the end of every day and there is no more chasing around to find the likes of Eddie Lawson.

So much has changed in the three decades since those days. Even if, fundamentally, in racing it's still all about winning and in the media it's still all about filing that copy or those photographs on time. Perhaps it's not as good fun as it used to be, but we all tend to look back through rose-tinted spectacles or in the riders' case, goggles and visors. Old principles never die.

Can you imagine – my opening assignment for Rothmans was to fly to Australia for the very first time and spend ten days with the new World Champion? I remember the impact Barry Sheene had made on the British public and media with those world titles in the seventies, but nothing prepared me for the impact Wayne and Donna had made in Australia. Pat Cash may have won Wimbledon that year, but Wayne was voted Sportsman of the Year in Australia. The Nine Network had brokered a deal to show all the grands prix live the following year and Phillip Island, better known for its penguins, was going to stage the very first Australian Grand Prix.

I had a wonderful time filming a documentary about the team at Calder Park. We surprised an old school friend of mine from Cumnor, Dave Fuller, and his family, turning up unannounced with Wayne at their house just down the road from Wollongong. Dave was surprised enough when I got out of the car, but when Wayne followed, he and in particular his sons were completely speechless. My first night in Wollongong was quite an eye opener when, on our visit to the North Gong pub, two ladies fell out of the door in front of us to continue a fight in the middle of the road. The whole trip in fact was a complete eye opener, with Wayne and Donna producing a Kylie Minogue/Jason Donavon style persona throughout the vast country.

Unfortunately, when Wayne returned to the track in 1988 it was not so easy. While World Champion Gardner fought a personal and often painful duel with the brutally quick but equally out of control Honda in 1988, Steady Eddie got on with the task of regaining the world title for Yamaha. The American riders had always been telling us that the finest corner in the world was the corkscrew bend at Laguna Seca in California and, as always, we described their claims as bullshit. We found out for ourselves that they were absolutely correct for once when the circuit just inland from Monterey on the Pacific coast hosted its first grand prix. To put it in a truly American way, the Corkscrew was awesome, with its blind approach before dropping off the edge of the planet downhill left, right, left.

Lawson won the race for the home crowd and six more grands prix wins did the trick. He claimed his third 500cc title after finishing second to Gardner in Brno, but it was the new kids on the block who drew the eye. Kevin Schwantz won the opening round in Japan riding the V-4 Suzuki. His bitter rival back home in the States Wayne Rainey won in Donington and Australian Kevin Magee took his sole grand prix victory at Jarama. Mamola brought the Italian Cagiva factory their first podium in Spa and sadly Freddie Spencer, beset by injuries, announced his retirement, although he changed his mind.

The highlight of the year was a fantastic four-rider battle in the French Grand Prix at Paul Ricard. To their credit, the BBC even delayed their coverage of a Formula One Grand Prix to continue with my commentary of a race that probably cost Gardner at least a fighting chance of retaining the title. He was leading at the start of the last lap when he slowed with a piston problem. Just 0.46 seconds covered Lawson, Sarron and Schwantz when they crossed the line with Gardner fourth.

The highlight of my new role with Rothmans was getting Wayne on Terry Wogan's much watched live show on BBC One. Immediately after the first day of practice ended for the British Grand Prix at Donington we flew by helicopter to Battersea helipad in London. A car rushed us to the theatre on Shepherd's Bush Green. We raced into the studio where they initially thought I was Wayne, who was then interviewed by Wogan while I sampled the delights of the green room. Back in the car, the helicopter took us down the Thames as the sun was setting and landed back in the car park at Donington. It was all over in less than four hours. Wayne got back to practice on Saturday morning and qualified on pole in the afternoon.

Sito Pons came out on top in the all-Spanish battle with Joan Garriga for the 250cc Championship. Toni Mang announced his retirement and Jorge Martínez continued his and Derbi's domination of the smaller classes with both 80 and 125cc world titles.

My phone rang early one December morning in 1988. A furious Wayne Gardner was on the line and very angry. He demanded whether I knew that Honda had signed Eddie Lawson and that he would ride a privately entered V-4 in a team sponsored by Rothmans and run by the legendary Erv Kanemoto in 1989? I certainly knew nothing about it but soon did.

A week before Christmas, photographer Malcolm Bryan and I were on the plane to Los Angeles to spend a secret couple of days with Eddie in his home town of Upland. I was nervous after witnessing Eddie's playful contempt for the media on far too many occasions, but he was brilliant. The perfect host who could not have been more helpful. Requests for pictures of the World Champion running alongside a giant freight train in the desert, driving across the salt flats and posing outside his magnificent new house were no problem. We went out to dinner with his friends who honestly really didn't know what Eddie did for a living. He told them he raced motorbikes but nothing about winning grands prix and world titles. In Europe he was a sporting superstar; back home in Upland a mate who liked to go out for a beer.

There was a double bitter pill for Wayne Gardner to swallow. The 1989 season ahead was going to be difficult and he had a new team-mate in the factory team. Mick Doohan was a tough, raw youngster from the Gold Coast who had impressed Honda in national races and some wild card appearances in the World Superbike Championship. They saw him as the future and how right their predictions turned out to be. Wayne's old crew chief Jerry Burgess was assigned to teach Doohan the ropes. The atmosphere in the garage was tense and I was caught in the middle. Wayne, the former World Champion and hero of Australia, understandably not wanting to help Mick take over his mantle. Rookie Mick was desperate to learn and never afraid to speak his mind, thinking we spent too much time promoting Wayne.

Two other riders who would have a massive bearing on the next decade fought a race-long battle at the opening round in Suzuka. Schwantz came out on top in a very personal fight with Rainey, who messed up his last lap calculations. Lawson finished third on his Honda debut with Gardner fourth after a hairy ride in which the Australian bruised one of his testicles so badly after contact with the tank there was talk of amputation. Two weeks later thoughts of such a painful operation were a very distant memory as Gardner's legendary status increased tenfold back home.

Phillip Island is a holiday island 90 miles down the Victorian coast from Melbourne. The famous penguin parade when hundreds of penguins waddle out of the sea onto the beach at dusk every night and the surf beaches attract thousands of tourists from all over the world, but it had never experienced anything like this. They love their sporting heroes in Australia and the island was almost sinking under the sheer volume of fans supporting one of their own. This was the very first Australian Grand Prix just two weeks after that opening round in Japan and Gardner – sore testicle or not – was expected to win. He did just that. The 2.765-mile Bob Barnard-designed circuit high on the cliffs above the Bass Strait was built for grand prix motorcycles to race on and how they lapped it up.

Gardner finally won a titanic battle with Rainey, Sarron and Magee and first the island and then the country went completely crazy. My sister-in-law at the time was a senior nursing sister in Perth. When Wayne crossed the line to win the 30-lap race, she was the first over the fence onto the track to celebrate. She was the first of many.

Incredibly, once again Barry Sheene had not forgotten me. Australian television viewers loved him, and he was the obvious choice as front man for the new Channel Nine *Wide World of Sports* coverage of grand prix motorcycle racing. He told them that 'Nickel Arse' was the only person to commentate on the 125 and 250cc races and so I got the job. Working with Barry, who commentated on the 500cc races with the legendary Darrell Eastlake and Formula One World Champion Alan Jones, was an education. I had to constantly keep my wits about me. They told me wrong times for crucial meetings with the producer, informed parking attendants I had the wrong pass and tried to drive our hire car high up the wall of the single-track tunnel that led to the paddock.

It had been a truly amazing weekend in Phillip Island, but grand prix racing has a nasty habit of kicking you in the teeth when you least expect it. Just seven days and thousands of miles later I stood on a desk in the tiny press room opposite the pits at Laguna Seca to announce that Wayne Gardner had broken his leg. He'd crashed in the third round of the championship and worse was to follow. American Bubba Shobert sustained career-ending head injuries after a collision with Kevin Magee on the slowing down lap after the race had finished.

Rainey gained revenge on Schwantz at Laguna Seca with a win. Steady Eddie was getting to grips with the Honda with another podium finish. However, it was put into perspective when I rang the BBC who told me they did not require a voice piece because everything was focused on the appalling Hillsborough football stadium disaster in Sheffield.

Lawson grabbed his first Honda victory at the opening European round in Jerez but together with the other championship contenders sat out the next round in Misano. The leading riders refused to go out because of safety concerns caused by heavy rain and the original race was stopped. The race was re-run and local rider Pierfrancesco Chili raced and won. Lawson sat on the pit wall signalling Chili every lap with a single finger that did not indicate he was in first place.

Freddie Spencer had been lured out of retirement by Yamaha team boss Giacomo Agostini to replace Lawson. He properly retired halfway through the season to be replaced by Luca Cadalora. It was an anticlimactic end to an amazing career. The crux of the championship came once again at Anderstorp three rounds from the finish. Rainey crashed two laps from the end fighting with Lawson for the lead. Lawson duly won and finished second behind Schwantz two weeks later in Brno. He arrived back in Goiânia for the final round with a 15.5 point advantage over Rainey after half points had been awarded in a rain-affected Spa race that had twice re-started.

If anything, Goiânia was even crazier than it had been during my first visit two years previously. Once again it prepared to celebrate with a new World Champion and Eddie came up with the goods. He finished second behind Schwantz to claim his fourth world title and, even more significantly, become the only rider to have won successive 500cc world titles on separate machinery. Media shy Eddie did us proud before an evening of celebrations that perhaps only Goiânia could host.

BBC Radio 4 had asked me to come on the Monday morning sports bulletin on the *Today* programme. The Harris family had grown up listening to the *Today* programme with the legendary Presenter Jack de Manio, my late dad's absolute favourite. Of course, I agreed.

The only place to celebrate a world title was the Zoom Zoom club. The owner would fire a gun into the ceiling to get the proceedings underway which usually went on until well after breakfast time. It was only when dancing stripped to the waist and full of the local brew, I realised that I'd messed up the time differences between Brazil and London. I was due to answer the phone call from

London in my hotel room in less than ten minutes' time. Still stripped to the waist and accompanied by Niall Mackenzie I ran and stumbled down the main street between the honking cars. As I reached my hotel room the phone was ringing. I answered in my best possible BBC voice, although perhaps a little breathless. I know my dad would have smiled.

Sito Pons retained his 250cc crown at Donington. American wild card John Kocinski won the first and third rounds but switched to the 500cc class halfway through the year. Safety concerns reared their ugly head when Venezuelan Iván Palazzese was killed in a multi-rider first-lap crash at Hockenheim. The organisers failed to stop the race immediately and were desperately lucky not more lives were lost. Álex Crivillé became the youngest 125cc World Champion riding the JJ Cobas. Fellow Spaniard Manuel Herreros took the 80cc crown without actually winning a race.

Pilgrim Fathers
1990–1992

EDDIE LAWSON RACED past Mat Oxley and me over the rise at Laguna Seca at around 150mph before braking hard for the tight hairpin at the bottom. Or at least the World Champion thought he was braking, but when he pulled hard on the front brake lever absolutely nothing happened. The lever pulled straight back to the handlebars. Changing down through the gearbox and stamping on the rear brake did little to reduce the speed. As the Yamaha raced over the grass towards the rapidly looming straw bales, Eddie jumped ship. He crashed feet first into the bales and lay there.

In front of us, at the very crest of the rise, the marshals didn't seem to be reacting. We screamed at them to wave their yellow flags to warn others racing over the rise that a stricken rider lay at the bottom of the hill, surrounded by scattered straw bales. But they shouted back that they had received no instructions on their radios. It was time to take matters into our own hands and Mat, a TT winner and great journalist, grabbed a yellow flag, started waving and the riders slowed. A potential disaster had been averted.

It was Friday afternoon at the second grand prix of the 1990 season. It was a crash that had a massive impact on the championship outcome and illustrated that still more could be done to improve safety. It was discovered that his brake pads had popped out, leaving him no front brake whatsoever. Eddie missed the next six races with a crushed right heel.

It was time for Eddie's apprentice to step up to the plate and he did just that. After proving he could win the world title on a Honda the previous year, Eddie had returned to the Kenny Roberts Yamaha team where Wayne Rainey was his team-mate.

Californian Rainey was on fire and all those battles with Schwantz and that early dirt-track training prepared him for the ultimate test. With Lawson absent, Rainey dominated the championship to claim his first world title when he won in Brno. In a faultless year he only finished off the podium once when he retired with front-brake problems in Hungary. The champion won seven grands prix and nobody could match him, not even his bitter rival Schwantz on the Suzuki. The hard-riding Texan won five grands prix, but injury problems blighted a serious challenge. Doohan was getting to grips with the fearsome factory Honda and won his first ever grand prix at the first one to be held at the Hungaroring on the outskirts of Budapest. Team-mate Gardner won in Jerez and brought Australia to a halt once again, beating Doohan by less than a second in a very personal victory at Phillip Island.

Frenchman Christian Sarron retired after a 15-year career that included a 250cc world title and a 500cc grand prix win, while that typical Aussie Kevin Magee was side-lined for the whole season after crashing at the second round in Laguna. The American domination spread to the 250cc class where John Kocinski fought off the challenge of Spaniard Carlos Cardús to claim the title. Loris Capirossi restored some European pride, becoming the youngest ever World Champion when he clinched the 125cc title after a last round shoot out with Hans Spaan and Stefan Prein. It was an amazing final round where the Italian riders ganged up to help the teenager and Spaan and Prein never had a chance. They celebrated in the pizzeria on Phillip Island by naming a pizza after the new World Champion.

The magnificent Spa-Francorchamps circuit, which had been there right from the start in 1949, staged its last grand prix in 1990. Two particular corners at this legendary Belgian venue just could not be changed to make it safer and, sadly but correctly, Rainey won its last grand prix and grand prix racing never returned to Spa. Rijeka, another stalwart from those early road circuit days, also staged its last grand prix on the new purpose-built track.

Eddie Lawson certainly never could be accused of making racing boring. In 1991, the four times World Champion left Yamaha and joined the under-achieving Italian Cagiva team who produced the most gorgeous-looking motorcycles on the starting grid. The 250cc Champion Kocinski gave the title back to the Europeans and joined Rainey at Yamaha. Rainey retained his title, but it was an awful lot closer than the previous year with Doohan and Schwantz pushing him to the limit.

It started in Suzuka where just over half a second separated Schwantz, Doohan, Rainey and Kocinski when they crossed the line to set a benchmark for the season. Rainey fought back and won at the second grand prix at the new Eastern Creek circuit in Sydney. The success of the Australian Grand Prix and Gardner had produced such a massive interest in the sport, it was thought that a more accessible circuit next to a big city would benefit everybody. It didn't and after six years the Australian Grand Prix returned to its rightful home on Phillip Island. The location, the facilities and the weather may not have matched Eastern Creek but when you have the greatest motorcycle racing track in the world overlooking the Bass Strait, such advantages count for little.

Rainey won for the third time at Laguna Seca but Doohan took over the lead in the championship for the first time when he brought Honda success in Jerez. Lawson gave Cagiva their first dry weather podium at

Misano before an epic duel that started back home in the States continued at the Transatlantic Races in England and then exploded onto the grand prix scene.

Quite simply, Rainey and Schwantz really did hate each other right from the start. They clashed every time they met. It's rumoured that Schwantz even tried to date Rainey's sister just to upset his rival but, on the track, Rainey held the upper hand with the world title that Schwantz wanted so so badly. They fought a ferocious duel at the frighteningly fast Hockenheim circuit which was only decided by 0.016 seconds in favour of Schwantz in front of 150,000 fans who certainly got their money's worth. Schwantz continued the charge with a record-breaking win in Assen, but Rainey held firm to retain his title with third place in the penultimate round at Le Mans, ironically won by Schwantz. In the end it was the consistent Doohan that pushed Schwantz back to third in the championship.

Both Rainey and Schwantz missed the final round with injuries sustained in testing when grand prix racing ventured into pastures new – Malaysia. The 2.178-mile Shah Alam circuit was close to the old Kuala Lumpur international airport that had almost been destroyed by a fire a few months earlier. I really did not know what to expect but immediately we all loved KL. The food, the nightlife and the friendly people were wonderful, but Shah Alam did offer a few worries for us Westerners.

They told me – although I assure you, I never went in and checked – that a python was asleep in the rafters when they opened the press office.

Our office was an old shipping container; the lack of flushing loos was a major problem for anybody who'd overloaded on that spicy laksa, while it was rumoured that the marshals would not help riders at a certain corner because the undergrowth was full of poisonous snakes. I survived, but only just, especially with a spicy-food induced issue which had to be solved by an injection at the medical centre. Kocinski grabbed his first 500cc grand prix win while he was replaced by Luca Cadalora as 250cc World Champion with Capirossi making it an Italian double when he retained his 125cc crown.

I will not pretend that I understood and really cared that much about what was going on behind the scenes. As long as the bikes were out there racing and I got paid, I was happy. I didn't sign up all those years ago to be a political correspondent, although even to me it was obvious that plenty was going on. At a chaotic press conference at Jerez in 1991 a Spanish company called Dorna Promoción del Deporte organised a presentation to the media to explain why their $30 million bid to buy the television rights to grands prix racing had been accepted by the FIM. Dorna had little or no experience in motorsport but, looking back, it was a pivotal moment both for the sport and for me.

The young Spanish translator struggled under the weight of questions to the non-English-speaking Dorna representatives. At one point, Dorna's director of television and marketing Jaume Roures slammed his fist on the desk in front of him. We assumed he was fed up with the anti-Dorna questions from the floor, only to find out later the real reason. He'd not heard a word of the press conference because throughout he'd been plugged into his tiny portable radio listening to the commentary of the Cádiz–Barcelona football match just down the road in Cádiz. His team, Barcelona, had to win to become league champions, but his outburst came when Cádiz scored their third goal of four. Not the best start for Dorna, but under the inspirational leadership of Carmelo Ezpeleta they also bought the rights to the championship, established a working relationship with the FIM and later gave me a job that most people would die for. Perhaps I should have paid more attention, but all my efforts were taken up with reporting events on the track and there were plenty.

Early in 1992 I was summoned to the Dorna headquarters in Barcelona. It was in the same location as the vast empire today, but it then consisted of just one basement with a few editing machines and an office above. They offered me a contract to do voice overs on the highlights after each grand prix. Sometimes I recorded them very early on a Monday morning in a tiny studio truck that drove to each European race, sometimes in a small studio in London and at flyaway races in a hotel room. It was a good grounding for what lay ahead.

Friday afternoon qualifying for the 1992 Dutch TT in Assen and everything in the garden seemed rosy for the Rothmans Honda team. Doohan had made a fantastic start to the season riding the more user-friendly V-4 Honda. He'd won the opening four grands prix followed by two second places and another win to arrive in Holland with a massive 53-point lead in the championship. However, it proved to be a qualifying session of total carnage and nobody really knew why. They certainly did not understand just what significance it would have for the ultimate outcome of the championship. Riders went down like flies for no apparent reason and heading the list was Doohan.

The championship leader had already crashed once that weekend and was unhurt. Doohan then went out in the final qualifying session to cement that championship lead with pole position. He fell on his first flying lap after bedding in some new pistons. Coming out of the first bend he was flicked out of the saddle at over 100mph and the tibia and fibula in his right leg snapped when he slid into the kerb. For mere mortals in would have been a catastrophe, but for a grand prix rider and especially Mick it all appeared pretty routine. I was privy to the team's discussions as to what the best course of action would be to protect that massive championship lead. Should he go to London for the operation to repair the damage and then be fit to race at the British Grand Prix which meant missing just two races and 40 possible points? Should he fly to America where Mick had already received top class treatment or – Mick's preference – have the operation conducted immediately at the local Assen hospital. The local hospital decision was taken with Mick even suggesting that he might be fit enough to ride at the Hungarian round in 15 days' time. Little did I realise as they wheeled Mick to the waiting ambulance that it would not be 15 days but nearly two months before I saw or even spoke to him again.

At first, the news from the local hospital was good. A successful operation with plates fitted to the broken tibia and fibula we were told. After a few days it was obvious that all was not well. A visit from Dr Claudio Costa, regarded by the majority of the paddock as the grand prix doctor, set the alarm bells ringing. There were major circulation problems with the broken leg. Mick knew something was seriously wrong when his foot started to turn black and he could smell the dying, rotting flesh around the wounds. Dr Costa tried to visit and treat him but was chased out of the Assen hospital because they did not want to hear his opinion. When talk of amputation was mentioned, it was time for Dr Costa to take drastic action to save first the leg and then the career of the championship leader. The Italian did both.

He bravely blatantly kidnapped both Doohan and Kevin Schwantz, who'd broken his forearm and dislocated his hip in a collision with Lawson, from the hospital. An air ambulance was waiting for the escapees when they arrived at the tiny Groningen aerodrome and they were on route to Dr Costa's clinic at Imola in Italy. If he'd not risked everything there was every chance Mick would have had to have his right leg amputated. As it was, it took another seven weeks of extensive and painful treatment to totally eliminate the possibility. At one stage Mick had his two legs sewn together to try and restore circulation from one to the other.

I knew it was serious but despite plenty of enquiries resulting in the compilation of some pretty bland press releases I had no idea what Mick was going through. All he wanted was to get back in the saddle and defend that championship lead. All he could do was lie in bed watching the grands prix on the television and see those precious hard-earned championship points drip feed away to Wayne Rainey.

Mick's gaunt grey face matched the mood of the riders when they arrived at the penultimate round of the championship at a venue nobody wanted to be at. Interlagos in the massive sprawling city of São Paulo was not even a good Formula One car circuit, and for grand prix motorcycles it was a disaster. Somehow it was approved as the venue for the Brazilian Grand Prix, despite unprotected walls and barriers encasing fast corners. The weather, chaotic organisation and the location – with the riders donating thousands of dollars to the desperate occupants of the muddy favela that backed onto the track – made it a thoroughly miserable weekend. Grand prix motorcycle racing never returned.

Mick had missed four races and seen that precious championship lead slashed to 22 points with two rounds remaining. Although he could hardly walk, he knew he had to ride to have a chance of winning his first world title. His legs were spindly remnants of what they used to be, and his right calf was still encased in a light cast. He showed me the wounds on his right leg that reminded me of the local butcher's shop back home, but nothing was going to stop him racing. It was a painful experience to witness first hand such a brave man go through so much pain to achieve absolutely nothing. His twelfth place in a tortuous 75 miles of pain and courage yielded no World Championship points. Rainey's third win of another injury hit season meant Mick was just hanging in there by two precious points for the final showdown at Kyalami in South Africa two weeks later.

Carmelo Ezpeleta later told me he actually obtained personal permission from Nelson Mandela for the race to go ahead at the re-vamped Kyalami circuit. This was a South Africa that had cast off the shroud of apartheid but there was still much unrest in the air. A massive fire in the VIP car park that burned out 42 cars cast a cloud of black spiralling smoke over the proceedings. It was a backdrop to a race that ended Doohan's heroic attempt to win the title.

Typically, Mick was a lot fitter than the previous race after frantic work by Dr Costa to strengthen the leg. Despite having to change his riding style to compensate for the lack of strong rear braking he qualified in third place after leading the way with only ten minutes remaining. Rainey was one place behind him and knew exactly what he had to do in the 28-lap race.

It's not a miracle when a new World Champion is crowned that magically a t-shirt appears over his leathers celebrating his achievement as he climbs the steps of the podium. It's not a miracle that a folder appears on every desk in the media centre with pictures and a biography of the new champion ready for publication. The scene after the race of the Rothmans Honda media staff cutting up 200 Doohan 1992 World Champion t-shirts and press folders told its very own sad story. Mick had failed by two tiny precious points to take the title his determination and broken body deserved. He finished sixth but third place for Rainey behind Kocinski and Gardner was enough. The Californian World Champion was quick to commiserate with the distraught Doohan. Racing is racing and Mick knew given the same opportunity that injury provided he would have been just as ruthless. Some of the Doohan World Champion t-shirts slipped the scissors and the next year were seen being worn in Greece. I have absolutely no idea how that happened. Those authentic Doohan World Championship winning t-shirts were soon to become a familiar sight when Mick finally clinched the title two years later.

Team-mate and fellow countryman Wayne Gardner was much happier. He signed off his grand prix career with a second place and was still the only Australian 500cc World Champion. A month earlier, just a couple of days after announcing that his battered body had had enough, he won the British Grand Prix at Donington and burst into tears when Donna flew in from Australia to surprise him at the press conference.

Not so happy was Eddie Lawson as he left the grand prix paddock for the last time. Never frightened to voice his opinion Eddie had upset a good few people in the paddock over the years who, as a result, perhaps forgot that this was one of the truly great World Champions in the history of the sport, with four 500cc world titles on Yamaha and Honda machinery, who had, in his last season, brought Cagiva their first Grand Prix win in Hungary. We'd all had our moments with Eddie, but I take people as I find them and found him easy to work with in his year with Rothmans Honda. In fact, just two weeks earlier Eddie had been the unlikely life and soul of an impromptu party in the São Paulo Novotel hotel after the Brazilian Grand Prix. At the end of a great night he paid for everything and admitted later he missed his plane home the next day still suffering. Typically, without a fuss Eddie was saying goodbye. Real geniuses are not known to be the easiest of people to deal with.

It had been a monumental season of drama, injuries, controversy and change. All the tension and excitement boiled over and exploded into an end of season party that I have never experienced before or since. A hotel near the Kyalami circuit was the venue and it soon got very lively. At one stage, who else but Kevin Schwantz and Randy Mamola appeared on the dance floor with the fire hydrant hose which they turned on full power. All the furniture and some of its occupants were swept to the back of the room. Outside a giant fountain became a massive swimming pool with the entire paddock, in various states of dress or not, diving in. After driving Wayne and Donna to the airport the next morning for the last time I went to find the hotel manager to apologise. He would have none of it and said it was the best night they'd ever had in the hotel and we'd be welcome back anytime. Sadly, it was our very last visit to Kyalami.

The Dark Side
1993–1996

A GREAT DEAL may have happened in 1993 but for most
people only one thing is remembered – the Wayne Rainey
crash at Misano that left the World Champion paralysed
from below the waist. Four months earlier at Jerez,
Japanese 250cc rider Nobuyuki Wakai had been killed
in an accident when he collided with a spectator crossing
pit lane. After hitting the spectator, who miraculously
was not seriously injured, Wakai crashed and hit his
head on a pit-wall step.

Those television pictures of Wayne tumbling alone into
the gravel trap at the first corner leading the tenth lap of
the Italian Grand Prix still come back to haunt you. The
doctors watching said they knew immediately he was
paralysed by the way he fell, but at the time the rest of
us just thought it was a question of whether he would
be fit for the penultimate round in seven days' time at
his home grand prix in Laguna Seca. After the race was
won by Rainey's team-mate, the 125 and 250cc World
Champion Luca Cadalora, I interviewed third placed

and championship leader Kevin Schwantz. We thought Wayne may have broken his collarbone and Kevin hoped his bitter rival would be back to continue their fight for the title.

An hour after the race had finished the paddock became eerily silent, despite the frantic effort by the teams to prepare the freight for the long flight to America. First rumours spread through the paddock about Wayne's condition. Then they were followed by facts. Wayne had been critically injured and was paralysed below the waist. Then there was silence.

Five days later practice got underway for the penultimate round in a weekend of desperate sadness at Laguna Seca. Despite the success of American riders on foreign soil, back home, the mainstream media and sports fans – and Eddie Lawson's mates – knew little about the sport. Kenny Roberts was determined to change this and had worked with many dedicated people to help promote the home grand prix, with World Champion Wayne Rainey as the figurehead. So there was a feeling of emptiness, especially for Kevin Schwantz who was the new World Champion. John Kocinski brought Cagiva their first dry race win, but it mattered little to most. A giant black cloud of grief hung among that familiar sea mist swirling around the hills overlooking the beautiful Monterey Bay a few miles from the inland circuit.

Two weeks later, the season ended with Brazilian Alex Barros winning the FIM Grand Prix at Jarama. It was a day in the Spanish sunshine that crowned two new World Champions, Tetsuya Harada in the 250cc class and Dirk Raudies in the 125cc class. Freddie Spencer had embarked on yet another brief return from retirement but finally called it a day after crashing in qualifying at Laguna.

It was also the end of a season that heralded my move to what we always jokingly called 'the dark side' – the Formula One World Championship. Two days after the Assen race I was at Donington Park organising a quick few laps around the circuit for a *Daily Mirror* journalist as pillion with Daryl Beattie who'd replaced fellow Australian Gardner in the Rothmans Honda team. A phone call from my Rothmans boss David Beck was more than a small shock. He told me Rothmans were pulling out of grand prix motorcycle racing and turning to four wheels as title sponsors of the Williams team. He left it to me to make the official announcement at the Barcelona Grand Prix a couple of weeks later, although by then everybody knew. Keeping a secret in a paddock of either two or four wheels was impossible. A couple of months later, David approached me to offer me the same media manager's job but in the Formula One World Championship. To be honest I did not take one second to decide.

*

I followed Formula One, but honestly, I knew little about it. I'd worked at the Silverstone Grand Prix a couple times in the media centre. The first time was when sadly the press officer Dave Fern's father died, and I was left in charge on race day. Just before the race was about to start somebody or something sliced through the television feed cable to the media centre. Which obviously resulted in no pictures and the caretaker media manager taking a fair bit of stick, especially from the Italians. Just when it was looking more than a little desperate, up stepped Bob Boot, whose company looked after the sound system throughout the circuit. He produced a simple wire coat hanger to return sanity and pictures to the media centre. The hanger acted as a television aerial and the BBC coverage was the answer, although some visits to the cricket during the race did not please those same Italians.

A year later, part of my new job was to lead the race winner from the podium to the media centre. That did not seem that difficult. Unfortunately for me, however, when Nigel Mansell won his home grand prix the place went crazy and he went for a ride round the circuit on the back of a police motorcycle, but we got there in the end.

I was determined not turn my back on the bikes, however, and worked out that I could attend around half the grands prix that did not clash with Formula One and the BBC were happy with me to carry on with my radio motorcycle race reports. I embarked on the craziest period of work and travel every weekend with amazing support from my wife Sheila and our daughter Sophie (although she was too young to realise it at the time).

It was grand prix motorcycle racing and football that helped me so much when I stepped over to the dark side for the first time. Damon Hill had always wanted to be Barry Sheene and was a very useful motorcycle racer before switching to four wheels. He and legendary three times World Champion Ayrton Senna were the Williams drivers for the 1994 Formula One season.

Damon and I could talk bikes all day long, but I was surprised by Senna. I was so nervous the first time I met and then interviewed him at a secret test at Estoril in Portugal a day before a massive media launch at the Palácio Hotel opposite the Estoril Casino. He was really helpful, and the interview and video of the team were ready for the 300 journalists who'd been flown in from all over the world.

I arrived a couple of hours early suitably suited and booted for the press conference. I was the first and the only person in the ballroom of the hotel when a door opened at the far end. I prayed to myself it was not Ayrton Senna, but it was. What the hell was I going to say to him as he approached the new boy with so little knowledge of his sport with an outstretched hand?

'Good evening Nick,' he said – Oh my God, he's remembered my name! I thought. He continued that John Kocinski had had a good season on the Cagiva, how do you think he will go this year? I was on safe ground, thanks to him, which made the events on 1 May at Imola even more personal. It was a day that even my experiences of handling tragic situations could not have possibly prepared me for. It was one of those days people can tell you exactly where they were when they heard the news. Ayrton Senna was dead.

It had been a tough start to the new season for the Williams team in Brazil and Japan. It was my first European grand prix, but I knew Imola well and was feeling more at home in the Rothmans double-decker bus at the top end of the paddock, but all was not well. I think we always thought that Formula One was safer than motorcycle racing. The events over that weekend made me think again.

On the Friday, right in front of us, Rubens Barrichello had a massive crash in the Jordan car and was lucky to escape serious injury. On the Saturday afternoon, Austrian driver Roland Ratzenberger was killed when he hit the wall at 190mph at the Villeneuve corner. It was the first Formula One death for eight years and the paddock was numb. Senna was devastated but made the decision to race the next day but with an Austrian flag tucked down the side of his seat to unfurl at the end of the race. That opportunity to honour Ratzenberger never came.

Sitting on the top floor of the bus watching the race I had no idea just how serious the situation was. When Senna disappeared out of the top of the television picture, I naively assumed he was on a wider line at the 190mph Tamburello curve. When the distressing pictures returned of the wrecked car and trapped driver, I realised something was seriously wrong. When Senna's PA rushed into the office looking for his passport, I realised that something was very seriously wrong and put our plans into action. An ashen-faced David Beck sat us down and told us Senna was dead, but that we could do nothing until it was officially confirmed. When the appalling news was confirmed, we were ready.

I immediately found myself in a completely different place. A zone in which I was totally oblivious to anything outside of my immediate focus. A zone, surprisingly, devoid of sadness and grief. The Williams media team Annie and Jane flew back to England to man the fort at Williams's headquarters in Didcot. I stayed most of the night in that tiny office in the Imola paddock speaking to the world. In a strange – and probably slightly morally uncomfortable way if I'm honest – I felt situated at the very forefront of the biggest sporting story for at least a decade. I remember the news producer at BBC World Service telling me through my headphones to speak slowly and with reverence because I was announcing to millions of people throughout the world that a true sporting legend had been killed. The phone never stopped ringing and I never stopped talking and typing.

The early flight out of Bologna the next morning was a very sombre affair but even then, through lack of sleep and so much flowing adrenalin, I didn't really process what had happened. It was Bank Holiday Monday back in England and I was alone in the office, the desk in front of me stacked with papers announcing Senna's death. Suddenly, for the first time and 24 hours after the crash, it struck home. The legend who'd put me at ease a couple of months earlier with his Kocinski question was dead. At last I felt sad, and also guilty that such a tragedy could feel like such a professional opportunity.

It was a strange feeling walking into the familiar surroundings of the Jerez paddock just five days later. It was the first European round of the 1994 bike season and after a quick hello everybody was busy. No Rothmans catering this time and I remember having a tin of cold baked beans in Peter Clifford's motorhome for my lunch. Life moves on at a great pace and everybody seemed to be doing very well without me and Rothmans, especially Honda and Mick Doohan.

Back in the corporate Honda colours because they could not find a team sponsor, Honda and Doohan totally dominated the 1994 championship. The fully fit Australian won 9 grands prix and finished on the podium in every one of the 14 races. He clinched the title with victory in Brno which luckily for me did not clash with Formula One. It was good to be there to celebrate with a team and rider who went on to crush all opposition for the next four years. There was no cutting up of t-shirts and media kits this time. The 1993 World Champion Schwantz sporting the number one plate on his Suzuki replacing the familiar number 34 was beset by the racer's curse of wrist injuries that would eventually lead to his retirement.

Cadalora brought the Yamaha team – still reeling from the Rainey accident – a couple of wins to finish runner-up behind Doohan. Wheelchair-bound Rainey made a brave and remarkable return to the paddock to manage the 250cc Yamaha team. Two circuits staged their last grands prix. Doohan won at both the beautifully situated Salzburgring in Austria and Hockenheim in Germany.

While Doohan and Honda had started their domination there was still a glimpse into where the future lay. At the Japanese Grand Prix an 18-year-old with long, flowing hair had shocked and battled with the established stars. Norick Abe finally crashed out fighting for the lead with three laps remaining. He would return and be remembered not just for that amazing hair. Italian Max Biaggi, who'd ridden for the Rothmans Honda 250cc team the previous year, brought the Italian Aprilia factory their first world title in the 250cc class. Japan's Kazuto Sakata made it an Aprilia double with the 125cc title.

I reunited with Barry Sheene and my old Channel Nine friends in Adelaide for the last round Formula One scrap between Damon Hill and Michael Schumacher. The crash, the accusations from both drivers as to who had caused it and the massive media interest stood me in good stead for what lay ahead.

I'd settled into Formula One and now felt comfortable, especially with the old-school British national newspaper media gang. Led by Stan Piecha from the *Sun* they travelled the world reporting, socialising and making me very welcome, because the Rothmans hospitality and especially the after-lunch or dinner schnapps were the very best. Also, they always wanted to know the football results and I made it my job to bring them into the media centre and read them out. Work hard and play hard was their motto and they certainly embraced those beliefs. On the work front they would decide what the story of the day was and then write it in their respective newspaper's style. They were not happy if someone broke ranks and followed a different line.

Doohan duly retained his title in 1995 on the Repsol-sponsored NSR Honda but not without a few scares along the way. The main threat came from his old team-mate and friend Daryl Beattie who found a new lease of life switching to Suzuki. It looked like business as usual when Doohan won the opening home round at Eastern Creek, but when he crashed at the opening European round in Jerez Beattie took over the lead in the championship. He then won the next round at the Nürburgring. Sting Doohan and he will sting you back. He proceeded to win four grands prix in a row to re-establish his authority. He was never headed again by Beattie who gained a superb but unexpected runner-up spot in the championship in front of Luca Cadalora.

The Spanish influence was bubbling upwards from the smaller classes. Alberto Puig and Àlex Crivillé finished first and third at Jerez but then I witnessed a horrendous 150mph crash at Le Mans which ended Puig's season. He crashed into the wall as he pitched the Honda flat out into the right-hand bend just after the start and finish, smashing his left leg.

For the first time ever, three brothers finished on each of the three podiums at a grand prix. At Suzuka in Japan Takuma Aoki was third in the 500cc race, Nobuatsu second in the 250 and the youngest Haruchika won the 125, going on to gain the title for Honda. Max Biaggi retained the 250cc crown for Aprilia, only finishing off the podium once in 13 races. Already the rumbling about him moving up with the big boys was being heard.

When Kevin Schwantz says he's had enough you know he means it. In Mugello that year, drained and pained by constant wrist injuries, he announced his retirement from a sport he'd graced for seven glorious years. The tall, lanky Texan who defied both logic and pain to become a cult hero and World Champion could take no more. His number 34 was also retired from 500cc entry lists to honour someone who had the skill and bravery to race a 500cc rocket ship that would take your breath away and make you close your eyes. That one world title and 25 grands prix wins was scant recognition.

I was still living out of a suitcase, combining both two and four wheels, and found a willing contributor to my efforts from a very unlikely source. At European Formula One races 'the boss' Bernie Ecclestone would always eat in the back room of the Rothmans Williams bus which was next to my tiny office. He would often poke his head round the door to both frighten me and make me laugh. On more than one occasion I had to put the phone down in mid flow of a radio report when I heard him coming up the stairs because I knew the station I was talking to did not have the rights to broadcast. Bernie liked his bikes and asked me to organise a lunch each year at Monaco for the riders who lived there. He was a brilliant host to the likes of Doohan, Beattie and the Aoki brothers. He always asked them why they were wasting their time in grands prix and saying they should switch to World Superbikes!

The majestic Doohan continued on his winning ways in 1996 despite the annoying presence of his Repsol Honda team-mate Àlex Crivillé. Hondas totally dominated the proceedings, only missing victory on two occasions. We'd all experienced Mick's temper and Australian sarcasm and Crivillé got the works at the final round in Eastern Creek in front of the home crowd. Crivillé crashed into his team-mate at the final corner of the race while he was leading. Both riders fell, opening the gate for Loris Capirossi to win his first 500cc Grand Prix. Two rounds earlier in Barcelona Doohan had finished second to retain his title in the race won by Carlos Checa. The Spanish challenge was mounting.

Crivillé had learnt to be thick-skinned when previously Mick had given him the works after a race in Brno. I was commentating live for BBC Radio 5 from the television screens back in their London studios. The problem was, I didn't know who actually won the 22-lap battle. Lap after lap, mile after mile, Crivillé just rode in the slipstream of his team-mate. Mick could not shake him off. You could almost see the steam coming out of his helmet. He was getting angrier and angrier because he knew what was coming. He was not wrong. Up the hill towards the final chicane and the finish Crivillé prepared to make his move. He timed it to perfection to steal the chequered flag from his team-mate by 0.002 seconds. Back in London I had no idea who had won and waffled away until the celebrations by one rider and the stare from the other made it all very clear.

The most popular win of the 1996 season came when the long-haired Norick Abe brought Yamaha rare success in his home grand prix at Suzuka. It was difficult to see anybody or anything halting the Honda juggernaut in the years that lay ahead. Biaggi continued to stake his 500cc upgrade by retaining the 250cc title, but it was tight. He won the final round at Eastern Creek to pip the Honda of German Ralf Waldmann. Haruchika Aoki finished second at the same venue to retain the 125cc crown, but a new name was emerging that would turn the sport on its very head. Little did I realise at the time.

In the media centre at Mugello after practice for the Italian Grand Prix the Italian media were clustered around somebody sitting on one of their desks. To be honest, I had no idea who the teenager was his with longish hair and a fresh face. I was soon put right by my Italian colleagues who informed me I should keep an eye on this teenager because he was very quick. They told me he was the son of the equally long-haired, three times grand prix winner Graziano Rossi, who was a great mate of Barry Sheene. Three months later Valentino Rossi won his first 125cc grand prix in Brno and celebrated by almost crashing into the pit wall. Rossi had arrived.

Chariot to Hell

1949–1996

AT THE END of the 1996 season the sidecars ceased to run as a grand prix class. They had been there right from the start in 1949. I think you either loved them or hated them, especially towards the end. For those 48 years they had provided some incredible racing, innovative engineering and, during those barren times in the solo classes, some Great British success to commentate on.

When Eric Oliver with journalist Denis Jenkinson as his passenger won that first 1949 world title it was easy to understand what sidecars where all about. A motorcycle and sidecar were a very popular mode of transport at the time and Oliver and Jenkinson's Norton-powered outfit was a souped up version. But racing being racing, in the search of more speed and stability they began to move away from the road-going designs.

In 1954, the first outfit where the driver knelt rather than sitting on the saddle appeared. BMW-powered kneeler outfits dominated the championship for 20 years. Then a Swiss driver changed the very face of the sport by taking the kneeler concept even further away from motorcycles. Suddenly, racing sidecar outfits were more like racing cars than motorcycles. The revolutionary outfit of Swiss driver Rolf Biland scrapped leading link forks and featured hub centre steering. However, while Biland was the master engineer and master driver, winning seven world titles, it didn't prevent interest in the class dwindling fast apart from in Britain, Germany and Holland.

I loved sidecars and the crazy guys who both drove and passengered. They were always situated down the rough end of the paddock. They were the ones usually in trouble with the police and the first to brew up the tea and open a tin of biscuits. Apart from the top few, they were the poor relations and reminded me so much of the struggles of those pioneers fighting to make a living in the early days. Sidecar racing was both exciting and dangerous. Many lost their lives including a great friend of mine, World Champion Jock Taylor, in a desperately wet weekend at Imatra in 1982 when he crashed going over the railway lines.

With such little solo success for British riders at a World Championship level for so many barren years it was sidecars with Steve Webster and Tony Hewitt that really saved the day. They attracted great interest back in Britain winning four world titles while still included in the World Championship Grand Prix series. BBC radio would always follow their progress through me on a Sunday afternoon. Their World Championship outfit was featured on the stage for the BBC Sports Personality of the year and footage of them racing across the wet Assen grass into a water-filled dyke was frequently shown.

The sidecar boys were always the best company on a night out, as long as you stayed out of trouble. I found out that for myself back in 1981.

I woke up on an April Sunday morning at the Donington Manor Hotel hoping and praying they had forgotten. They had not. After far too many pints of IPA in the Redgate Lodge at the circuit the night before I had jokingly suggesting that anybody could be a sidecar passenger and especially at the TT in the Isle of Man. Give me the chance and I'll take it, I told the sidecar boys as I ordered another round. They did just that and there was no way out.

I'd been in the chair of a racing sidecar outfit just once before when Jock Taylor took me gingerly round a damp Donington for a *Motor Cycle News* feature. This was already looking far more serious. Trevor Ireson lived just down the road from me near Swindon and for the last two years had won both sidecar TT races with passenger Clive Pollington. It was decided that I would replace Clive for the first lap of TT practice on the Tuesday evening in the Isle of Man. Somehow, we convinced the

Auto Cycle Union that I was eligible for an International Competition Licence. I bought a new pair of bright white basketball boots to celebrate and was ready to go. There was just one more hurdle to cross.

Ten days before the TT lap, I was in Jarama for the Spanish Grand Prix. To get a colour front-page picture of me and Trevor for the TT edition of *Motor Cycle Weekly* we needed to take a posed picture in the Jarama paddock. That was the plan, but Trevor and Clive came up with a different idea. Why waste that colour front page with a paddock shot? Surely it was an action picture that was needed. In the Saturday afternoon qualifying for a grand prix they got their wish and *Motor Cycle Weekly* got their picture. It was pure lunacy, totally illegal and bloody dangerous. Halfway through qualifying, Trevor and Clive raced into pit lane. Clive jumped out and disappeared to the back of the pit lane garage. 'He' emerged two minutes later and qualifying continued round the 2.058-mile circuit.

For three laps fellow competitors and spectators alike were amazed at how the sidecar wheel was at least a foot off the ground at most corners. Surely with such an experienced passenger on board this should not happen. It didn't once Trevor had screamed back down pit lane; the passenger had jumped off and disappeared only to return dressed in the same style leathers and helmet to continue in a more dignified manner.

I don't know how they persuaded me to fill in for those three terrifying laps. Perhaps it was their test to see if I had the balls for the ultimate test, the 37.73-mile lap of the TT Mountain circuit. I lay on my hotel bed that night thinking that was the craziest thing I'd ever done in my life, but I still had the TT to come. Trevor and Clive, and certainly not Trevor and Nick, had qualified in eighth place for the Spanish Grand Prix the next day.

I knew when I opened my eyes for the very first time with the 750cc Yamaha outfit airborne as we powered over Ago's leap at the bottom of Bray Hill that all the advice that had been drilled into me about hanging on was so true. The many laps of the TT Mountain circuit in the car with both Trevor and Clive had not prepared me for this. Their advice just to lay back and enjoy it seemed a distant cloudy memory as I used every part of my body to stay aboard as Trevor braked hard for Quarter Bridge. What had I let myself in for? But why worry, there were only another 36 miles to go!

Mercifully it was a dry, sunny Tuesday evening as I sneaked into the paddock. No notebook and pen as my working tools this time, but helmet, leathers and bright white basketball boots. Clive had kept an eye on me all day making sure I ate some lunch and was kept busy with little jobs. Graeme Crosby asked me if I owed him any money, Mick Grant's wife Carol could not stop laughing and Roger Marshall said I was a braver man than he.

More sensible advice came from the sidecar boys. Dick Greasley told me to relax as much as possible to ease the tension on my wrists. Passenger Chas Birks taped up the laces on the white basketball boots. Didn't want them to get caught up in the wheel halfway round. Trevor seemed totally relaxed at the prospect of having such a novice as his partner. 'Relax, and if you want to stop just shake your head, but for Christ's sake hang on,' was his advice.

The position I'd practised with Clive – laying in the chair holding the front and side handholds with my legs trailing out of the back – had seemed fine in the garage. It was a very different story once out in the real world. My wrists were already throbbing as we braked for Quarter Bridge. The throbbing just increased as I hung on for dear life through Braddan Bridge and Union Mills onto the flat-out section from Glen Vine to Greeba Castle. Suddenly, as we hit another bump and my neck threatened to wrench itself from the rest of my body, I at last fully understood what I'd let myself in for. Too late.

By Crosby I could hardly breathe. I felt sick. I ached from head to foot as we seemed to hit bump after bump at 140mph. Only later did I realise there was worse to come. We raced flat out past the pub and speed trap at the Highlander into the dip, braking for Greeba Castle. I was ready to shake my head and say enough but was saved by old memories. Thirteen years earlier I'd sat on that wall watching Agostini and Pasolini and now it was me. I had to hang on to at least the pub at Ballacraine. We arrived and there was no thought of a pint as I used every protrusion on my body – yes, every part – not to join the radiator at the front of the chair. Onto the Glen Helen section and more bumps when suddenly out of the blue an outfit appeared in front of us. To my amazement we overtook it in the Doran's Bend section and from that moment I knew I had to complete the lap whatever the consequences to my body and brain.

Out of Sarah's Cottage where Hailwood and Ago had crashed on my first TT visit 16 years earlier, we raced onto the Cronk-y-Voddy Straight. Trevor had told me on the earlier car journey how much this section had been smoothed out. He said that he would urinate blood for at least a couple of weeks when he got home after practice and the races because of the bashing his kidneys received. If this was smooth, what is the infamous Sulby Straight going to produce, I thought as my thigh smashed into the wheel arch once again.

Trevor's words that Barregarrow Hill was a beauty and that I'd love it seemed a long time ago as we screamed through the bottom almost touching the kerb. I was trying to rest my neck and wrists as we raced between the houses in Kirkmichael village at what seemed around 600mph. Trevor had a long hard look to see if I was OK when I followed Dick Greasley's advice about relaxing and nearly left him alone as we hit another mighty bump and my feet appeared above my body.

With teeth gritted I told myself I was doing all right and was going to make it, but then I sank to my lowest point when the 16-mile board flashed by. I thought we must be near Ramsey and well over halfway through the torture, but we still had over 20 miles to go! No time to mope as we flopped over Ballaugh Bridge, through Quarry Bends towards the dreaded bump-ridden Sulby Straight. It did not let us down. Trevor's assessment was just about perfect. Just suck up your balls and hang on. You will feel like you've completed ten rounds with Muhammad Ali by the same you reach the smooth bit. The smooth bit was like arriving in heaven after a trip through the fires of hell and it was on towards Parliament Square in Ramsey.

As we came out of the square Trevor gave me yet another of those long glances and indicated I should look behind. Unbeknownst to me, Mick Boddice and Chas Birks had been following us since Glen Vine to check I was OK. They gave me an encouraging wave and I thought I was home and dry but was so wrong. The whole mountain section became a blur. There was fierce acceleration up towards the Gooseneck and beyond between the fences and grassy hillsides. It was becoming a very personal battle to hang in there and I was praying with my eyes closed for it to finish.

Then the plot changed (but was just as painful) when we started the downhill descent. The bumps were now trying to throw you out of the front instead of the back. I opened my eyes as we raced through Keppel Gate and for five glorious seconds caught a glimpse of Douglas Bay below, bathed in the early evening sunshine. For the first time since the lap had started, I knew I was going to make it.

Any breath I had left in me was knocked out of me as we dropped down to Creg-ny-Baa where we slowed to obey the oil warning flags and I caught a glimpse of spectators drinking a pint and enjoying the sunshine at the pub. Trevor gave me the last glance and indicated to hang on because he was going to give me a taste of what it was really like to be a proper passenger. Oh my God, had we only been playing at it? For the first time he unleashed the sheer power of the 750cc two-stroke Yamaha engine, revving to 11,500rpm and a speed of around 150mph as we catapulted towards Brandish where the braking from that speed caused more problems than the acceleration. We continued on our merry way through Hillberry and Signpost and even the bumps at Bedstead could not ruin the promise of a pint and a hot bath. Through the dip at Governor's Bridge and we were in the promised land: the Glencrutchery Road. The torture was over.

My prayers had been answered. I wanted to pat Trevor on the back as we cruised past the grandstand,

and I wanted to wave to our photographer, but I could manage neither. I fell out of the chair into Clive's arms. He took off my, well actually his, helmet and I sat on the wall thanking God that the pounding, buzzing and pain had finally stopped. It may have seemed like a lifetime, but the lap had taken 24 minutes 41.2 seconds at an average speed of just under 92mph. Jock Taylor and Benga Johansson's winning speed for the three-lap sidecar race six days later was 107.02mph with a fastest lap of 108.02mph. I still had a long way to go and without any shadow of a doubt could only ever complete one lap at a time of the mountain circuit.

Back in the Fold

1997–1999

THE 1997 GRAND prix season had a familiar ring to it. Total Honda domination spearheaded by Doohan. His Repsol Honda team-mates Crivillé and Tadayuki Okada had their moments, but the momentum of the Doohan charge was unstoppable. It was only at the last race of the season that he failed to finish on the podium, crashing out while leading comfortably at Phillip Island. He won a record 12 races and retained his title 4 races before the season ended. Any chance Crivillé had of catching his team-mate was wrecked by a qualifying crash in Assen which caused him to miss the next five races. He fought back with a win at Phillip Island.

Kenny Roberts finally left Yamaha to set up his own team and build Modenas-badged bikes. Rainey took over at Yamaha but could do nothing to halt the Honda charge.

There was massive interest in the smaller classes where two young Italians were making all the headlines. The 250cc World Champion Biaggi fell out with Aprilia and returned to Honda to retain his title, but only just. Three riders, Biaggi, Waldmann and Harada, could still clinch the title going in to a tense final round at Phillip Island. His second place behind Waldmann was enough. Biaggi waved goodbye to the 250cc class after four successive titles. The 500s beckoned the Roman and his impact was both immediate and impressive.

Following that first grand prix win the previous year, Rossi simply steamrollered the 125cc opposition to win his first world title. Riding the Aprilia, he lost the tag as Graziano's son by winning a record-breaking 11 grands prix. He was on his way, and from now on Graziano was known as Valentino's father. Biaggi had already joined the elite and it would not be long before Rossi followed. But he had some business to attend to before taking on the big boys.

Biaggi rattled Doohan right from the word go in 1998 after a 500cc debut to remember. Riding the Erv Kanemoto-prepared Marlboro-sponsored Honda NSR he became the first rider for 25 years to win on his 500cc debut. It was just what the championship needed and provided an insight into what to expect in the future. Doohan was fired up and fought back after the Suzuka shock with wins in Johor and Mugello. The threat to his title was not only the upstart Biaggi but his old foe and team-mate Crivillé. After his second win of the year at Paul Ricard, the Spaniard led the title chase for the

Double Vision – sometimes the camera does lie with double World Champion Freddie Spencer in action on both the World Championships winning 250 and 500cc Hondas.

With the Bass Straight shimmering in the background Wayne Gardner sends Australia crazy with his second win in succession at Phillip Island in 1990.

World Champion Wayne Rainey leads Kevin Schwantz at Jerez in 1993. Schwantz reversed the order at the chequered flag.

Graziano's son – not for long. An angelic looking Valentino Rossi made his grand prix debut in 1996.

The Master Craftsman – Mick Doohan brought Honda five successive World 500cc titles.

The moment of truth – Valentino Rossi fights off bitter rival Max Biaggi to win on his Yamaha debut at Welkom in 2004.

Like father like son – Kenny Roberts senior celebrates with Junior after he grabbed a front row start at Barcelona in 2006.

A smiling Casey Stoner brought Ducati their first premier class title before he moved onto Honda to win their first 800cc crown.

Before the hurricane and the white horse arrived – Valentino Rossi leads
Yamaha team-mate Jorge Lorenzo at Indianapolis in 2008.

Never to be forgotten – The ever-smiling Marco Simoncelli.

Pulling the pin – Marc Marquez celebrates victory at Aragon in 2013 on route to that first premier class World title.

I can't believe what you are saying – Marc Marquez looks perplexed as he listens to Valentino Rossi at the infamous Sepang press conference in 2015.

The wait was finally over and Danny Kent celebrates that first British World title for 38 long years at Valencia in Spain in 2015.

35 years after Barry Sheene stood on the top step of the podium in Sweden, Cal Crutchlow celebrates the first British success in the premier class at Brno in 2016.

The final farewell – Dani Pedrosa, Valentino Rossi, Marc Marquez and Andrea Dovizioso seem to be enjoying the goodbye video as much as I am.

very first time. At last a real fight for the championship and Doohan responded as we knew he would – by winning races.

There was controversy in Barcelona when Biaggi crossed the line first but was disqualified for ignoring the black flag. Doohan retained his title at the next round with victory in Phillip Island and let everybody know he was still the king with his eighth win of the season at the final round in Buenos Aires. Biaggi completed a brilliant debut season in second place in front of Crivillé.

Rossi stepped up to the 250cc class but found the going much tougher against two hardened warriors who taught him a great deal. Capirossi returned from the 500s to partner former champion Harada at Aprilia. They produced one of the most controversial finishes to a season in the history of the sport. The tactics of Capirossi that afternoon in Buenos Aires are still discussed over many a beer in the grand prix paddock today.

Harada and Capirossi were separated by just four points coming into the final bend of the season. Harada led and would be crowned World Champion, but Capirossi came from a long way back in second place to hit Harada. The Japanese rider crashed; Capirossi stayed on to take second place and the title. He was at first disqualified but later re-instated on appeal and crowned World Champion. Rossi won for the first time in Assen and eventually finished runner-up, one point in front of the luckless Harada.

At the start of the 1999 grand prix season my beloved Oxford United were in big trouble and I had by then become a director. Administration loomed and I was in a board meeting of gloom and doom when my phone rang. 'How is Mick Doohan?' was the question from the BBC. I'd been here before and hedged my bets. Away from the gloom of Oxford, Mick was in the Jerez sunshine practising for the third round of the championship but obviously all was not well. I immediately phoned Mat Oxley at the circuit and the news was not good. The World Champion had crashed at 120mph at turn three. It was early days, but it appeared Mick had broken his right shoulder, his leg and left wrist. The woes of Oxford United were forgotten immediately.

This was Mick, surely he would return even if it were next season? The surgeons fitted two plates and 12 screws into his left leg and a plate in his left forearm, but his battered and scarred body cried 'enough!' Both Mick and his body had nothing else to prove and just before Christmas he announced his retirement from the sport. That raw talented production bike racer from the beaches of the Gold Coast had evolved into one of the truly great World Champions. Time after time Mick proved he had the courage and ability, but it was his determination that stood him above the rest. Only Agostini and Rossi have equalled his feat of winning five successive titles. His 12 race victories in 1997 were a record and he won more 500cc races for Honda than any other rider. Mick only wanted one thing and that was winning grands prix races. Nothing or nobody could stand in his way. Of course, he could be difficult and intimidating but winning world titles was never easy. Without that pressure and pain Mick is great company today and a highly successful businessman, although I still wouldn't want to negotiate a contract with him.

Doohan's departure opened the floodgates and it was team-mate Crivillé who stepped out of his shadow. Sixth place in the penultimate round at Rio de Janeiro in Brazil brought him and Spain their first World 500cc title. It was just reward for Crivillé who'd so often had to play second fiddle to Doohan, but a new grand prix winner was making big waves and he had a familiar name.

Kenny Roberts Junior could never be like his dad – nobody could. Kenny Junior was the opposite in many ways but one: he could race motorcycles and win grands prix. Kenny arrived with his crew chief Warren Willing from his dad's team to put Suzuki back on the map. He won the opening two grands prix, beating a fit Doohan fair and square before his Jerez accident. He finished the season with victory in Argentina to finish second in the championship in front of Okada and Biaggi who'd switched to Yamaha. In Valencia there was no Honda on the 500cc podium for the first time since 1993 – times, once again, were a-changing.

Rossi was ready to join the 500cc fray in 2000 after becoming the youngest ever 250cc World Champion with victory in Brazil while Emilio Alzamora took the 125cc crown without winning a race.

Rothmans pulled out of Formula One and I was ready to return full time to my first love. What a time to choose as the new millennium, with an explosive new cast and revolutionary technical changes, loomed.

A Star is Born as Barry Departs

2000–2002

THE SCREAM OF a highly tuned BMW Formula One car engine sliced through the icy Catalan air. It may have been Barcelona, but this was January 2000 and there was snow on the ground as we drove past the grand prix circuit. I was being driven to the town of Vic, the home of Manel Arroyo, the Dorna director of communications, after being picked up at the airport. I thought our meeting would be in his Barcelona office, but he'd fallen off a trail bike and damaged his leg and so the venue was the lounge of his house in the foothills of the Pyrenees.

This really was a moment of change – hearing the new engine in action that would power the Williams Formula One car for the following season on the way to a meeting that would shape my life for the next 18 years underlined that. I'd shared every emotion with my Williams team of friends and colleagues for the last amazing six years, but now I was set to return to a job and sport I loved so much.

I'd already agreed to work for Dorna promoting grand prix racing in Britain where it was playing very much second fiddle to the World Superbike Championship. Over strong Catalan coffee and biscuits Manel also asked me whether I would be interested in commentating on the Dorna live television world feed from every grand prix and hosting all the press conferences. I could have flown home after the meeting without boarding an aeroplane. I'd miss Formula One, but this is where I wanted to be, back on two wheels. Little did I realise on that cold January day that I would witness grand prix motorcycle racing being turned on its head and scaling heights I could never have imagined.

The new millennium heralded the departure of many of the old brigade and the arrival of a new breed of young, brash talent that captured the imagination of the world. The king had already announced his abdication, and with Mick Doohan's retirement the World Champion Àlex Crivillé was only going to win one more grand prix. Mick's trusty team headed by crew chief Jerry Burgess had been assigned by Honda once again to produce a new World Champion with 125 and 250cc World Champion Valentino Rossi taking his first steps in the 500cc class. The Italian brewing giants Nastro Azzurro were the title sponsors of the new team, something which certainly suited the Australian-dominated team and the media.

Biaggi stayed at Yamaha alongside Carlos Checa with Australian Garry McCoy and last year's Valencia winner Régis Laconi remaining with the satellite WCM Yamaha team. With so much new talent emerging and with Suzuki not able to provide the same scale of investment as the other Japanese giants, Kenny Roberts Junior knew this might be his one big chance to re-write the history books. He took it. The RG 500 Suzuki was not the best bike out there, but the combination of Warren Willing's technical team to get the best out of it coupled with the skill, tactical nous and a sheer bloody mindset inherited from his father did the job.

The season started at Welkom in South Africa at the government-funded Phakisa Freeway circuit. It was an interesting 150-mile drive from Johannesburg to Welkom across the Free State. Vast open spaces were interrupted by shanty towns before you reached the abandoned mine-shaft headgear and slag heaps of the old gold-mining town of Welkom. Many of those seams of gold had long run out and this was a town of around 200,000 people fighting for its very life. Every morning the roundabouts were packed with people seeking work, hoping to be picked up for labouring jobs. Sadly, although the apartheid regime was long gone there were still certain people living in the past. Being told by the young black waiter not to be seen giving him a tip, the use of the word 'kaffa', the ignoring of instructions from the black security guards round the television compound and a diner in a local restaurant with a gun stuck in his belt were a reminder of days gone by. The grand prix was like a breath of fresh air to the town and gave many, especially the young people working at the circuit, some hope for the future.

Little did I realise on my full return to grand prix motorcycle racing, when I hosted a rainy Dorna press conference held outside, just how significant this weekend in Welkom had been. Dorna had launched the MotoGP logo and concept. The MotoGP class would replace the 500cc class that had been there from the very start and this was just the beginning. It was obvious that the two-stroke days were numbered. Road bike sales were all about four-strokes and so in order to keep the existing manufacturers, attract new ones and meet the World Superbike challenge head on, it was time to change. And it would take time, but the seeds had been sown.

Australian Garry McCoy won my first race back at the microphone, and commentating was pure joy as he made my job so easy. Garry – compact and an ex-speedway rider – rode the 500cc Yamaha in a way that defied all logic. He slid the grand prix bike like a speedway machine on the shale, often with smoke pouring from the rear tyre, and tattooing big black tyre marks on the tarmac in the process. It was easy to get very excited.

Rossi made his 500cc grand prix debut but, after setting the fastest lap, crashed on the twelfth lap.

Roberts picked up his second win of the season at Jerez where the race was run in two parts and Rossi stood on the 500cc podium for the first time. Race victories were spaced out with World Champion Crivillé winning for the last time in Le Mans; Norick Abe repeated his Suzuka victory of four years ago and Loris Capirossi and Alex Barros brought the Pons Honda team wins at Mugello and Assen respectively. Rossi won his first 500cc Grand Prix at Donington, Biaggi brought Yamaha some much needed success at Brno, but the consistent Roberts was set to take the title three rounds from the finish in Rio. Sixth place was enough for him to celebrate with his father, but his greatest win came just eight days later. Kenny went out to show everybody at the Pacific Grand Prix at Motegi in Japan just why he was a true World Champion. He beat Rossi by over six seconds at the home of Honda. As different as chalk and cheese off the track, but uniquely the same once in the saddle, Kenny Senior and Kenny Junior are the only father and son pair to celebrate world titles. What a combination.

The 250cc Championship was settled in the finale of all finales on the last lap of the last round at Phillip Island and between two team-mates. After shadowing his Yamaha team-mate Shinya Nakano for 24 and three-quarter laps, Frenchman Olivier Jacque pulled out of his slipstream racing down the Gardner Straight towards the chequered flag to claim victory and the world title by 0.014s. It was a masterclass of patience by the Frenchman, but you had to feel sorry for Shinya.

Two grands prix in 2000, both in Britain, made me realise just how far grand prix racing had dropped behind the buoyant World Superbike Championship in the British publicity stakes. The outspoken and flamboyant World Superbike Champion Carl Fogarty had lured the fans away from grand prix, where British riders were struggling.

The Barry Sheene-type adulation that World Champion Fogarty had generated convinced the BBC to show the Superbikes live. I was at Silverstone for the British Formula One Grand Prix and early on the Sunday morning tuned in to watch the second race at the second round of the Superbike Championship from Phillip Island. Fogarty was involved in a horrible crash and, sadly, so bad were the injuries to his upper left arm and shoulder that he never raced again. For the BBC it was a disaster because Fogarty had been the main reason for their decision. When Rossi started making the headlines, however, their interest and eventually their allegiance switched to grands prix.

The British two-wheel grand prix at Donington attracted a paltry 18,500 spectators, though those that did come were treated to a podium finish by Jeremy

McWilliams in the 500cc race riding the Aprilia twin. A month later I went to the first of two World Superbike rounds to be held at Brands Hatch. The place was packed and the atmosphere electric – especially when Fogarty rode a couple of demonstration laps. Grand prix racing had a lot of catching up to do in Britain.

Rossi and Biaggi really did not like each other one little bit. On or off the track, it did not matter. An early spat in a restaurant when 250cc World Champion Biaggi was alleged to have ignored or even mocked a young Rossi was where it all started. It just carried on from there. It was exactly what the 2001 championship needed. Throw in another fiery, hard-riding Italian Loris Capirossi and even the British public were getting interested. The first race of the season set the scene perfectly.

Rossi made a bad start in the 21-lap race at Suzuka and was behind Biaggi who was hell-bent on not giving up his third place, especially to Rossi. The young Honda rider was equally intent on chasing down the leaders and would enjoy passing his great enemy. As they raced down the main straight towards turn one Rossi made his move but Biaggi slammed the door in his face. Rossi was forced to take evasive action, racing onto the grass at 150mph. For two more laps Biaggi held him at bay, but an aggressive, fired up Rossi eventually passed the Yamaha. A pass he celebrated with a none too friendly one-finger salute. Rossi was on fire and won that opening grand prix which he followed with victories at Welkom and Jerez. His very first podium finish at Suzuka gave Honda their 500th grand prix win. Thirty-nine years, 11 months and 16 days had raced by since Tom Phillis brought Honda that very first grand prix win at the Montjuïc Park circuit in Catalunya.

After those opening three wins, I'd organised a photoshoot on the London Eye with Valentino followed by a press conference. The young Italian had a flat in London and had intimated he was living there. I duly picked him and his great friend Uccio up from there and gave them a lift to the Eye. We had many London press conferences and public events in Leicester Square for the next few years and Vale always told us he was living in London. It was only later I found out that he would often fly into Gatwick the morning of the event, come up to London on the Gatwick Express – enjoying his relative anonymity in the UK at the time – and fly back that night.

After meeting the press in a pub near the Eye, we jumped in a taxi bound for the BBC studios at White City. Both Vale and Uccio were like a couple of kids planning the school prom, constantly on the phone to Italy and laughing. They'd found out there was a Rossi fan club in Hawaii and planned a special presentation at Rossi's home grand prix in Mugello. It started off by just flying a couple of the fans over for the race, but as the conversation and laughter became more animated it turned into something much bigger. Over the race weekend at Mugello it went on to having his helmet and leathers in a Hawaiian flower design. It ended with the complete pit crew wearing Hawaii shirts, the fairing of the bike in Hawaiian livery and a rubber swimming pool with plastic palm trees next to the track. This was a phenomenon of fun and self-promotion the sport had never witnessed. Others had tried but did not have the talent where it really mattered out on the track. Rossi just had buckets full of both.

The 22-year-old nicknamed himself the Doctor because the Rossi surname was so common in the profession. It stuck for ever. Even before the Hawaiian show there had been earlier 125 and 250cc race-winning celebrations. They included a pillion ride for a blow-up doll, a stop at the trackside marshals' portable loo during the slowing down lap and dressing as Robin Hood on the Donington Park podium. The Rossi juggernaut was up, running and soon unstoppable. The fans and media could not get enough of it.

On the track, Biaggi was hanging in there despite the brilliant start to the season by Rossi. How the Italian media fuelled the fire between their two modern-day gladiators from Rome and the Adriatic coast respectively in this passionate land. It was bound to happen, and tempers boiled over once again after the grand prix in Barcelona. I walked into the press conference room after the race to find Max sitting alone dabbing what appeared to be a cut over his eye with a handkerchief. He told me he had been bitten by a mosquito, but it later transpired there had been an altercation on the steps to the podium after Rossi had finished just over a couple of seconds in front of him. It was never established who or what actually hit Biaggi, but it was certainly not a mosquito. The FIM were not happy, but it just added to the tension and rivalry. The fans were returning to the sport in their droves.

After Barcelona, Biaggi won in Assen and the Sachsenring but Rossi fought back with wins at Donington, Brno, Estoril and Motegi. Sete Gibernau won his first grand prix for Suzuki at an emotional Valencia Grand Prix just after the attack on the Twin Towers in New York. He stopped to plant an American flag in the gravel trap on his slowing down lap while team-mate Kenny Roberts wore a New York Fire Department baseball cap on the podium after finishing third. With three races remaining we flew to Australia to witness both history and the future come together in one breath-taking weekend.

Those magnificent, unpredictable 500cc two-strokes were on their final tour of duty after nearly 30 years of entertaining, scaring and bringing such admiration to the few that managed to tame them in action. They were determined to show us what we would be missing on a circuit that was built with them in mind before the four-strokes arrived next season. They did not let us down.

A truly epic battle around Phillip Island ensued with less than three seconds separating the first nine riders across the line. What a way to bow out while the future was clear for all to see. Valentino Rossi won his first 500cc world title after beating Biaggi by 0.013 seconds. Mum Stefania was there to watch him but dad Graziano hated flying and celebrated at home the world title he himself had never quite managed to win. Rossi celebrated by finishing the season with victories in Sepang and Rio.

Honda's latest prodigy Daijiro Kato dominated the 250cc class while Manuel Poggiali fought off the challenge of Youichi Ui to clinch the 125cc title after finishing fifth in Rio. Ui pushed him to the limit and could not hide his tears in the Rio post-race press conference. Jeremy McWilliams brought Britain a rare grand prix triumph with a 250cc win at Assen. It was the first British 250cc grand prix victory for 18 long, frustrating years.

Even Rossi was not sure what bike to ride at the start of the ground-breaking 2002 season. He loved the NSR two-stroke 500cc Honda that had brought him that first world title the previous year. His first test on the 990cc four-stroke RC211 V Honda had not been a great success, but this was the year of change, the year the four-strokes returned to the new MotoGP class. The new regulations allowed 990cc four-stroke machines to take on the proven 500cc two-strokes. The new four-strokes were big, powerful and very loud but could they match the nimble and more agile two-strokes? It should have been an intriguing contest, but it turned into a non-event – the four-strokes were back and winning right from the start. The manufacturers were happy.

It all started at a wet Suzuka. Rossi won from pole on the four-stroke Honda followed by the four-stroke Suzuki of Akira Ryō and four-stroke Yamaha of Carlos Checa. Even in the rain the two-strokes were nowhere in sight and were blasted into the history books. Despite the valiant efforts of Capirossi and Barros on the West-sponsored Pons Honda NSRs, they only got one sight of victory and messed it up big time. The new Sachsenring was tight and twisty, never allowing the four-strokes to throttle up to their true potential. This was the last chance of a rousing send-off to those 500cc rocket ships that had entertained us royally for so long. It all looked so promising.

With just three laps to go, Olivier Jacque riding the two-stroke Yamaha and Barros had fought off the four-stroke challenge spearheaded by Rossi. Jacque was edging away at the front as they raced towards the first corner, a horrible deceptive downhill right hander. Barros was desperate not to let the Frenchman get away and left his braking very late, too late and clattered into

Jacque as they tipped into the corner. Two-stroke history ended in the gravel trap surrounded by broken fairings and angry words.

The chapter had closed, and Rossi crossed the line to win his eighth grand prix of the season. He won three more, clinching the title with four rounds remaining in Rio. Honda were so impressed by Barros that they gave him a four-stroke for the last four races and he duly won in Motegi and Valencia. Honda had totally dominated the new era, with Biaggi's wins in Brno and Sepang their only defeats. At Phillip Island there was an all two-stroke front row headed by McWilliams on the Roberts Proton, giving Bridgestone their first premier class pole, but the result was the same as usual: victory for Rossi and Honda. We had witnessed the final two-stroke MotoGP pole position.

I said goodbye to Barry Sheene at Phillip Island. Deep down, I knew it was the final goodbye, but would not admit it to myself at the time. Two months earlier a simple fax from Barry had shocked the grand prix paddock in Brno. Straight to the point as always, Barry stated the facts that he had been diagnosed with cancer of the oesophagus and upper stomach. He added that it was a pain in the arse and that he was going to overcome it as he had done with anything thrown at him before.

Barry flew into Phillip Island on the windy Thursday afternoon before the grand prix and I waited at the helipad for him to arrive. It was a frail figure that walked up the slope from the pad with the wind coming off the Bass Strait at his back. We shook hands and embraced. He was so thin but typically full of outward optimism for the future. I saw plenty of Barry that weekend while he was working for Australian television. The last time I spoke to him was on the grid just before the start of the MotoGP race when I interviewed him. Less than four months later, Barry died in hospital on the Gold Coast. A true legend had gone. An utterly focused man, who would let nothing get in his way, had succumbed to an illness that even he could not fight. Barry had provided me with the opportunity to follow my dream. There will never be another like him.

Welkom Yamaha

2003–2004

THE FOUR-STROKE PHENOMENON was working with both Ducati and Kawasaki joining the fray in 2003. Honda ruled the roost but wanted even more: a Japanese MotoGP World Champion. They thought they had found their man in Daijiro Kato who had finished seventh on his MotoGP debut season the previous year after dominating the 250cc class in 2001. They were also keen to boost their sales in the USA and brought in AMA (American Motorcyclist Association) Champion Nicky Hayden to join Rossi. Gibernau left Suzuki to join Kato at Gresini Honda and even Biaggi switched factories to ride for the Honda Pons team.

Honda's dream was shattered at the very first race of the season in Suzuka. This race day was a big occasion for me. The BBC had signed a contract to show the MotoGP races live while they still had one more year of their contract with World Superbikes. Their usual commentators Steve Parrish and Charlie Cox were seeing out the Superbike contract while the BBC took

253

the Dorna world-feed commentary off me and Matt Roberts. Suzi Perry and producer Belinda Rogerson had flown in to present their programme and conduct the interviews. It was a proud day for me after all those years growing up listening to and watching all the major sporting events courtesy of the BBC. Though it turned into a tough start.

On the third lap of the race, Kato crashed into a trackside wall at 130mph and lay unconscious on the side of the track. The Japanese rider never regained consciousness and was only kept alive by a life support machine. When it was finally switched off, he was officially declared dead. It was the first death at a grand prix race for nearly ten years and the Suzuka circuit has never staged another grand prix. The paddock, Honda and Japan were stunned at the death of a true World Champion. To this day Japanese racing has never fully recovered from the loss of a rider who usually had a smile, even though he was a shy character, but most importantly was a proud and dedicated father of two. The fact that Rossi won the race and Loris Capirossi brought the Desmosedici Ducati a podium finish on its MotoGP debut mattered little as we prepared for the next grand prix in South Africa three weeks later.

Sete Gibernau was not only a natural ambassador for the sport and the riders, but also a very good grand prix rider. The grandson of the founder of the Bultaco manufacturing dynasty had a rocky ride to the top tier, but his victory in Welkom was a true indication of what the Spanish rider was all about. Riding without his Gresini Honda team-mate Kato he beat Rossi fair and square in a heart-stopping duel. Inspired by the memory of and in dedication to his team-mate, he produced the ride of his life. Kato would have been so proud of him and suddenly Gibernau was a championship contender.

Rossi retaliated with victory in Jerez. The estimated crowd was 130,000 with 20,000 extra tickets being sold following Gibernau's Welkom success. Gibernau fought back with victory at a wet Le Mans but once again the champion struck back with a home win at an even crazier home grand prix at Mugello. Not only did those tens of thousands of patriotic fans packing the glorious Tuscan hillside celebrate the Rossi victory, but a second place for Capirossi on the bright red Ducati designed and built just across the hills in Bologna and a third place for Biaggi. Just seven days later those Ducati celebrations exploded into a sea of red flags and smoke to light up Barcelona with Capirossi bringing the iconic Italian factory their very first premier class victory.

Gibernau was at the absolute peak of his career. Wins over Rossi in Assen and at the Sachsenring moved him up to second with the title still in sight, until the champion decided it was time to up the pace. It was a pace nobody could match as Rossi and the RCV Honda moulded into one to disappear over the horizon. The Italian was playing with opposition that was itself of the very highest quality. He won six of the remaining seven races including a memorable ride at Phillip Island. Despite suffering a ten-second infringement for a yellow flag incident he battered the opposition led by Capirossi. He celebrated with a massive bed sheet borrowed from his hotel and emblazoned with the classic Barry Sheene number seven to celebrate the life of his father's great friend.

I would never have made it as a national newspaper journalist because I did not believe enough in rumours. The BBC were unhappy that I'd not pushed Honda's Carlo Fiorani hard enough at an interview in Rio when the rumours were raging through the paddock and beyond that Rossi was considering leaving Honda. How could that be true – surely this was the perfect combination of man and machine? Why change it? But they did.

Perhaps Vale needed a fresh challenge and also wanted to show Honda that, without him in the saddle, winning the world title would not happen. Perhaps Honda wanted to prove that their RCV four-stroke was such a brilliant motorcycle that there were plenty of riders who were quite capable of replacing the champion and repeating his success. Like so many seemingly loving marriages, you just can't believe it when the partners announce they are splitting up. Even before a rather flat announcement at the press conference after the final round in Valencia, it was common knowledge that Rossi was on his way to the under-achieving Yamaha team. If he wanted a new challenge, he had certainly got one. He brought the majority of his championship-winning Honda team with him, led by crew chief Jerry Burgess. In 2004 we would discover just how good Valentino Rossi was.

Manuel Poggiali appeared to be on the Rossi route to MotoGP, adding the 250cc title to his 125cc title, with Dani Pedrosa also on a similar path capturing the 125 title in Malaysia.

Yamaha were in a mess. They had not won a race since Biaggi brought them success at the end of the 2002 season in Malaysia. The M1 four-stroke just could not match the Honda or even Ducatis. Discussion in the paddock and in the media speculated whether Rossi's master touch could magic a long-awaited grand prix win. No one even mentioned a world title. They did after the opening grand prix of 2004.

There had been many great moments previously and there were still plenty to come but on 18 April at the Phakisa Freeway Racing circuit in Welkom, South Africa, Rossi joined that exclusive club of the true greats. He sat alongside the likes of Duke, Hailwood and Agostini at the very top table. No one gave him a chance in the 28-lap race around the 2.636-mile circuit, although the warning signs were there when he grabbed an impressive pole position and was joined on the front row by the Hondas of Gibernau and Biaggi.

From the start Rossi was at his absolute limit sliding, out of the saddle and braking late while Biaggi was smoother. They were still bitter rivals, no olive branches having appeared in the intervening years. Biaggi was the last Yamaha winner, Rossi the last Honda winner and now they had swapped camps. This mattered to them both so much and much more than it had in many previous duels. Six laps from the finish Biaggi tried to break away but Rossi hung onto his back wheel like the proverbial limpet. Three laps from the finish Rossi made his move with a classic block pass on Biaggi at the penultimate tight right-hand corner. Welkom had never witnessed anything like this before. The 45,000-strong crowd went wild while the worldwide television audience held its breath. Rossi led by inches as they crossed the line to start the last lap. Biaggi gave everything to grab back the lead, but despite setting the fastest lap of the race this had been signed off from above as Rossi's day.

With the place in total turmoil, the 25-year-old Italian crossed the finishing line with two-tenths of a second advantage over Biaggi, who played such a massive part in the proceedings. The winner was totally overcome with emotion and exhaustion. Rossi parked his M1 Yamaha against the guard rail and kissed the number 46 before sinking to his knees. The shoulders of his blue sweat-laden leathers shook with emotion as the tears flowed in the privacy of his crash helmet. We had all witnessed something very special.

Sadly, it was the swansong for the Welkom circuit. The usual political turmoil plus rumours that the promoter had disappeared meant we never went back. I was truly sad because I honestly felt that the grand prix brought more than simply just racing motorcycles to this struggling city burdened by unemployment, the threat of Aids and old-fashioned prejudice – it brought some much needed optimism to the wonderful young people we worked with at the circuit, but it was to be no more. One thing is for certain, Welkom went out on a high, but I often wonder what we left behind.

Despite that opening win Rossi knew the Hondas would be after his blood and he was not wrong. Gibernau was on fire and took over the championship lead after wins in Jerez and Le Mans. Rossi and Yamaha fought back with victories in Barcelona, Mugello and Assen. In a horrifying 190mph crash at Mugello, Shinya Nakano escaped serious injury when his rear tyre delaminated coming over the rise just after the start line. Makoto Tamada brought Bridgestone tyres their first four-stroke win in Brazil and repeated his success at Motegi. Former

World Superbike Champion Colin Edwards stood on a MotoGP podium for the first time, finishing second behind Rossi at Donington.

I had no idea where Qatar was. A bit of research revealed it was a peninsula in the Persian Gulf. Once only known for pearl fishing and its desert landscape, it was now regarded as the richest country in the world following the discovery of natural gas. Fifty-eight million dollars had been spent building a race circuit in the desert and we were on our way for round 13 of the 2004 MotoGP World Championship.

It proved to be a country of such great contrasts. On a trip into the desert and the magnificent sand dunes we witnessed the birth of a baby camel, only for the Bedouin shepherd to reach into his flowing robes to find his mobile phone to announce the new arrival. The six-star Ritz Carlton Hotel, full of ageing football stars seeing out their careers in lucrative Qatar, was our home for the week.

The trip to the Losail International Circuit took us first through the dusty, traffic-ridden outskirts of Doha, past the mosque and filling station. After filling up the hire car for less than a fiver, we would play spot the camels on the drive through the desert to the circuit. Very hot, very dusty, very windy, great facilities and no crowd was the recipe for the next three days.

Rossi arrived with a 39-point lead in the title chase with four rounds remaining. He left with that lead slashed to 14 and thirsting for revenge after a weekend of controversy in the sand. Rossi had only qualified on the third row of the grid for the 22-lap race around the 3.343-mile technically superb but slippery and dusty Losail circuit. On the eve of the race, Rossi's crew went over and over his grid position on a paddock scooter to give their rider a marker to ride over in the morning warm up to practise a line into the vital first corner. Some thought they were laying down rubber to enable their man to get better grip off the line. Amidst allegations and confusion, Rossi's team's conduct was deemed to have infringed the general sporting code and their rider was sent to the very back of the grid.

Rossi was furious and carved through the pack in the opening laps of the 22-lap desert encounter. He was fourth in four laps and only had one thought – to win the race, despite the penalty. Two laps later, at the last left hander, he slid onto the green AstroTurf, the Yamaha flicked sideways and he crashed, gashing two fingers on his left hand. Gibernau won, picked up 25 precious points, meaning Rossi's lead was down to 14 points with three rounds remaining, and we were on the plane to Malaysia.

At this time, Valentino would always turn up late for press conferences, especially the Thursday pre-event conferences in the circuit media centre press conference room. Five days after the Qatar race, we didn't even wait for him in Sepang. We would start without him, not that he ever seemed to worry.

I'd already asked Gibernau if there would be any repercussions from the Qatar grid incident. He was explaining that he had already moved on from Qatar when Rossi arrived, dark glasses and all making him look all the more menacing. When I asked him the same question, his answer indicated he did not feel the same way. He chillingly stated that Sete Gibernau would never win another grand prix and his prophecy turned out to be 100 per cent correct. To say the champion was fired up would be a vast understatement. He won the Malaysia race with Gibernau down in seventh. Rossi celebrated by borrowing a broom from a trackside marshal on his slowing down lap and started to sweep the track mocking the Qatar decision. He was on a roll and nobody, Gibernau or the authorities included, was going to stop him.

Seven days later he won at Phillip Island to win his sixth world title and bring Yamaha their first MotoGP four-stroke crown. This was his greatest ever season. Yamaha was dead and buried before he arrived, but by explosive ability, enthusiasm and a sheer bloody-minded attitude Rossi had pulled them out of the pit onto the top step in a season of brilliance.

He completed the year with victory in Valencia where 12 months earlier he'd announced his departure from Honda to Yamaha. There was only one party that regretted that particular decision.

In the smaller classes, MotoGP stars of the future were making a name for themselves. Pedrosa won the 250cc title to become the first rider for 44 years to win 125 and 250cc titles in successive seasons. Andrea Dovizioso was 125cc World Champion and a certain Casey Stoner brought the first 125cc grand prix win for KTM in Malaysia.

Family Values
2005–2006

ROSSI AND GIBERNAU were at it right from the word go in 2005 but it ended with exactly the same result as before. The Spanish Honda rider knew he had to win first time out with the support of the home crowd in Jerez. It came down to a last bend confrontation, the inevitable collision and victory for Rossi. Gibernau strode up pit lane after finishing second to express his views on the incident. Rossi and his team just smiled, they knew they were on top of their game, and Rossi often played with the opposition as he cruised to the world title. Eleven grands prix wins brought him the crown with four rounds to go at circuits old and new. One notable exception came in the shape of Capirossi on the Bridgestone-shod Ducati with back to back wins in Motegi and Sepang.

Marco Melandri joined Gibernau at Gresini Honda and took second place in the championship after a superb season which included victories at the last two rounds. Barros won in Estoril and Laguna Seca returned to the calendar after an 11-year absence with a home victory.

There was no better place to be on that scorching July afternoon in 2005 than in California, in pit lane with Nicky Hayden's legendary father Earl witnessing and sharing with him the triumph of his son at his home grand prix. Earl, who'd fathered and nurtured three sons – Tommy, Roger Lee and Nicky – into brilliant motorcycle racers. Earl, who travelled the world with his son Nicky in a warm, friendly and polite way that was not always the case with grand prix riders and their fathers. This was a long way from Owensboro nestling alongside the Ohio River in Kentucky in every sense.

The brothers learnt to ride on the farm and Earl also ran the local second-hand car franchise, Second Chance Autos. He would relate how he'd send Nicky round the back of a customer's house who had fallen short on the hire purchase agreement. While he kept the customer talking, Nicky would jump in the car and drive away. Valentino Rossi remembers meeting them for the first time on their first ever visit to Japan at probably the busiest location in the whole world, Tokyo railway station at 9am on a Monday morning. Wherever they went, they won friends. After Nicky's first grand prix win there were no blow-up dolls on the pillion or dressing up on the podium, but a pillion ride for his father who'd made all this happen.

This was just the start and there was much more to come. Dani Pedrosa retained his 250cc crown and was on his way to MotoGP. Tom Lüthi brought some much appreciated success to Switzerland with the 125cc title.

The two new circuits on the 2005 calendar were soulless, concrete, government-funded mausoleums that didn't last for long. Of course, it was exciting to fly to China and the Formula One track outside Shanghai. The facilities, as you might have guessed, were unbelievable. But carp-filled pools in the paddock, fancy wooden arches and a massive half-filled media centre with its lifts and glass doors just did not hide the lack of interest from the Chinese public and the depressing, ever present smoggy weather. Formula One remained, but MotoGP stayed for just four races.

The other new circuit lasted just three years, which was shame. The 3.318-mile Istanbul Park circuit in Turkey was a fantastic track for racing high powered MotoGP motorcycles, but from the moment you arrived you just knew it would not last. Again, at the beck and call of Formula One the facilities could not be faulted, but the track was in the middle of nowhere on the Asian side of the Bosporus.

We arrived there tired and grumpy from Australia after five races in six weeks. The surrounding area reminded me of pictures from an Eastern European war zone. Just getting to the circuit from our so-called hotel included fighting for space down an unmade road with huge monster-like articulated lorries who would have eaten hire cars for breakfast if you gave them the chance. Getting back in the dark was even worse. Rather like Shanghai, the empty seats in the pristine grandstands told their own story and it was obvious the money would run out. It did after just three visits or perhaps even earlier.

On our last visit in 2007 there was far more interest in the press conference held by Formula One supremo Bernie Ecclestone than the MotoGP race that weekend. He told the assembled media he now owned the circuit because of the money owed to him. In the middle of the second practice session on Friday afternoon he appeared in our media office with notebook and lawyer in tow measuring up and checking all the fittings which he now owned. It was a totally bizarre scene. He didn't recognise me, and I felt free to carry on with my radio broadcasts without constantly looking over my shoulder.

We never returned to this gateway to Asia and the vibrant, exciting city of Istanbul. My undying memory of the Turkish experience was witnessing the first MotoGP race winner Marco Melandri sliding the Gresini Honda at over 160mph through the turn 11 right-hand bend on our very first visit. It was named the fastest corner of the year and made it worth fighting those articulated trucks to get there.

After hosting 229 solo grands prix, the layout of the legendary Assen circuit was also changing. The riders and the purists were not happy when told the first section of the track was being shortened in 2006. Rossi signed off with his third win in four years on the old circuit.

I'd never seen Nicky Hayden get angry, but I can promise you he was angry, very angry with his new team-mate as they both struggled to stand up in the gravel trap at the Parabolic Interior corner at Estoril in Portugal. Even on the television screens you got the gist of what the American was screaming at a startled Dani Pedrosa. Who could blame him for such an uncharacteristic outburst of abuse and gesticulating?

Hayden had arrived at this penultimate round of the 2006 World Championship with the rare but real chance of pushing Rossi off the top step for the first time in five years. Riding the RCV Honda he'd worked hard to develop with crew chief Peter Benson, the Kentucky Kid arrived on the Portuguese coast with a precious 12-point lead over his former team-mate Rossi. It was a chance he would probably never get again and the last person he thought would wreck it was his own team-mate.

The 2.599-mile Estoril circuit that nestles between golf courses a couple of miles inland from the seaside town of Cascais was the venue for the most dramatic penultimate round that ultimately, although we did not realise it at the time, played a massive part in the outcome of the championship. It all started quietly enough. Rossi led with his Camel Yamaha team-mate Colin Edwards protecting him, acting as tail-end Charlie in second place. The Honda duo of championship leader Hayden and Pedrosa had settled into the chasing pair with still a long 23 laps remaining when they started the fateful fifth lap.

Turn six at the end of the slightly kinked back straight was a tricky, deceptive left-hand bend and Pedrosa got it so, so wrong. The 250cc World Champion left his braking far too late, ran onto the kerb, locked the front wheel and crashed, with his sliding Honda skittling down Hayden. That 12-point championship lead disappeard in a cloud of sparks and then Portuguese gravel

This was Rossi's big chance, but it was not that easy. Any thoughts he'd had of a comfortable 25 points and a 13-point lead going into the last round were scuppered by the satellite Hondas of Toni Elías and former 500cc Champion Kenny Roberts Junior. Crossing the line with one lap to go, Roberts was leading and eased off. In the heat of battle, he'd miscalculated the number of laps and thought he'd won; surely now Rossi would grab maximum points. He led coming out of the final corner onto the long start and finish straight with Elías in tow. At the vital moment the Spaniard Elías pulled out of his slipstream as the chequered flag fluttered to win by 0.002 seconds, grabbing his one and only MotoGP win. Rossi's 20 points gave him an 8-point lead as the final round in Valencia approached. Nobody gave Hayden much of a chance.

It had not been an easy season for Rossi chasing that sixth consecutive world title. It appeared his main threat would come from Capirossi on the Ducati, but injuries from a first bend crash in Barcelona wrecked his chances. Hayden I knew would be consistent, but there was an extra edge to his confidence and riding. He won outside of America for the only time in Assen when countryman Colin Edwards crashed out of the lead within sight of the chequered flag. The whole paddock, apart from Honda, fely sorry for Colin. He never won a grand prix, which was scant reward for a funny guy and great rider. Hayden made it two in a row at Laguna, but Rossi closed the gap with a win in Malaysia, one of five successive podiums before the Valencia showdown.

When the sun shines off the Mediterranean, 100,000 fans pack the Ricardo Tormo circuit and the legendary fireworks fill the sky, there is no better place to decide a world title. Sunday 29 October 2006 was one of those days in Valencia. Just to add to the fun, former World Superbike Champion Troy Bayliss returned to replace the injured Gibernau at Ducati and Hayden had found a way to forgive Pedrosa. If Hayden won the race and Pedrosa was second, the American would be World Champion by a single point even if Rossi finished third. Sounds easy enough, but it all turned out very differently.

Rossi qualified in pole for the 30-lap race with Hayden in the middle of the second row. They could not have made more contrasting starts racing towards that vital first corner at the tight and twisty circuit. Hayden flew like a missile from the second row while Rossi's Yamaha rather lamely lifted the front wheel. When the dust settled, Hayden was safely tucked in behind the Ducatis of Bayliss and Capirossi, but the champion was struggling down in seventh. An overheating Yamaha engine took the edge off acceleration and Rossi was having to ride hard, too hard to stay in contention.

On the fifth lap at the infamous second corner that had claimed many a victim, Rossi pushed beyond the limit and crashed. He quickly remounted 20 seconds at the back of the field with a bent footrest and gear lever, broken clutch lever and damaged handlebars. This time even Rossi could not perform a miracle. Hayden's pit board screamed at him that third place would be enough, and it was. Bayliss crossed the line for a worthy only grand prix win with Capirossi second, but 100,000 eyes focused solely on one man as Hayden took third place and the world title.

Mum Rose, dad Earl, brothers Tommy and Roger Lee and sister Jenny celebrated with their man in pit lane as did the world of racing. Immediately after the emotional podium ceremony, Earl was knocking on the door of Rossi's motorhome to commiserate with the Italian. MotoGP is a highly dangerous, tough, ruthless way of earning a living. Because of the very nature of their chosen profession, 'gentleman' and 'decent' are not words you hear too often to describe riders and especially World Champions. Off the track, Nicky was both of these. His tragic death in a cycling accident in 2017 just outside the Misano circuit in Italy was met with worldwide grief. Nicky Hayden was a very special person both on and off a motorcycle and is so missed by all.

Casey Stoner had arrived in the MotoGP class riding the LCR Honda and took second place in Turkey. Another future MotoGP World Champion Jorge Lorenzo was crowned 250cc Champion with Álvaro Bautista taking the 125cc crown.

Minds into Nines
2007–2009

AFTER FIVE YEARS of destroying lap records and top speeds, the 990cc four-strokes were reduced down to 800cc in 2007. With top speeds approaching 220mph at certain circuits there were major concerns that tracks could not safely cope with such missiles. In principle it sounded like the correct decision, but in practice the 800cc machines were lapping as fast and, in many cases, faster than their bigger brothers. Riders know the score and so quickly learnt that by braking later into corners and then negotiating them quicker produced the faster lap times. One rider in particular took to the 800s like a duck to water. Stoner's time had come.

The Australian joined Capirossi at Ducati when Gibernau retired. The first race of the season was an eye opener for every reason. Stoner led each lap on the Bridgestone-shod GP7 Ducati to show Rossi what to expect for the remainder of the season. He set a new lap and race record and his top speed of 201.8mph was exactly the same as race winner Rossi's the previous year on the 990cc Yamaha. So much for slowing down then with 800s.

The stage was set for the Australian and the new 800s. Try as they might, Pedrosa and Rossi could not stem the flow of bright red Ducati blood and Stoner was in a class of his own. Honda had to wait until the tenth race of the season for their first victory of the season with Pedrosa victorious at the Sachsenring. Rossi won for the fifth time in Jerez but eventually had to settle for third place in the championship and a single point behind Pedrosa.

At Brno on the Thursday afternoon I met Vale walking the circuit the wrong way round, head bowed and deep in thought. A tax bill from the Italian authorities was reported to be costing him around 90 million euros. Those trips on the Gatwick Express were catching up with him. He returned the next year with no tax worries, ready to fight to regain the crown he'd worn for so long.

Stoner stormed away at the front to bring Ducati their first premier class title with ten grands prix wins and his points total equalling Rossi's record-breaking 367 set in 2005. He'd scored points at every single round. To add salt to an already painful wound for Honda, Stoner clinched the title at their home in Motegi when he finished sixth in the race won by his team-mate Capirossi. It was a staggering performance by Stoner that caught everybody by surprise.

The next race was at Phillip Island where Stoner and Australia celebrated with another win. Former World Supersport Champion Chris Vermeulen also brought Australia added success with Suzuki's first grand prix win in the four-stroke era and first win for six years with victory at a wet Le Mans. Lorenzo prepared for his MotoGP debut the next year, clinching his second 250cc crown with Gábor Talmácsi bringing Hungary their one and only world title in the 125cc class.

Flying into Doha International Airport was always interesting. Miles and miles of sandy nothingness is suddenly broken by the dazzling lights of Doha's ever increasing skyscrapers that you feel you could lean out and touch on the way down. In March 2008 though, coming into land for the opening round of the championship in Qatar, it was not the lights of Doha that pierced the darkness below but an amazing silhouette of the Losail International Circuit totally surrounded by pitch black darkness.

I'd learnt not to doubt the Qatar organisers when they built the Losail circuit in double quick time to stage that first race in 2004, but to light up the entire 3.343-mile circuit to race at night – surely this was even beyond their expertise and very deep pockets. The flight over the desert was proof they had both. The first ever floodlit World Championship motorsport race to be staged on tarmac was ready to go after just 175 days of frantic work under the desert sun. The US Company Musco Lighting had already lit up the Daytona International Speedway in Florida and their engineers spent 1,300 working hours ensuring MotoGP would make history. It was a massive task.

Forty-four 13-megawatt generators provided enough electricity to light up 3,000 homes at the same time. They generated enough power to light a street running from Doha to Moscow. The complete lighting system included over 1,000 structures, 3,600 separate bulbs and over 300 miles of wire to link it all up. There was enough light to illuminate 70 full-size football pitches. The riders, before the first test under the lights, were concerned about glare off the track surface and on the visors of their helmets. Once again, it had all been thought out. A number of the bulbs were specially designed to aim light away from the actual track. It was directed onto secondary reflective surfaces, which reconfigured and redirected the light back onto the track surface. The beam that was aimed onto the track was a narrow ribbon of light that could be aimed with accuracy to within one-tenth of one degree.

When that massive red ball of the sun dropped below the desert skyline and the equally big and round yellow moon's rays illuminated the miles of empty sand, the sound of MotoGP engines craving action broke the silence. The 3.600 bulbs sprung into light and I knew history had been made. The opening Thursday night practice session for the new season was underway.

Six months later there may have been no floodlights, but MotoGP history was been written once again at the most iconic motorsport battleground of them all – the Indianapolis International Speedway in America. What a place. Vast grandstands surround the most famous banked racing oval of them all.

The biggest sports stadium in the world with a capacity of over 250,000 features the famous line of original bricks forming the start and finish line. The annual Indy 500 car race was one of the biggest sporting events of the year in the States and one of biggest in world motorsport. I could smell the petrol and tyres, and hear the roar of the crowd above the announcer's excited voice the first time I stepped into this vast empty arena, but what were we doing here at the home of four wheels? On 14 August 1909, the first ever motorsport event to be staged at Indianapolis was seven motorcycle races. They had been invited to return in preparation for the hundredth birthday celebrations the following year. The 2.620-mile grand prix track in the centre incorporating part of the oval was not that exciting but, for me, just being there at 'the Brickyard' was enough.

Rossi, right from the word go and even before, was determined to win the title back in 2008. He'd switched to Bridgestone tyres in the winter although it was the same old story under the Qatar floodlights with Stoner starting his defence with a win. Pedrosa took the lead in the championship for the very first time with victory in Jerez but it was his bitter rival from their 125 and 250cc days that was making the headlines.

Jorge Lorenzo made a sensational debut to his MotoGP career partnering Rossi at Yamaha. He was in pole position at the first three races and won the third in Estoril. Rossi fought back on our last visit to China to secure his first win in eight months. He was back in business and finished on the podium at the next four including wins at Le Mans and Mugello. Stoner was not done and won three in a row at Donington, Assen and the Sachsenring. The showdown between Rossi and Stoner came to a head at Laguna Seca on a scorching hot Californian afternoon in July and I'd lost my voice.

Probably the most talked about, controversial, brilliant, magnificent or just plain dangerous Grand Prix – it just depended whose side you were on – certainly took your breath away. I had plenty of breath left that Sunday afternoon. I'd started croaking on Friday, was hoarse by Saturday qualifying and could produce no more than a whisper on Sunday when Rossi and Stoner arrived on the start line for the 32-lap race.

Stoner had dominated so far, leading Rossi by almost half a second after his fifth successive pole. Great World Champions are prepared to risk everything when it really matters, and this really mattered to Rossi. At 29 years old, he produced a frightening display of utter ruthless determination that demonstrated just what an eighth world title would mean to him. Rossi knew he could not allow Stoner to get away and every time the Ducati got in front he fought back immediately. It was a mighty head to head and on the fourth lap Rossi left nobody and especially Stoner in any doubt about just how far he was prepared to go to win.

They were side by side on the brakes before plunging down the legendary step off the Edge of the World into the Corkscrew. Rossi was forced onto the outside and then onto the dirt and dust of the inside as they switched left to right coming out at the bottom, but he was still leading, with Stoner having to run wide to avoid collision.

This was not just a fight for a grand prix win or even the world title. This was all about pride between two great riders at the very peak of their powers. It was spellbinding to witness, even if I could only listen to Gavin Emmett and an injured rider John Hopkins on the microphones. Stoner knew he had the extra speed and bided his time. The outcome was decided on lap 24. Stoner lined up Rossi at the final corner but was a fraction of a second late on the brakes. He ran on into the gravel to avoid hitting the back of Rossi's Yamaha and went down at walking pace. He remounted to finish second, but the battle was over and so was the war.

Rossi won the next four grands prix, including a hurricane-threatened Indianapolis opener where I told viewers I thought I'd seen a white horse in pit lane. Luckily with the hurricane approaching and a long delay after the race had been stopped, I didn't think many people had tuned in but those who were still awake let me know. The race never re-started with advertising hoardings being tossed around in the threatening winds. It was an advertising banner being blown up pit lane that reminded me of a white horse after a long wait talking about nothing. I've never been allowed to forget it.

Rossi regained the title with victory in Motegi, while Stoner finished the season with a win in Valencia but second in the championship. That Corkscrew confrontation three months earlier had been the pivotal moment of an amazing season.

Marco Simoncelli won the 250cc world title and Frenchman Mike Di Meglio the 125s. Fifteen-year-old Scott Redding brought some real joy to Donington by winning the 125cc British Grand Prix. He was the first British winner in the class for 35 years and the youngest ever grand prix winner at the tender age of 15 years 170 days. Third that afternoon was a certain Marc

Márquez taking his first ever step onto the podium. Many were to follow.

Rossi barely had time to celebrate because challengers old and new were lining up in 2009 to take him on. First it had been Biaggi and then Gibernau, but this time it was his new team-mate Lorenzo who was the target of the mind games. They always tell you the first person a rider wants to beat is his team-mate. Rossi and Lorenzo followed that principle throughout the season and especially with some classic confrontations in Barcelona, Sachsenring, Brno and Indianapolis. Unlike the other two, Lorenzo stood firm. The result was some fantastic battles out on the track and plenty of words off it. It was classic Rossi on both fronts. This was the season of the first sole tyre supplier in MotoGP and it was Bridgestone that saw off Michelin to win the contract.

Once again there was a pivotal moment, although it came a lot earlier in the season than the previous year. The outcome was the same. It was Lorenzo's home grand prix in Barcelona and the 22-year-old was having a superb second MotoGP season already having won in Motegi and Le Mans. With the home crowd at fever pitch, Lorenzo outbraked Rossi into turn one of the final lap. Despite the considerable efforts of his team-mate, he stayed in front as they raced downhill into the frighteningly fast right-hand bend that led onto the start and finish straight. The packed crowd in that towering double-tier grandstand overlooking the finish line were on their feet when Rossi decided it was time to assert his authority once again. Somehow, he managed to position his Yamaha on the inside of Lorenzo's similar steed at 120mph when it just seemed an impossible move. Nothing is impossible when Rossi wants to put the 'youngsters' in their place and remind them who is the master. He won by 0.095 seconds. It was the Corkscrew all over again.

Rossi won six races to retain the title. Lorenzo pushed him hard with four wins but was 45 points adrift of his team-mate at the finish. The champion had clinched his ninth world title and scored his one hundredth grand prix victory, but still those challengers continued to line up. Hiroshi Aoyama won the very last 250cc Championship before it switched to Moto2 while Julián Simón was crowned 125cc World Champion with Bradley Smith second.

Royal Flush
2010

IT WAS A Monday morning in September 2010 and the same plain table and uncomfortable plastic chair in the café upstairs at Bologna airport, along with the same numb feeling of sadness coupled with that inbuilt desire to get on with it and tell the story properly. I'd been here before, drinking the same cappuccino at the same table and chair after the death of Ayrton Senna at Imola and the life-changing accident of Wayne Rainey at Misano. It did not get any easier, but Colin Fenton's words of advice all those years ago still rang true. It's your duty to tell the story correctly in respect to the person who has died.

Twenty-two hours earlier one of the nicest guys I'd ever met in the paddock and a grand prix winner with the potential to chase a World Championship lost his life in the Moto2 race at the San Marino Grand Prix in Misano. Shoya Tomizawa died after he crashed coming out of the Tramonto corner onto the back straight and inexplicably slid back into the path of the distraught

Scott Redding and Alex de Angelis who could not avoid the stricken Japanese rider. The teenager had already written his place into the history books by winning the very first Moto2 race five months earlier under the Qatar floodlights and finishing second three weeks later in Jerez.

In all walks of life when somebody dies, and especially in tragic circumstances, we all say what a great person they were, which is the natural reaction, but in Shoya's case it was absolutely true. While retaining that inbuilt Japanese politeness he was a bubble of enthusiasm and fun in the paddock even with somebody nearly 50 years his senior. You just could not help liking him and the wave of grief that hit the Misano paddock that afternoon reflected this. I'd only really met him after he won that opening round in Qatar but already he'd made a great impression on me and many others.

As we left the paddock that night with darkness drawing in over the nearby Adriatic Sea all the Japanese riders, mechanics, journalists and photographers assembled to pay a silent tribute. It was a reminder to us all – and especially to those of us who report the action without being actively involved – that this is still and always will be a dangerous sport. It may have been the first death on the MotoGP track for seven years but never forget that it can happen. It made me realise that just watching the action on a couple of television screens in a darkened windowless room gave no real indication of just how fast and dangerous this sport was. I vowed to get outside, get trackside whenever I could. It was a necessary reality check to reflect what was actually happening and not just what we commentated on via those television screens.

I would like to say I'd been closely following the progress of a certain Marc Márquez and had already marked him down as a future World Champion when seeing him first race in the 125cc World Championship as a baby-faced 15-year-old, but I'd be a liar. My first recollection of Marc was him being told off, or probably scolded at his age, by Judith, the Dorna press officer, for chasing the kangaroos at the Phillip Island wildlife park in Australia. I commented that I thought he looked 12 years old when he took his first podium finish at Donington Park in 2008.

Two years later I certainly knew who he was when he won the 125cc World Championship. The floodgates were about to open. It was 2010 and the year of change, and none more so than in that new Moto2 class which replaced the two-stroke 250s that had been there from the very start in 1949. Four-stroke 600cc powered by mandatory highly tuned Honda engines was the new concept. They were CBR 600 RR engines prepared by Trevor Morris, who'd been around longer than me, and his team. Some purists hated the change, but it was considerably cheaper, encouraged new frame design and produced some superb racing. It would not be long before Moto3 followed suit, making the three classes all four-stroke and hopefully cheaper to support, although new expenses always creep into whatever racing budget you are preparing.

Former MotoGP winner Toni Elías was crowned the first Moto2 champion, riding the Moriwaki framed Honda, with former 125cc champion Julián Simón second and Andrea Iannone third. It was a good start to the new era.

Jorge Lorenzo captured his first premier class title the same year on the YZR Yamaha after finishing third in Malaysia behind his team-mate Rossi, who typically stole the limelight in Sepang but not the title. The Doctor had endured a tough year and the Bye Bye Baby message on his helmet at his home track in Misano told the story. He was on his way to the Italian dream team with Ducati. Where Ferrari had failed to lure him to Formula One despite some impressive tests, Ducati got their man and Italy held its breath.

The other grand prix in Italy at the magnificent Mugello circuit had been a disaster for Rossi. He crashed and broke his leg slowing on a cold rear tyre in practice at the Biondetti chicane to prevent that serial follower of faster riders Héctor Barberá from following him. The tears flowed on the banked Tuscan hillsides that surround the circuit as the bright yellow helicopter took off en route to hospital with a stricken Rossi on board. He acknowledged those tears with a wave of the hand which just produced more tears. Typically, he was back in action just over five and a half weeks later to finish fourth at the Sachsenring; no wonder Ducati were licking their lips.

The British Grand Prix returned to Silverstone after a 23-year residence at Donington Park while newly built Motorland Aragón replaced the much photographed, much planned and much celebrated but never actually built Balatoring in Hungary that had appeared on the original grand prix schedule. The first question was – where is Aragón? Once established that it was in cowboy country in the desert between Zaragoza and the Mediterranean coast at Reus, the important questions followed.

However glamorous your job may seem from the outside it's still the basics that matter. Flying all over the world commentating on World Championship motorsport may seem a perfect way to earn a living, but scrape the surface and it was those basics of food times, football and beer that kept what at the time was a predominantly male group of travelling souls ticking over.

Topics of conversation vary when you are on these long flyaway trips. Football and the opposite sex have been high on the agenda on flights to the far flung corners of the globe for as long as I can remember. That probably does not come as the greatest surprise to those long-suffering loved ones back home who maintain regular life ready for our return with bags of laundry and excuses of jet lag when a meal out is suggested. After all, give us a break, we have been eating out every night for the last three weeks talking about football and the opposite sex!

Occasionally conversations do vary to a more practical level, touching on how bad the traffic might be into the circuit, what time lunch will be and, most importantly, the availability of the nearest loo to our commentary position. Four hours of live television, punctuated with the need to consume vast quantities of bottled water, cause their own special problems, especially to somebody in the grey hair age range.

Even the most modern of circuits have caused some tricky moments. Mugello, the Ferrari F1 test track and magnificent home of the Italian MotoGP race, had facilities to die for – apart from a good old-fashioned sit-down loo. A hole in the ground is a hole in the ground despite being surrounded by gleaming while marble and bright lights. The search for a proper sit-down job became the focus of our investigative powers. Two were eventually discovered. The first in the medical centre and the second behind the commentary boxes. The only problem was that the one behind the commentary box had no lock because it was a disabled toilet. A nameless colleague from the BBC was caught in a compromising position by the cleaner while sampling its delights. He had devised an intricate locking method of wrapping his belt round the door handle combined with a broom handle, but it failed miserably in his hour of need.

To our delight our first visit to Aragón produced no such problems, in fact the complete opposite. There was a very posh loo just outside our commentary box which was convenient in every sense of the word. The loo was always immaculately clean and there was a selection of those little bottles of hand wash and even aftershave, which I'm told you have at your disposal when you travel on business and first class flights. The other wonderful feature was that nobody else seemed to use it. You could quietly sit there planning your day ahead with nobody entering to bother you. All it lacked was a British morning daily to prepare you perfectly for the hustle and bustle of the paddock.

There was enormous excitement in Aragón when King Juan Carlos of Spain announced that he was going to attend the very first World Championship race at the circuit. There was a flurry of activity in the paddock with scary-looking soldiers and dogs checking every nook and cranny before the arrival of the king in the morning.

I'd already had the pleasure of meeting the king's personal bodyguard a couple of years earlier when His Highness had attended the Spanish Grand Prix in Jerez. Once again, the availability of the nearest ablutions came into play. To relieve yourself at Jerez it was a 75-yard walk along the balcony from the commentary position. As you can imagine it was journey that I'd embarked on many times, but there was a problem the morning of the race in Jerez. The problem was in the shape of a swarthy stocky man, dressed in a shiny but perfectly fitting suit which matched his highly polished black patent leather shoes. He politely, but with no hint that you could disagree, informed me that the balcony was closed for the morning before the king arrived. I explained my predicament and to my amazement he agreed to accompany me to the ablutions together with a friendly little cocker spaniel who seemed more interested in the food smells from the nearby hospitality units than sniffing out explosives. Our little parade set out along the deserted balcony overlooking the pits and returned a couple of minutes later. I thanked and shook hands with the suited gentleman when I noticed the pistol-shaped bulge from the inside pocket of that well-fitting jacket.

On the Sunday morning of the Aragón race the place was buzzing before the arrival of the king. I decided that before the morning warm-up sessions for the races got underway, a visit to my own little secret haven of rest and tranquillity was the perfect start to a long day. On arrival it was obvious that somebody had gone to an awful lot of trouble on my behalf to make it a perfect start to my day; you could see your face in the polished porcelain, those little bottles around the sink positively glowed and, the nicest touch of them all, a vase of fresh-smelling flowers completed the picture. I was in heaven and still nobody to disturb me but with the warm-up about to start it was time to return to that smellier, dirtier commentary box and start work.

As I crossed the corridor to the commentary box Gemma, the Dorna head of communications, was purposely striding towards me with a sheet of paper in her hand. In fact, it was not just a sheet a paper but a laminated sheet of paper – like a notice, even an official notice that was waiting to be pinned up somewhere.

As she swept by on her important mission I managed to read some of the big black writing. My Spanish is poor, but I got the gist. The words 'Strictly Private' and 'King Juan Carlos' stood out clearly on the clean white sheet. I tried so very hard not to laugh and uttered my customary *hola*, about the only Spanish word she could ever understand from my Oxfordshire lips. I was doing OK but faltered as she stopped at the door of my haven of rest and took the drawing pins out of her pocket. By the time the laminated notice had been placed on the door I was finished. Actually speaking while taking gulps of air between the convulsions was impossible.

She looked aghast at me and simply said, 'It's too late isn't it?' A mere nod of the head was all I could muster in answer to her polite but scarily stern observation; the pinning up of the royal proclamation had come just a little too late for its instructions to be followed by one particular member of the commentary team.

I spent the next four hours dreading the arrival of that man in the shiny suit and patent black leather shoes into the commentary box. I dreamt of dark damp prison cells in the castle above the nearby town of Alcañiz, a public trial for treason in Madrid and even a medical examination to prove just what I'd been doing in that private room. He never arrived, and we got back to discussing the important things – football and the opposite sex.

Marco

2011

HONDA – WITHOUT a world title for four long, barren years – had been eying up Casey Stoner for a long time and inevitably they got their man in 2011. The ground had been cleared with race boss Livio Suppo leaving Ducati to join Honda in a similar role. Suppo understood Stoner and got the best out of him. Stoner trusted the Italian and joined him to partner Dani Pedrosa, surely the unluckiest rider in MotoGP history.

While others bounced and slid, Dani always hurt himself when he crashed, whether it was caused by himself, often by others and just as often by pure bad luck. I remember just five days after clinching the 125cc world title back in 2003 in Malaysia, he celebrated his first ride as World Champion at the first practice session in Australia with a helicopter ride to hospital in Melbourne. It looked a pretty innocuous crash as he slid into the barrier at the bottom of Lukey Heights on a typical damp Phillip Island morning, but this was Dani. Two broken ankles ruled him out for the remainder of the season. Seven years later he was fighting for the 2010 premier title with his old nemesis Lorenzo when a mechanical problem with the throttle threw him high into the Japanese air just three laps into practice at the Twin Ring Motegi circuit. You didn't have to be a rocket scientist or surgeon to guess the outcome; another broken collarbone and flight back to Barcelona for the luckless Pedrosa.

What a contrast 2011 turned out to be for the two big shakers of the sport. The so talented Stoner took to the 800cc Honda like a duck to water. Rossi, with the nation resting on his broad shoulders, buckled on the uncompetitive Ducati.

Rossi had arrived into the dream team a couple or at the least a year too late. Ducati, fired up by that initial 800cc success, were resting on their laurels. The bike had always been difficult to ride, and while they struggled Yamaha and Honda as always were catching up and then overtaking them. It was such a bitter pill to swallow for the passionate Italian fans watching their hero struggle so much and Stoner just piled on the pressure and there was nothing Rossi could do. Ten wins for Stoner to join the exclusive club of Geoff Duke, Giacomo Agostini, Eddie Lawson and a certain Valentino Rossi as winners of the premier class for two different manufacturers.

Rossi finished seventh with one podium finish. The Australian simply rubbed more salt into an already very painful wound at Jerez. A humbled Rossi came to his pit-lane garage to apologise after bringing them both down when he torpedoed the Ducati into the Honda at the first corner in the earlier race. Only Casey would have had the balls to suggest to 'God' that perhaps his ambitions had outweighed his talent. Rossi's chance for revenge on the track never materialised.

Stoner clinched the first 800cc title for Honda in the proper place. Not the Honda headquarters at the Motegi Twin Ring circuit, but seven days later at home in Phillip Island where he secured his fifth victory in a row at his home race on his twenty-sixth birthday.

Race day ended for his nearest challenger Lorenzo with Yamaha team manager Wilco Zeelenberg trawling through the gravel trap looking for the top of his rider's third finger on his left hand after a crash in the morning warm-up. Lorenzo high sided from the Yamaha at the fast final corner onto the Gardner Straight. His hand was caught under the sliding bike at well over 100mph. When he finally came to a halt in the gravel trap he stood up and took off his bloody glove to reveal the tip of his third finger had gone after being grounded into the tarmac. Wilco's later search was not successful.

Stoner had finished third the previous week behind Pedrosa and Lorenzo at Motegi in a race he nearly didn't attend. The original Motegi race in Japan was postponed after the earthquake and resulting tsunami on 11 March.

A new date was set for the end of September amid worries
about a radiation leak at the Fukushima Daiichi nuclear
power station. Initially Stoner said he would not attend,
but together with all the top riders made the journey to
receive an amazing welcome from the Japanese people.
It was the first major sporting event to be held in Japan
since the disaster and the welcome was both warm and
grateful. Some took the risk more seriously than others.
Lorenzo admitted he only showered in bottled water
while Ducati arrived with a monitor from Italy which
duly registered less radiation at the circuit than at home
in Florence.

Yamaha celebrated their 50 years of racing with Ben
Spies winning Assen and a poignant visit by Wayne
Rainey to Misano, the first time since his 1993 crash.
We'd seen plenty of Wayne since the accident but this
was different. You would never have guessed Wayne was
returning in a wheelchair for the first time to a place
that must have such dark memories. A place where he
smashed his body and changed his life for ever. Wayne
was as friendly and dignified as ever as he celebrated
Yamaha's successful 50 years.

The highlight of the celebrations for me was an
amazing evening at the Indianapolis Show Ground to
witness Kenny Roberts reunited with the TZ 750cc
Yamaha round the Indy mile dirt track. Witnessing the
master in action sliding the two-stroke projectile was a

reminder of just why he was so special, not that anybody needed reminding. Nothing had changed and you could have turned the clock back 40 years watching 'the king' who'd turned grand prix racing on its head returning to his roots. This where it had all started.

German Stefan Bradl went one better than his dad Helmut, who finished runner-up in the 1991 250cc Championship, by clinching the Moto2 Championship. Helmut was always in his garage quietly offering advice and encouragement.

Márquez's frantic challenge ended as he crashed during practice in Malaysia when the marshals failed to display warning flags at a wet part of the Sepang circuit. Márquez missed the last two races with a career-threatening eye injury but returned with a vengeance the following year.

The steady Nico Terol was the very last winner of the 125cc Championship before Moto3 arrived in 2012. The 125s went out with a bang and the race at the Sachsenring was a reminder of what a class of close racing it had been for 62 glorious years. Even the Tissot still and video cameras could not separate Héctor Faubel and Johann Zarco when they crossed the line and the race was awarded to Faubel because he'd set the fastest lap of the race.

'He's gone' was the simple text from Frine in her media centre office that finally confirmed what we already knew but could not broadcast. Marco Simoncelli was dead. The 2011 season was totally overshadowed by the events of Sunday 23 October in Sepang. The friendly lanky Italian with the big hair and big voice had been brought up and developed around the mini bike tracks on the Adriatic coast of Italy, an area that simply lives and breathes motorcycle racing and produces World Champions by the bucket load. Just seven days before that terrible day I'd had a good chat with Marco when the former 250cc World Champion had finished in second place, just his second MotoGP podium, in Australia. He told me he was planning that first MotoGP win before the end of the season.

It was a typical sweltering day at the circuit next to Kuala Lumpur International Airport and we were in good spirits on the Sunday morning. Our commentary box was, as usual, the tiny sweat-dripping windowless cell-like television interview room behind the podium. Fellow commentator Gavin Emmett and I were feeling good because we were going home the next day after three weeks on the road. We were joined in our cell by the injured Yamaha rider Ben Spies to provide expert analyses on this penultimate round of the MotoGP World Championship. Sepang had really taken off as a MotoGP venue after so many sterile Formula One car races. The packed grandstands and noisy crowd created a crazy, exciting atmosphere that really summed up the difference between the two- and four-wheel World Championships at the time.

That atmosphere and good feeling evaporated in the blink of an eye on the second lap of the race. Simoncelli went down at turn 11 and Rossi and Colin Edwards could not avoid him as – like Tomizawa the previous year – he slid back into the track. We were shaken but carried on commentating as the red flags to stop the race came out immediately. It was clear from the very moment of impact that this was very serious and when no action replays appeared on screen we were under no illusions about the severity of the situation.

Behind the scenes in the medical centre so much was going on to try and save Marco's life and all we could do was keep talking and talking. Ben Spies was visibly shocked but helped us manfully to keep going before a call on his mobile took him back to the Yamaha garage to receive the news we all dreaded. With no information in our headphones we just kept going, explaining why the race had been stopped and emphasising that there was still no definite news about Marco's condition although obviously he had been seriously injured.

When the pictures on the screen switched to a distraught and dignified Dorna CEO Carmelo Ezpeleta stopping in every pit lane garage to speak to every rider we all knew that Marco had gone. With no official confirmation we could not announce this to 20 million viewers worldwide and just kept talking and reminding viewers of the situation. By this time the 67,000-strong crowd outside who'd had no announcement about the race re-starting or abandonment were getting angry and agitated. A couple of plastic bottles were thrown from the grandstands and we just kept talking until Frine's text arrived.

It was almost a relief to make the formal announcement that we had all been dreading since those very first live pictures of the crash that seemed now so many hours ago. The end of the programme was so dignified and brilliantly put together by the Dorna producers to provide an instant fitting tribute.

I was totally numb as I left the bubble of the commentary box into a grief-stricken media centre, ready to host one of those press conferences that everybody dreads. But it has to be done. I was proud of how we handled the events of that black afternoon. Whatever experiences you may have of similar situations, and sadly I had plenty, nothing prepares you. I just hope we gave Marco the dignified respect he so richly deserved.

The rider who'd ruffled more than a few feathers of the established stars, especially those of Lorenzo and Pedrosa, with his hard riding style never regained consciousness from the crash. Without a doubt, that hour in Malaysia while we waited for the confirmation was the most demanding one I've ever experienced in a commentary box, but as always Colin Fenton's words from all those years ago helped.

There was more sadness and reflection to come, especially with the news eleven months later that 77-year-old John Brown had passed away after a long illness at home in Kettering. My hero, who had fuelled my love affair with grand prix racing with his reports from across the globe in *Motor Cycle News*. My *Motor Cycle News* colleague, who helped and guided me into all aspects of grand prix reporting, but most of all my friend and the leader of the three musketeers. Sadly, I missed his funeral, where the third member of the musketeers Paul Fowler gave such an emotional eulogy, but we assembled in the bar of the Sama-Sama Hotel in Kuala Lumpur at the same time as the funeral and raised a glass to a true legend. JB would have approved.

Over to Dylan Down in Pit Lane

I WON'T PRETEND, try as I might I never really got to grips with all the technical stuff. Thank goodness for people like our pit lane reporter Dylan Gray. Whether we were teasing him about our air conditioned commentary box in Sepang when he was suffering the humidity of pit lane, or comparing the warm commentary box in Phillip Island to the icy cold pit lane, or lying to him that we were being fed by an endless supply of coffee and biscuits, Dylan would just relish the opportunity to explain to the audience what was going on. I even forgot his name once handing down to him in pit lane, but he just loved being in among the real action.

Dylan's enthusiasm was limitless, as was his patience with the old duffer in the commentary box. He would always tell us that pit lane was where the stories on track began and where new and exciting technology lay in wait for its rider's approval. Pit lane truly was an eye-opener as to how many small factors can decide who takes the glory and is forever in the history books, and who is forgotten within a season for being 0.5 seconds slower over a 70-mile race.

He explained that this last decade leading up to the World Championship's seventieth birthday had seen many such cases as Dorna took calculated risks and sometimes controversial decisions that came in for immense criticism at the time from fans and paddock veterans alike. However, looking back now, even the most die-hard critics would agree that what happened was necessary to reach the mind-boggling heights of competitiveness that exist today.

Dylan pointed out that it was what happened back in 2009 that was the most relevant. This was the year the championship switched to a single tyre supplier, in this case Japanese tyre giant Bridgestone. Dylan explained that having everyone on the same rubber was a huge step, as tyres are one of the biggest deciding factors of any racing championship. Millions of dollars are spent on the machine and the rider, but the single most important variable, the tyres, last less than 45 minutes and can change drastically from one make to another.

Dylan was convinced that the switch back to 1000cc engines at the start of 2012 was also a very important step. With the financial crisis affecting many manufacturers' budgets, the decision to change to a simplified larger engine capacity had been taken in 2009 to shore up grid numbers. After that, teams did not have as much creative licence to do as they pleased inside the engine, being limited to a standard cylinder bore and maximum number of four cylinders. Put simply, manufacturers were indirectly told to not spend so much.

This rule change, however, did not result in a grid full of competitive machines. After Suzuki dropped out in 2011, only Honda, Yamaha and Ducati were the full factory participants. Even with the satellite factory teams such as Tech 3 Yamaha, LCR and Gresini Honda and the Ducati teams of Pramac, Aspar and Cardion AB the grid was at risk of dwindling to only 12 bikes; hence the purposely named 'Claiming Rule Teams' were born. The CRTs consisted of highly-tuned road-going engines in prototype chassis, which were more than a few horsepower down from the full-fat prototypes. For the die-hard bike techy though, it was a dream come true; a dream of tuning David to beat Goliath. However, Dylan explained that, even though they were allowed a softer tyre than the factory bikes, that would prove an impossible task through lack of sheer horsepower.

Yet among all the frustration and lacklustre results emerged something much bigger: the desire of the whole MotoGP paddock to make it work. 'It' being the championship as a whole. Mechanics and riders who had once enjoyed glory were putting their heart and soul into privately funded and prepared machines they knew couldn't win. This is something Dorna was well aware of, appreciated, and used as leverage.

Dylan recognised that the championship organiser knew that technology costs had to drop even further and that the playing field had to be levelled to get a grid full of bikes that could fight for the podium. Near-uncontested races and strung-out fields did finally help convince the existing manufacturers that something had to give. Come 2014, the so-called 'Open Class' replaced the CRTs. The Open Class gave every factory the option to enter bikes with spec software and concessions to engine development and fuel allowance among others.

To Dylan this sounded like an obvious choice, but Honda, Yamaha and Ducati remained under factory rules, especially as their highly developed in-house software was at that point significantly better, though both did take the opportunity to field tuned-down versions of their bikes in the class alongside Ducati. As results would show, a performance gap to the factory bikes still existed after the change, which continued to infuriate some. Especially the riders dealing with criticism such as: 'but he's on the same bike as Marc Márquez'. No, he wasn't. It was an Open Class machine.

The proof of the pudding was in the eating, as Dylan explained. The changes did work and lured both Suzuki and Aprilia back to the championship a year later, as well as KTM by 2017; the year the championship became what Dorna CEO Carmelo Ezpeleta had set out to create. Everyone was using the same electronics, the same tyres (now Michelin), and just enough concessions were given to the factory teams needing some extra help in reaching the top, such as more engines and testing allowances. But with the big emphasis in MotoGP racing being on 'moto', manufacturers naturally do not sit still and always look to drop those extra thousandths of a second.

Gone too Early
2012

AS THE 2012 season got underway there were rumours, but there always are in a MotoGP paddock. They suggested that Stoner was not happy and even considering walking away. I honestly did not believe them; after all, he'd won two of the three opening grands prix. Casey was pretty intense while at work in the MotoGP paddock and didn't always give out the vibes he was the happiest man on the planet anyway. The fourth round of the championship was at Le Mans – not the Steve McQueen 24-hour car race Le Mans, but the Bugatti circuit which, when two wheels turned up, was a very different place despite using the same start and finish area beneath those towering grandstands.

None of us really liked going there very much despite the superb job by promoter Claude Michy to put on a great show for the ever increasing public and some tremendous racing. This was 24-hour car racing terrain and we never felt very welcome. We suffered from rude officials who would lock and change gates and parking areas overnight; policemen who would change routes and entrances each day and offer no assistance when, seeking an alternative route to the previous day, you found you had a large, usually stripped to the waist and full of alcohol Frenchman jumping on the bonnet of your car.

The media conference room was pokey and to be found one floor above the musty, rambling media centre. This time, I was summoned to the back of the stage amidst the stacked chairs and tables before the usual pre-event press conference got underway. Repsol Honda press officer Rhys Edwards asked if Casey could make a statement before the conference got underway and we agreed. I naively assumed it was an announcement that the World Champion was going to sign a new contract with Honda and that – despite the rumours – he had no intention of retiring. But I was so wrong. Nobody in that packed media centre had an inkling of what was going to follow.

Casey calmly announced that he would retire at the end of the season. There was total silence for a couple of seconds before the media rose as one to applaud a rider who had provided them with more column inches and air-time than most. Basically I think he'd just had enough. Twenty of his precious 26 years had been spent travelling the world racing motorcycles. Brought up on the dirt tracks of Australia, his parents Colin and Bronwyn had sold everything in Australia to enable their son to start road racing in Britain. They'd lived in a caravan in the Lake District and when he did start racing on the tarmac it was obvious to all that he was something special.

I remember interviewing him when he was 16 years old at a British Championship launch at Donington Park and then watching him struggle through his first season of 125cc grand prix racing. Even then Casey seemed a bit of a loner. He joined a group of us on the annual visit to the market in Kuala Lumpur during the weekend of his first Malaysian Grand Prix. I wanted a pair of fake Adidas training shoes and left the bargaining to a young Casey who relished his role. The stall keeper did not have a chance and it was that stubbornness and the ability to walk away if he did not get he wanted that brought him those two world titles and the bravery to say 'that's it' when he'd had enough. Sheer ability was without a doubt his biggest asset, but that bluntness and also his mocking of Rossi struggling on the Ducati that Casey had won the world title on did not make him the most popular rider with the fans. Yet on the track nobody could deny his true greatness.

My friends – all ex TT and Manx Grand Prix riders – were always a little sceptical about Stoner on our weekly get-together in the Bear and Ragged Staff until they witnessed him in action first hand in the pouring rain at Silverstone the previous year. While others fell by the wayside in the teeming rain and freezing cold, Casey Stoner rode the Honda like a jet ski through the spray to victory in a true masterclass that any grand prix star old or new would have been proud of.

Casey told the stunned assembled media he'd fallen out of love with grand prix racing, blaming the commercialism, lack of paddock access and the dumbing down of technical innovation for his decision. Dorna were furious at his accusations, pointing out that they had ploughed big sums of money into supporting his grand prix career especially in the early stages. Rossi just sat there and said little – he had more pressing problems on his mind.

In the ideal world, Stoner would have retained his world title as his retirement present but it was not to be. A horrendous crash during qualifying at Indianapolis left him with a damaged ankle, although typically he finished fourth in the race before being forced to miss the next three races with the injury far worse than first feared.

He returned in time for his last ride at Phillip Island. There could only be one corner at this magnificent weather-beaten cliff-top venue that could be named after the Australian World Champion. Gardner and Doohan already had a bend and straight named after them but anybody who'd had the privilege of watching Casey slide first the Ducati and then the Honda, leaving a massive black tyre mark on the tarmac at the 120mph turn three, a left hander overlooking the choppy Bass Strait, knew there was only one corner it could be. After the naming ceremony the weekend followed the same pattern as the last five with a commanding victory in front of the home crowd. Two weeks later he finished third in the final grand prix race of his career and Casey left the paddock he'd begun to hate for the final time to enjoy life on his farm in Australia. His wife Adriana and new daughter Allie were the focus of his attention plus a fair bit of hunting and fishing. He dabbled with four wheels in Supercars, completed test rides for first Honda and then Ducati, but vowed never to return to the MotoGP race track.

The other big story for me that year was Cal Crutchlow finishing third in the MotoGP race at Brno in August to become the first British podium finisher in the premier class for 12 long years. Crutchlow had come through the historically tough route of British Superbike Championship, World Supersport Champion and finally World Superbike Championship before joining the Monster Tech 3 Yamaha team in 2011. It was a brave decision and it would have been easier and certainly more financially viable for him to stay where he was, but Cal was made of sterner stuff and loved nothing more than proving people wrong.

British World Superbike Champions James Toseland and Neil Hodgson had found moving up to MotoGP a step too far for various reasons. World Superbike legend Colin Edwards never won a grand prix and Crutchlow struggled to adapt in that first season but podium finishes in Brno and Phillip Island in 2012 set the ball rolling for the Coventry-born rider who turned down a professional football career with his home-town club to go motorcycle racing. The foreign media loved Cal and he played them brilliantly at the sometimes rather sterile pre-event press conferences with off the wall and controversial comments which always put me a little on edge when he sat in front of me. He was never afraid to speak his mind and express his opinions on subjects such as contracts, crashes and other riders that most of the others would steer clear of.

Lorenzo had regained his world title with a second place behind Stoner at Phillip Island after a tremendous year-long battle with Pedrosa, but times were changing. Márquez clinched the Moto2 and the double World Champion would join Pedrosa in the Repsol Honda MotoGP team in 2013. Rossi's two-year Ducati nightmare was coming to an end and soon the nine times World Champion announced he was returning to Yamaha the next season. Both would return to successful days. Ducati with a total reorganisation of their racing team structure and Rossi on a machine capable of winning grands prix.

Pull the Pin
2013

MÁRQUEZ ARRIVED IN the premier class in 2013 like an unexploded hand grenade thrown into the pack. It did not take long for the pin to come out. After finishing third in the opening round under the Qatar lights in a battle with Rossi that was just the hors d'oeuvre to the main meal that lay ahead, Márquez won the second round at the new Circuit of the Americas in Texas. Surely that would do to start with for the youngest ever winner in the premier class, but the Spaniard already had his sights on becoming the youngest ever premier class champion.

He cared little for reputations and two weeks later pushed Lorenzo out of the way at the final corner in Jerez to finish second. To add insult to injury that final corner had just been named after World Champion Lorenzo and he was not amused by the young whippersnapper who already had sights on his crown. In Mugello, Márquez walked away from a 220mph crash and it was team-mate

Pedrosa who led the way by seven points from Lorenzo with 'rookie' Márquez a further 23 points adrift when we arrived in Assen for a remarkable Dutch TT.

Rossi returned to race-winning ways on the Yamaha at last, but it was team-mate Lorenzo's bravery that showed just how true a World Champion he was, and the pain he would endure to prevent Pedrosa and I think particularly Márquez stealing his crown. Lorenzo crashed in the wet second practice session and it was immediately obvious to us on the screens that he'd broken his collarbone. That horrible dropped left shoulder walk through the gravel trap said it all. As is the way these days he was flown to Barcelona to have a titanium plate fitted with ten screws to repair the snapped collarbone and we surmised that he could return to the next round in Germany a couple of weeks later. Lorenzo had other ideas and was flown back on the Friday night prepared to race the next day. He was passed fit after the warm up and finished an incredible fifth after 26 painful laps – nobody ever suggested being a World Champion was easy.

His heroic efforts where blown apart when he crashed while looking so comfortable at the Sachsenring two weeks later, re-breaking his collarbone, and there was no way back this time around. Championship leader Pedrosa also crashed in practice, missing the race and leaving the gate open for Márquez who needed no written invitation. Including Germany, he won five of the next eight races and finished second in the other three. But this was Márquez and there had to be some fun and games on the way.

He popped a dislocated shoulder back into place to finish second at Silverstone after a warm-up crash. Trackside marshals had to scatter when Márquez's sliding Honda almost hit them while they moved Cal Crutchlow's stricken Yamaha from the gravel trap after he'd crashed 30 seconds earlier. Márquez was fined with a two-point penalty for ignoring the yellow flags signifying Crutchlow's crash. Two rounds later, Márquez was involved in a controversial collision that put out team-mate Pedrosa when he won in Aragón. Márquez clipped the back of his team-mate's Honda as he passed him, slicing through the rear wheel sensor operating traction control and Pedrosa crashed. Márquez arrived at Phillip Island with a 43-point championship lead with just three rounds remaining.

My maths ability has never been in question – I am hopeless. From private maths coaching to get through the 11-plus at Cumnor Primary School to trying to work out World Championship points or number of laps remaining, my struggles with arithmetic amused Gav alongside me in the commentary box, which was rather an estate agent's description of where we sat to work in Phillip Island. To be blunt, it was a shed in the paddock close to the gentleman's urinals, again with no windows and two small screens to check the timing and watch the action.

Phillip Island had been re-surfaced and Bridgestone knew their tyres would not last the race distance so a flag to flag race with a compulsory pit stop was planned. Riders had to come in to change tyres on laps nine or ten, which provided yet another complication for Mr Einstein in the commentary box. I marked down each lap as the riders raced down the 210mph Gardner Straight to the Doohan Corner and smiled when they started to roll into pit lane to change the tyres. When Márquez raced through at the end of ten laps I was convinced once again I'd run out of fingers and miscalculated, but the confusion and then anger on pit wall suggested that somebody else had also run out of fingers. Unbelievable in the age of computers, traction control, fly-by-wire throttles and seamless gearboxes that Repsol Honda could not count up to ten and bring their man in at the right time, handing 25 precious points to Lorenzo. Not that it mattered in the end.

Márquez became the youngest premier class World Champion after finishing third at the final round in Valencia. After the podium celebrations he came to the media centre and conducted two press conferences, first on the race with Lorenzo and Pedrosa and then as the new World Champion. He then did it all again in Spanish before leaving one and a half hours later, still in his leathers, to start the celebrations proper.

Just 20 years old, this was somebody very special both on and off the track. His pure ability coupled with that win at all costs attitude that stands out World Champions from the runners-up was there for all to witness and appreciate. Off the track he was friendly and he understood and was prepared to meet those often laborious duties as a World Champion and ambassador for the sport. His mentor, the former 125cc World Champion Emilio Alzamora, had already done a brilliant job.

Rossi finished fourth on his return to Yamaha but dropped a bombshell at Valencia. The pre-event press conferences as the end of season approaches always get a little tastier, and a question from the floor just when we were ready to pack up changed the mood. Rossi admitted the speculation in the Italian press about the sacking of his long-time crew chief Jerry Burgess was true. Somebody within the Rossi inner circle had leaked the news and Rossi had only just had time to tell Jerry. I can't believe that Valentino would have leaked the story as some people suggested. This was the legendary Australian who'd guided the Italian to world titles with both Honda and Yamaha and stood by his side in the two-year Ducati nightmare. He was also the crew chief who'd brought world titles to Australia with Gardner and Doohan.

I'd first met Jerry when he was with Suzuki at the TT in 1981, and over the next 35 years lost an absolute fortune to him betting on any England–Australia cricket match. Ashes, one day, T20, you name it, and Jerry was usually collecting the money and the beer. I even took him and the Australians in the Rothmans Honda team to Lord's to watch an Ashes game in 1993. To their absolute delight it was the afternoon in which England captain Michael Atherton slipped over and was run out one short of his century. Gav and I got our own back 16 years later when we stuffed a note into Jerry's top pocket as he was about to accompany Valentino onto the Sachsenring podium after their 2009 German Grand Prix victory. He read it as he climbed the steps to be informed that Aussie Michael Hussey had been bowled out by Freddie Flintoff, that England were on route to victory and payment would soon be due.

World Champions and great World Champions like Valentino Rossi are totally ruthless in their pursuit of success which sets them apart from many of the others who never make it. Of course he did not take the decision lightly and had every right to instigate the change but the way it happened left a nasty taste in the mouth. To someone of my age, it should have acted as a warning, but it didn't. Nothing can remain the same forever however much you are enjoying it.

War

2014–2015

SURELY NOBODY THOUGHT that Márquez's success was a flash in the pan after he won the first ten races of the 2014 season. By the end of the year he'd won 13 races, and nobody could get near him, although Rossi with new crew chief Silvano Galbusera at the helm finished second, scoring 2 wins and 13 podium finishes. When younger brother Álex won the Moto3 title after a fantastic last race fight with Jack Miller and the Márquezs' great family friend Tito Rabat clinched the Moto2 crown, we started to believe that they had taken over the world.

Rossi's victories are always greeted with such adulation and celebration and his win at Phillip Island in 2014 was no exception as the familiar bank of yellow number 46 flags fought for space in the usual ocean breeze. The 35-year-old legend never doubted he would continue grand prix racing for at least two more years and everybody connected with the sport breathed a huge sigh of relief. Never since 1949 had a single person had such an effect both on and off the track. Nine world titles on the track said it all, but his popularity worldwide was totally unprecedented. He was quite simply the most popular competitor in World Championship motorsport on two or four wheels, the number one sportsman in Italy and high up the Forbes list of sporting millionaires, even after his much publicised dust up with the Italian tax authorities. Vale put grand prix motorcycling in a place it had never been in before. I remember going to Silverstone in 2011 to the launch of the new £40 million pit-lane complex. The true greats of world motorsport had assembled for the opening ceremony. But forget the likes of Jackie Stewart, Nigel Mansell, Damon Hill and even John Surtees – it was a 32-year-old Italian from the small town of Tavullia that they had all come to see.

One company happy with Rossi's decision was BT Sport, who had taken over amidst plenty of glitz and glamour from the BBC as the rights holders to MotoGP in Britain. It was sad but so predictable that the BBC, with their reputation and bigger audiences, failed to match the financial clout of the satellite companies. It was suggested that BT were paying £8 million a year for the rights, which was four times bigger than the BBC could muster. It had already happened to football, rugby, cricket and Formula One to name but a few in Britain, and MotoGP had already followed suit in Italy and Spain by switching to satellite broadcasters. The BBC's arrival with live MotoGP coverage in 2003 when Suzi Perry and producer Belinda Rogerson arrived at Suzuka on the day of Daijiro Kato's fatal crash had boosted the sport's viewing audience so much in Britain and spearheaded the interest they had themselves instigated from World Superbikes to MotoGP

I was personally sad because my fellow Dorna commentator Gav had left to join the new BT team and I missed him, not that I would ever tell him. Gav was totally disorganised in most aspects of normal life, in total contrast to how he worked. Gav, who was never wrong about anything. I spent many a long journey, especially queuing to get into circuits, with Azi Farni and Gav arguing often about their two great passions, Liverpool and Leeds United, but more often the colour of the grass or if we were going to get there in time. Gav, who would often not actually be there when I announced him at the start of the programme, and Gav, who I'd shared some great and tragic moments with in the commentary box.

Steve Parrish was also somebody I missed when the BBC departed. I'd suggested Steve as my co-commentator to BBC radio for their coverage of the British Grand Prix in the late eighties. It was Steve's first job with the BBC and he went on to become their lead television commentator for many years. He was the joker of all jokers, with legendary stories of blowing up a brothel in Macau and putting a snake in the helmet of one of his rivals to name but a few. One of my very first features in *Motor Cycle News* was about British Champion Steve and his sponsor Dave Moore. I could have never written the Barry Sheene biography without Steve's considerable help and love of his best friend.

I have commentated on every single one of Rossi's 89 premier class victories. He makes it so easy because something is always happening, within the race, celebrating or on the podium; there was an infectious fizz to every victory in so many different ways. You just got sucked in. However, it was not Rossi's win that day in 2014 at Phillip Island that made it a special afternoon for me – it was third placed Bradley Smith, taking his first MotoGP podium.

Nine years earlier on a warm summer's evening I'd sat in the garden of the Bear and Ragged Staff with 14-year-old ginger-haired schoolboy Bradley and his dad Allan. They wanted to go grand prix racing and the former schoolboy motocross star who was still at Theresa May's old School in Wheatley did just that. I was never that confident at that age, even travelling to London, but a year later 15-year-old Bradley was leading me through Munich and Shanghai airports on route to the Chinese Grand Prix. He won three 125cc grands prix and finished runner up in the 2009 World Championship before moving on to Moto2 and then MotoGP with the Tech 3 team. I can't pretend following his journey was not special and I'm certain I was more than a little biased when commentating on those grands prix wins, but that same passion as when watching Oxford United and those early days following Mike Hailwood and Oxford Cheetahs just never goes away.

Nothing prepared us for 2015. Nothing prepared us for the war of words that spilled out onto the race track between three of the greatest riders the world had ever witnessed. There had been few real indications of what lay ahead in the most controversial, headline-grabbing, head-on clash in the history of the sport. Forget Read and Ivy, Sheene and Roberts, and Rossi and Biaggi – this was war and the world just lapped it up. This was Ali and Frazier but at 200mph.

Re-united team-mates Lorenzo and Rossi never pretended to be friends. We'd had the Berlin-type wall down the middle of the garage and there'd been plenty of words, especially when Rossi felt he was being forced out of Yamaha to join Ducati. Both were desperate to win back their world title from Márquez, who naturally had upset them both a couple of times on the track, though it had never got really personal. Rossi in particular appeared to get on well with Márquez, who'd admitted he was the Doctor's biggest fan and as a youngster had had pictures of him on his bedroom wall back home.

The first dark clouds of war appeared over the isolated Gran Chaco plains of northern Argentina during our second visit to the Termas de Río Hondo circuit for the third round. Just getting there from Austin the previous weekend was a nightmare. It was a two-and-a-half hour wait to get off the ancient creaking jumbo, which was much happier doing its day job of ferrying American troops around the world. Then it was on through the two-man passport control at the tiny Aeropuerto de Tucumán. That was just the start.

'Don't stop at any traffic lights in Tucumán,' was the warning from the hire car man sat in his gazebo warmed by a log fire before the 60-mile car journey in the dark to Termas de Río Hondo. Asking directions from the gentleman in the hut at the entrance to the airport proved a waste of time as he giggled away with smoke which was definitely not tobacco pouring out of the window.

Soon afterwards we did stop at one of the many traffic lights. Don't stop may have been the warning but when the donkey and cart crossed the road in front of us we had to. Immediately a group of men appeared and without any encouragement started to clean the windscreen of the hire car. When we shook our heads at the suggestion of payment a large brick in a large hand appeared from nowhere on the clean windscreen and we scrabbled through our luggage to find some money, not having the faintest idea of what we actually gave them.

Termas de Río Hondo had never witnessed anything like MotoGP. Famous for its thermal hot springs and, to be honest, little else, it was like a crazy town from a black and white cowboy movie. Fans from all over South America poured into the main square on bikes, scooters, pick-up trucks and donkey carts. The music and festivities kept me awake all night long until some borrowed ear plugs from Bradley Smith did the trick. I thought the whole Argentine Grand Prix embodied what MotoGP was all about. It was a pain and expensive to get to, the steps into the media centre were scarily rickety, Jeremy McWilliams did discover maggots in his steak and the mosquitos were having a field day. However, this was not some empty, boring government-funded race track but a vibrant, fun-loving place that just wanted to party and celebrate the return of MotoGP to South America.

This was the second year in Argentina. The track was tough on tyres and played a massive part in the outcome of the race. Márquez, on the softer tyre, built up a big advantage but Rossi on the harder compound was catching fast. The first collision between the two came on the penultimate lap, Rossi fought back and was back in front and Márquez came again but once again Rossi held the line. Márquez's Honda's front wheel hit the swinging arm of Rossi's Yamaha and down Márquez went. The crowd went crazy, especially when Rossi appeared on the top step of the podium wearing a Maradona-emblazoned Argentina football shirt. He was never one to miss a trick. The battle lines had been drawn.

This was Rossi's chance – perhaps even his last chance – of winning world title number ten and he was on it. The Yamaha was good, he was fit and prepared to fight both on and off the track as only true World Champions can. It was an amazing contest and just got better and better as the season progressed, although nobody was prepared for the finale where the sporting world first held its breath and then took sides.

The Yamaha duo of Lorenzo and Rossi were on fire and at the top of their game with World Champion Márquez hanging on by his fingernails. The second coming together came at Assen. Lorenzo arrived in the north of Holland after four straight wins and looked unbeatable, although Rossi had finished on the podium at every round since his win in the open race in Qatar. This gave him a single-point advantage over his team-mate in the championship as the halfway stage approached. Márquez was struggling on the Honda and languishing in fifth place, 69 points down despite his customary win in Austin.

The World Champion looked much more like his old self and much more at ease with the RCV V4 Honda round those fast classic Assen curves as he and Rossi produced a breath-taking encounter. It came down to a shootout at the infamous final Geert Timmer chicane surrounded by a gravel trap that sucked in riders like a bunker surrounding a golf green. With the chequered flag being prepared Márquez closed in on Rossi through the 130mph Ramshoek left hander as they prepared to brake for the right, left, right chicane. On the brakes Márquez started to push the Honda up the inside of the Yamaha. Rossi knew exactly what was coming, leant into the corner and there was an inevitable collision. Márquez wobbled but stayed on and Rossi was forced to race headfirst into the dreaded gravel. It all happened in the blink of the eye, but Rossi already had the throttle open to lift the front wheel of the Yamaha as it dragged its way through the gravel, emerging back onto terra firma like a horse-riding gladiator amidst a shower of stones and dust to win by over a second. Rossi was ecstatic, Márquez furious and the 100,000 celebrated with their hero who was now the most successful rider at the 'Cathedral' in World Championship history.

With two rounds to go we arrived in Malaysia with Rossi leading Lorenzo by 11 points. Márquez was out of the reckoning 74 points down on Rossi but was about to play the lead role in deciding the outcome of the championship.

We were buzzing when we flew into Kuala Lumpur airport from Melbourne early on the Monday morning, still shaking after a truly amazing Australian Grand

Prix the previous afternoon. No less than 52 overtaking manoeuvres, more than a season's tally in some motorsports, in a breath-taking 75 miles around the finest battleground in the world. Márquez, Lorenzo, Andrea Iannone and Rossi produced a 200mph contest that showed the world and pushed my voice to the limit to reveal just what MotoGP is all about, and all viewed from our new commentary position looking over turns three and four with the surf crashing into the rocks below. The shed had finally gone and it just did not get better than this. Márquez took the chequered flag with Lorenzo and Iannone completing the podium and Rossi fourth.

I loved going to Malaysia to finish those long three weeks away in Japan and Australia. Some people flew off to sun-blessed beaches for a couple of days before the race, as the Sami-Sami Hotel near the international airport was not their place to relax, but for me it was perfect. There was a pool, a gym, a great breakfast, plus it was only a 35-minute train journey to sample the delights of downtown Kuala Lumpur with its markets and food. Throw in a lively bar, despite the band, and Premier League football on the telly and it was the perfect place to spend a few days. So I was releaxed but totally unprepared when I arrived at the Sepang circuit on Thursday afternoon for the usual pre-event press conferenece.

At first I honestly thought he was joking. There had been rumblings in the Italian press – who like a good rumble – that Rossi was unhappy with Márquez in Australia, claiming he'd deliberately slowed the race until getting away three laps from the finish to enable countryman Lorenzo to finish second.

It all started amicably enough on the Thursday afternoon at the pre-event press conference, with Rossi as championship leader sitting in the middle flanked by Lorenzo and Márquez. After some pre-fight pleasantries to my questions, Rossi then turned on Márquez like a hungry tiger pouncing on a piece of raw meat. He repeated his Phillip Island accusations and then launched into a more personal attack on the Spaniard, scorning his claim that he'd been a Rossi fan with those pictures on his bedroom wall. Some journalists thought that Rossi was joking, but he was deadly serious. He continued the character assassination and produced lap charts to support his Phillip Island conspiracy claims, kicking off a frantic media scrum that engulfed him as soon as the official conference had finished.

For the last 15 years when Rossi spoke the world listened and Márquez was visibly shocked, especially by the personal nature of the attack. This was not such new territory for the nine times World Champion. He'd softened up the likes of Biaggi and Gibernau in public before humbling them on the track, but Rossi was soon to find out that Márquez was made of sterner stuff. In fact he only had to wait three days for a brutal 20-lap encounter in a searing heat that matched the mood.

We'd moved into another even smaller windowless room where we could not turn off the air conditioning to commentate on a race that without a shadow of doubt was the most talked about in the history of the sport. Márquez's team-mate Dani Pedrosa on his day is unbeatable and this was his day. No accusations here about slowing the pace as he simply cleared off to claim a faultless victory. Lorenzo moved past Márquez – Rossi fans would claim too easily – into a safe second to clear some space for a battle between Rossi and Márquez that would decide the outcome of the championship. Rossi's chances of that incredible tenth world title blew up in a cloud of controversy, collisions and court rulings.

It was such a shame, but on the other hand it was also mighty exciting and never more so than on the fifth lap which will never be forgotten. Rossi had ignited the fuse with those personal attacks and Márquez rode as a furious man seeking revenge. They swapped third place nine times on that memorable lap using every tactic and a few more to stay in front.

Rossi was getting more and more frustrated as Lorenzo pulled away in second place and Márquez was more and more determined to prevent Rossi reaching Lorenzo to wreck his championship aspirations. Something had to give, and it did one lap later coming onto the back straight in the shadow of those massive grandstands jam-packed with fans witnessing a duel in which neither rider was prepared to give an inch. This had become very personal and much more than a championship decider. Rossi knew that Márquez could power past him coming onto that straight leading into the final hairpin and started to slow the pace, pushing Márquez on the outside wider and wider. There could only be one outcome as the Honda hit the Yamaha. Some claim Rossi tried to kick Márquez but footage suggests that his foot was knocked off the foot peg in the impact. Márquez went down, Rossi stayed on and claimed third place behind Pedrosa and Lorenzo at the finish. That's where the real off-track fun and games started.

I sat in the packed press conference room with everybody else and waited, waited and waited. After 30 minutes I told the journalists to get on with their work in the sprawling media centre next door, promising them as soon as there was any news, I would call them in. In the room behind the press conference room Pedrosa and Lorenzo, still in their champagne-soaked leathers, also waited as just up the corridor Rossi and Márquez put their respective cases to Race Direction. The meeting seemed to last forever. Pedrosa and Lorenzo were getting more agitated. They wanted to get changed and get back to the hotel to prepare for the flight home. Officials were running around like headless chickens and though the media have never been known for their patience, you had to have sympathy for Race Director Mike Webb. Whatever their decision, a lot of people were going to be very unhappy.

At last they emerged to announce that Rossi had been docked three penalty points by slowing to cause the crash. For a brief second we thought Rossi had escaped, but the realisation that three plus one equals four meant that he would have to start in last position on the grid in the final round at Valencia. Rossi had received a single penalty point after slowing Lorenzo in qualifying at Misano nearly two months earlier. That one point proved the tipping point. He would still lead Lorenzo by seven points going into the Valencian lion's den but, even for Rossi, riding through the field around the tight, narrow Ricardo Tormo circuit was a massive ask. Rossi had started at the back before and been able to ride through the field but this was Valencia. Overtaking was hard and often dangerous because of the nature of the track. Big risks would have to be taken to even reach the leaders let alone overtake them.

Rossi left the circuit immediately, missing the press conference. Race winner Pedrosa was furious that he'd been allowed just to walk out. The press centre exploded in a frantic frenzy of babbling phone calls, flash bulbs, television cameras, arguments, discussions and loud disbelief from the Italian corner. Back at the Sami-Sami the teams assembled in the restaurant that evening ready to fly back home later that night after three weeks on the road. The two Yamaha teams sat at separate tables, Lorenzo's team quietly celebrating and Rossi's silent and bitterly disappointed, wondering perhaps whether their leader's chance had gone for ever.

There were very few grey areas in the incredible ten days that followed before we arrived in Valencia for the showdown of all showdowns. I suppose two-thirds of the world supported Rossi and one third Márquez, although that changed once we reached Spanish soil. When I say 'the world', I mean the world, because I'd never witnessed anything like it. I'd been close up to the Damon Hill/ Michael Schumacher showdown in 1994 at Adelaide, but this was something much bigger. Social media went completely crazy with record figures for a sporting event. Over 700 journalists descended on Valencia and many more missed out because the media centre simply could fit no more in. Race day was completely sold out within minutes of the Malaysia clash, Formula One drivers such as Mark Webber hired private jets to be there and even the dear old BBC Radio 5 thought it worth a 30-second voice piece, and perhaps an audio clip from the winner probably sandwiched between some obscure athletics event and a story about Lewis Hamilton's dog – thank goodness county cricket had finished for the season.

The millions of Rossi fans bayed for Márquez's blood, endorsing their man's claims about Phillip Island and blaming him for the Malaysia clash. Márquez's fans bayed for the blood of Rossi, agreeing with the Race Direction decision and continuing with their claim that Rossi had deliberately kicked their man, causing the crash.

It was difficult to form your own judgement amidst so much anger and ill will. Had Rossi for once attacked the wrong person in the press conference? Had he lost his cool on the track in Malaysia with the title in his sights? Had Márquez slowed the race deliberately in Phillip Island and could he have backed off in the clash with a title contender in Sepang? The only thing for certain was that the ultimate argument would be decided at the 2.489-mile Ricardo Tormo circuit on the outskirts of Valencia. Lorenzo was the favourite, but Rossi knew all was not lost.

On arrival in Valencia the atmosphere was both electric and toxic as the accusations and counter accusations continued to flow. Honda withdrew their claim that they had footage of Rossi's alleged kick. Some suggested that Rossi's influence on social media could affect their bike sales – such was the power of the Doctor. Rossi had an appeal to the Court of Arbitration turned down; Dorna cancelled the pre-event press conference fearing another clash; Yamaha did the same with their sixtieth anniversary gala dinner and all the MotoGP riders were summoned to the headmaster's office of Carmelo Ezpeleta and FIM President Vito Ippolito to be reminded that it would be more than detention if the unsporting behaviour continued. Security around the three protagonists was tight and extra police were drafted in to quell any crowd trouble. Happily they were not needed. Such was the power and support for Rossi that 750,000 fans signed a petition urging Race Direction to change their minds, but they stood firm and the end of his title dream was in sight.

Lorenzo didn't need to be asked twice to seize the chance he could never have imagined when they'd arrived in Malaysia two weeks earlier. He grabbed the lead in the 30-lap showdown on the first lap and in true Lorenzo style was never headed. He slowed as the tyres faded on the Yamaha and claimed he could not read his pit board properly, but he crossed the line to clinch his third premier class world title and there was nothing team-mate Rossi could do, although he tried so hard. He fought through the pack to fourth place but fell just six points short of his goal. Second place would have given him the title but the wall in front of him was the Honda duo of Márquez and Pedrosa who had no intention of budging and he was never close enough to challenge them, despite such a Herculean effort. While matters were out his hands it would have been a very different story if Márquez and Pedrosa had pushed Lorenzo back to third.

The Rossi fans once again claimed the Spanish trio were following some form of patriotic team orders to keep their man at bay. Márquez had stalked Lorenzo for much of the race but never attempted to pass, which was not in his usual DNA but, in his defence, he had to fight off Pedrosa in the last couple of laps. The accusations and theories continued for months to come but 2016 already loomed. Lorenzo was the undisputed World Champion and testing for the new season started just two days later in Valencia. Life in MotoGP moves on at a hectic, unrelenting pace, but nobody involved will forget those two weeks of outright war.

Danny Demolishes the Demons

2015

WITH ALL THAT going on in the premier class, I was frantically trying to concentrate for a very special, long awaited celebration in Valencia. Thirty-eight years and 64 different riders from 12 separate countries had won grand prix world titles since the last British World Champion. I was in the middle of my motocross adventures when Barry Sheene won the second of his World 500cc titles in 1977 and incredibly that was it. A proud nation who had totally dominated those pioneering days of the World Championships both with riders and motorcycles had not produced a World Champion for 38 years. While the country celebrated the exploits of Carl Fogarty, James Toseland, Neil Hodgson and Jonathon Rea in World Superbikes, I clutched at the straws of those grand prix victories of McWilliams, Redding and Smith. They were a lifeline and both Smith and Redding came close to world titles in the 125 and Moto2 classes respectively but that final breakthrough came from an unexpected source, 21-year-old Danny Kent.

The Wiltshire rider had so impressed at the end of the first Moto3 season in 2012, riding the Red Bull KTM to wins in Japan and Valencia. Inexplicably he then departed to Moto2 only to return a year later with his tail between his legs after a disastrous season with the Tech 3 team. He slowly but surely regained his confidence on his return to the smaller class riding the Husqvarna-badged KTM with a couple of podium finishes before switching to Honda power and the influence and support of Stefan Kiefer and the Leopard Racing team.

Danny always had a bucketful of talent but was so often held back by self-doubt. In 2015 everything just gelled, especially in the first half of a remarkable season when he won six races, some by big margins and others by playing that Moto3 waiting game. After his comprehensive eight-second victory in front of the ecstatic Silverstone crowd I was working out where to start planning the long awaited celebrations. Kent had opened up a massive 70-point lead in the championship, but it's never that easy.

In the end it came down to that weekend in Valencia and the final round. The Moto3 race was first on race day and while others and the majority of the sell-out crowd waited in noisy anticipation for the eagerly awaited clash of the MotoGP titans, the equally noisy

British and Portuguese fans prepared for another battle that meant so much.

Miguel Oliveira, after an amazing second half of the season, had closed Kent's advantage at the front to 24 points. Portugal had never won a world title and Oliveira was their only grand prix winner. Kent was wobbling but knew if he stayed out of trouble and kept a calm head whatever Oliveira did at the front, he would take the title. Danny did just that despite a near coming together with his so-called team-mate Hiroki Ono on the very last lap of the season. Oliveira did what he had to do by winning but Kent ended those 38 barren years of agony with the ninth place to clinch the title. Unfortunately, there was no time for myself and fellow jubilant commentator Matt Birt to celebrate or even shake Danny's hand because the Moto2 grid was already lining up while Rossi, Lorenzo and Márquez were preparing for battle later in the afternoon.

It was a remarkable achievement by Kent in the most competitive of competitive classes in grand prix racing. A British World Champion was the icing on the cake in a memorable year. Forget the Rossi/Márquez shenanigans, this was the year that British grand prix racing placed itself back on the World Championship map and it felt so good, although a little overwhelming after so long making excuses in the shadows. We celebrated Kent's world title and a superb sixth place in the MotoGP

World Championship by Bradley Smith, which included a second place in difficult conditions riding the Monster Tech 3 Yamaha at Misano. Scott Redding finished third in that same race while Cal Crutchlow grabbed a podium finish in Argentina on his debut season with LCR Honda and it didn't stop there. Former World Supersport Champion Sam Lowes's second season in Moto2 ended in a superb fourth place which included victory in Austin. Britain was back and more was to follow in 2016.

Waiting for Cal
2016

NOBODY HONESTLY THOUGHT 2016 could match the sheer drama of the previous year, whether for the right or wrong reasons, but it did. This time the excitement and suspense were definitely for the right reasons, and endorsed everything Dorna had been trying to achieve with the rule changes and restrictions. There were nine separate winners in the 18-race season with all four major factories taking wins, and included in those nine winners was a certain Cal Crutchlow.

I'd always joked that I would not retire or even die until I had witnessed and even commentated on a British rider winning a premier class grand prix. I think you could count on the fingers of one hand anybody in the Brno paddock who'd been at Anderstorp in Sweden on 16 August 1981. I was one of those fingers who'd flown to Gothenburg and then driven to the 2.505-mile Anderstorp circuit that doubled up as the local aerodrome, its entrance in a trading estate surrounded by dark, ominous-looking woods occupied by gangs of

Hells Angels during the race weekend. Little did I ever think I was witnessing a historic moment.

I duly phoned over my report of Barry Sheene's close fought victory in the 30-lap, 500cc race and the world title for his great friend Marco Lucchinelli and brought back the picture of the pair of them laughing on the podium with both heads in one winner's garland. That was that, and despite some moments of hope from the likes of Niall Mackenzie, Ron Haslam and Jeremy McWilliams, no British rider had even got close to repeating Sheene's victory. Barry himself had passed away 13 years before we arrived for the Czech Republic Grand Prix on 21 August 2016 at the undulating Brno circuit which was such a total contrast to the flat, featureless Anderstorp aerodrome.

It stopped raining an hour before the 22-lap MotoGP race started but the 3.357-mile circuit was still very wet. This would be the track's first ever wet premier class race since it had been built 30 years ago to replace the old road circuit. Wet weather tyre choice was going to be crucial and Crutchlow gambled on the harder compound Michelin on both front and rear, guessing the track was going to start drying, and he was right.

Crutchlow was fifteenth at the end of the first lap, but as the track started to dry, he was picking off the men in front of him. We were concentrating on the riders at the front, but as always fellow commentator Matt Birt had spotted the progress of the LCR Honda, though honestly neither of us gave a real thought to such a historic moment that was unfolding in front of our very eyes. Crutchlow changed that mindset pretty quickly when he effortlessly eased into fourth place on lap 12 and set after the leaders. Four laps later he was leading and pulling away at the front.

My first reaction was to panic, but then get ready to celebrate. Panic because I was totally unprepared and had no statistics for a British victory. I just kept reminding myself to keep concentrating, not to go over the top, don't go completely silly, as Cal started his last lap. No wonder LCR team owner Lucio Cecchinello could not watch, but I had to and commentate at the same time.

Cal said afterwards he was cruising but I can promise him there was no cruising in the commentary box as he crossed the line over seven seconds in front of Rossi. That 35-year wait was over and already all the facts and figures were pouring in on my phone from the king of MotoGP stats Dr Martin Raines back home in Yorkshire. What a moment to savour, but amidst all the excitement and in many ways relief I thought back to Barry and that afternoon in Anderstorp. He would have just loved that Brno race. Did I stick to my promise not to go over the top and completely silly? Probably not, and who can blame me? This was a very special day.

Two weeks later Crutchlow came close to writing a completely new chapter in the history books when he finished second at the British Grand Prix at Silverstone. He started from pole, the first since Sheene at Silverstone in 1977, and a record crowd of 74,000 were urging him on to become the first British rider to win the premier class race at his home grand prix since switching to the mainland from the Isle of Man. However, he had to settle for second behind Maverick Viñales after a right old battle with Rossi, Márquez, Pedrosa and Iannone. But we did not to have wait long for his second victory to come along; rather like a London bus – none for 35 years and then two in a couple of months.

In a typical Phillip Island weekend of four seasons of weather in three days it was dry but cold for the race. Crutchlow relished the conditions, gambled on a hard front tyre and when Márquez, who'd regained his world title seven days earlier in Japan, crashed at the hairpin right in front of our commentary box, Crutchlow grabbed his chance with both hands. The Brno win was no one-hit wonder for the British rider who proved he could also win in the dry. I think I was a little calmer this time round.

Michelin replacing Bridgestone as the sole tyre supplier meant it was never going to be an easy 2016 season, and up until Assen it was following a predictable pattern. Márquez, Rossi and Lorenzo shared the spoils in the opening seven races, but with the rain falling in the Netherlands the season turned on its head.

Australian Jack Miller should have been racing in those wild party days of the seventies and eighties. After finishing runner-up behind Álex Márquez in the Moto3 World Championship, he bypassed Moto2 and came headfirst into MotoGP in 2015. He was a throwback, a true Aussie 'larrikin' who liked a beer and a party and who could ride a motorcycle especially well in the wet. It was wet, very wet in Assen and Miller was superb to win comfortably on the Marc VDS Honda after Rossi crashed to start a truly remarkable record-breaking sequence of winners. Jack was such a popular winner and celebrated in true Aussie style, drinking the winner's champagne out of his boot on the podium.

Márquez won the next round – a flag to flag confrontation at the Sachsenring. Italian Andrea Iannone lived up to his 'crazy' nickname. He flew off to Ibiza in a private jet to celebrate, immediately after giving Ducati their first victory since Stoner six years previously in MotoGP's first race at the re-vamped Red Bull Ring in Austria for 19 years. Crutchlow won in the Czech Republic and two weeks later young Spaniard and former Moto3 World Champion Maverick Viñales brought Suzuki their first win since 2007 at Silverstone. Pedrosa then won in Misano before Márquez, on track to regain that world title, was victorious in Aragón. Márquez clinched the title with victory in Japan, but two weeks later in Malaysia the ninth winner of the season came in the shape of Andrea Dovizioso with his first premier class win since Donington Park way back in 2009. Brad Binder became the first South African World Champion in any class since that old scrapper Jon Ekerold in 1981 when he captured the Moto3 title. A truly remarkable season for all the right reasons.

Forever Dangerous
2016

EVEN IN THESE days of instant medical attention, amazing rider protection and safe circuits there was a brutal reminder that grand prix motorcycle racing is still very dangerous when Luis Salom was killed in Barcelona. The friendly Spaniard who came so close to winning the Moto3 world title both in 2012 and 2013 crashed his Kalex into the wall on approaching the downhill turn 12 in the second Friday afternoon Moto2 practice session at the 2016 Grand Prix of Catalunya.

Experiencing a sudden loss in this way was not a new experience for the majority of the grand prix paddock but still the shock shook the very foundations of the community that consisted of around 3,000 people at a European race. The response from everybody was a stark difference from how such incidents were treated in those dark early days. After consultations with the riders, the circuit layout was changed overnight to incorporate the Formula One chicane between turns 12 and 13, taking out the dangers of the wall that had been protected by an air fence. Tragically it was too late to save Salom but was a real indication of just how things had changed.

Many older people, and Casey Stoner, moan that the sport has changed so much, 'it's just no fun anymore', that the riders are more like robots and have no time for the fans. I read a letter in *Motor Cycle News* claiming that modern-day riders have no character and nobody like Mike Hailwood is around anymore. Hailwood, the letter explained, could play the drums, saxophone and piano and today's modern-day riders have no interest in such things.

It was 1.30am on a Monday morning at a pretty deserted Melbourne airport in Australia as we made our way through the empty corridors to find the flight to Kuala Lumpur airport en route to the 2016 Malaysian Grand Prix when I first heard the sound of a piano. I took little notice because it had been a long, hard and exhilarating day in Phillip Island and piped airport music was not exactly going to stir the soul. Rounding the corner, I saw, all alone at a keyboard, Johann Zarco happily playing away without another person in sight and totally absorbed in his music. Frenchman Zarco, the current Moto2 World Champion, who had been disappointed not to retained his title with a twelfth place that afternoon, but who would make amends six days later in Sepang before moving on to MotoGP.

We nicknamed Zarco 'the professor' for the way he would explain and analyse in detail every question in press conferences and television interviews. On the outside, the piano-playing softly spoken Frenchman was the college professor explaining to his students what had happened in qualifying, but on the inside, he possessed that ruthless streak that had already upset some of his Moto2 colleagues and next season would begin to rattle the big boys in MotoGP, and especially Valentino Rossi. Only once did I see Zarco swap those two personalities when he turned on an Italian journalist who was asking some probing questions about the fatal Salom crash. Zarco told his interlocutor that he'd asked a 'shit' question, and I thought he was going to jump over the media conference desk and sort out the questioner, until Márquez stepped in to calm things down. No piano playing this time.

I was lucky when hosting the official press conferences that 90 per cent of the time the riders were happy to be there after success in qualifying or the races. My role was to set the ball rolling and it was only when we got to questions from the floor that things tended to be a bit tastier. Mandatory press conferences for the riders came into play at the end of the eighties. Before then, it really was a case of every man for themselves. Some such as Barry Sheene relished the opportunity and used it so much to their advantage while others such as Eddie

Lawson just were not interested and – usually with a smile on his face – made life as difficult as he could for the media. Eddie felt that what he did out on the track was enough. It was a very different paddock in those days. More open, more friendly and on the surface a great deal livelier but it changed, as did the world.

Social media and the internet have made international sportspeople millionaires but at a price. Millions worldwide follow their every word and breath on Twitter, Instagram and Facebook, and pictures and videos of them in action are beamed around the world in seconds, and they dare not step out of line in the same way their forefathers did on a very regular basis. The global success of MotoGP fuelled so much by the Rossi phenomenon has certainly not produced robots but riders who are more careful about what they say, what they do and where they go away from the paddock. Their commitments to the media and sponsors are a big part of their lives and a MotoGP weekend. For most of them, actually getting out there on the track is a relief. For once they are alone and making their own decisions. Their fate is in their own hands and not at the whim of the sponsors and the media. In that sense, they are no different to those earlier pioneers, the hell raisers of the seventies and eighties. Probably a fair bit richer though.

Hair-Raising Marc
2017

FOR THE LAST couple of months of the season, the paddock used to be a snake pit of rumours about who was going where the following season. When Bradley Smith told me on the afternoon of the first race of the 2016 season that he was joining the new KTM team in 2017 I realised that it had all changed. Halfway through 2016 it all seemed sorted for the next year. The big move was Lorenzo to Ducati, replacing Austrian Grand Prix winner Andrea Iannone who was on his way to Suzuki where he was joined by Álex Rins. Maverick Viñales, fresh from that maiden MotoGP victory at Silverstone, replaced Lorenzo, joining Rossi at Yamaha. Former Moto2 World Champion Pol Espargaró left Tech 3 Yamaha to join KTM and was replaced by current Moto2 Champion Johann Zarco. Chop and change it may have been, but new boys had to wait because two of the stay putters fought for the title.

Journeyman was a description of Andrea Dovizioso that really did not do him justice, but the Italian had been round the houses and back, winning grands prix in all three classes in a decade of competing in World Championship racing. A former 125cc World Champion, runner-up on a 250 and MotoGP grand prix winner on both Honda and Ducati machinery who found something else in 2017. The Desmosedici GP 17 Ducati machine helped, but Dovi, the most amiable and likable guy in the paddock, discovered some inner strength that made him realise he could win more races, especially in head to head situations, and actually challenge for the title. While his new much publicised team-mate Lorenzo struggled to make the transition from Yamaha, Dovi took the fight to Honda and World Champion Márquez. It was an intriguing contest. Last lap confrontations in two races with the king of risk takers in such situations summed up the new Dovi.

The Red Bull Ring had taken over the mantle as the fastest circuit in the calendar from Phillip Island and 90,000 people, three times as many as watched the Formula One race a few weeks previously, packed the grandstands and hillsides. The previous year Dovizioso had to finally settle for second place behind team-mate Iannone. This time it was World Champion Márquez, who simply relished such situations, especially if they went down to the last corner as it did, who was the foe. Inside going into that final downhill and outside coming out from Márquez, we expected nothing less and neither did Dovi who took the chequered with an uncharacteristic wag of his finger to the World Champion.

Two and a half months later, in the Japanese rain at Motegi he fought off a ferocious last lap challenge from Márquez and came out on top again. With three races remaining, Dovizioso trailed Márquez by just 11 points in the championship, but going into the final round at Valencia Márquez's lead had increased to 21 despite another wet weather victory for the Ducati rider in Malaysia. Once again it was a final round decider in Valencia and third place was enough for Márquez with the pressure off when Dovizioso slid off in the gravel. It was a typical Márquez moment and save, which summed up his season and probably his career.

Zarco was leading, but the pace was slowing and so Márquez raced past him down the start and finish straight into that deceptively fast 100mph left hander. He was wary of the Frenchman who'd made such an impression in his first MotoGP season, including some tyre-mark impressions on opponents' machines. Zarco was certainly no respecter of reputations and Márquez knew that, yet went too fast into the corner and the front end of the Honda slid away, but this was nothing new for the Spaniard. The left knee went down, pushed the Honda upright and he continued on his merry way and on towards the world title. He'd done it so many times previously that we were just not that surprised.

When the Flag Drops the Bullshit Stops

2018

IT TAKES A brave man to admit it's time to stop after 38 years of globetrotting and adulation. I was not that brave. I failed to read the signs that were shining so bright to others. Perhaps I didn't want to see that the adventure was about to come to an end because the consequences were just too painful to bear.

On the first day of practice for the 2017 British Grand Prix at Silverstone I was summoned to the paddock office of Dorna's communications director Manel Arroyo, where we'd often sat and discussed, among other things, the fortunes of Barcelona FC, where Manel was a director, and Brexit. The Dorna director of communications gently told 70-year-old Nick it was time for them to move on and my services as the MotoGP race commentator were no longer required in 2018.

I was much angrier with myself than upset with their decision. I wanted to stay for at least another year. I should have read so many signs but just ploughed on regardless in my little bubble thinking that everything remains the same for ever. Of course, I was hurt when others told me some of my colleagues said they had been covering up for my mistakes, but that's the very nature of the job and I was furious that I'd not realised the end was nigh.

There were seven grands prix remaining and I won't lie, they were a nightmare. A total mish-mash of emotions while I was determined to carry on commentating in the only way I knew how – passionate and loud. I was dreading the final grand prix of the season and my career in Valencia when I boarded the EasyJet flight to Spain on the Wednesday afternoon. That feeling just doubled in its intensity as we drove into the Valencia paddock to start a truly remarkable, emotional and uplifting weekend.

I was truly staggered by the response from the viewers worldwide and everybody involved in MotoGP, including the riders. I honestly never had any idea just how popular my commentaries and press conferences had been and it was a weekend that I will never ever forget. Messages poured in from all over the world; I was interviewed by every television and radio station involved in the sport and written features appeared from France, Australia, India and home in Oxford. The riders' thank-you video led by Valentino Rossi and Marc Márquez attracted 1.2 million viewers on Facebook. Around 20 million viewers watched the final live broadcast as I said goodbye to the cameras from the commentary box. There were gifts, dinners and I could not walk ten yards without being asked for a selfie.

I'd planned to slip away on Sunday without a fuss and booked a flight. The Repsol Honda team asked me to conduct my final television interview with Marc Márquez on Sunday evening if he was crowned World Champion and so the flights were changed in case. Marc won the title with that third place and I stayed. Once again, as the World Champion waited patiently for first the prize giving to start in the centre of Valencia, followed by the interview, I appreciated just how far the sport had developed on and off the track. It was around seven hours since the title had been won and Marc was understandably desperate to meet up with his loyal team to celebrate, but he carried out all his commitments, including a wonderful interview where he told me it was his hairdresser that had done so much to put him on track to win the title. Halfway through the year she told Marc his hair was beginning to fall out. There was no history of baldness in the family and so he rushed to the doctor who told him it was stress that was causing the problem. The stress of trying not to be Marc Márquez and ride conservatively and not take risks. He went back to his old ways, won the title and kept his hair.

The next day, as others prepared for what was always regarded as the first test of the new season after the Valencia grand prix, I flew home for the last time. At Valencia airport I almost missed my flight to Madrid performing selfies and signing autographs. I sat shattered but exhilarated on the short flight to the Spanish capital. The 38-year journey was finally over; nobody would recognise me in Madrid. As I climbed the stairs into the terminal, two six-foot African American guys approached me. 'Oh my God are you Nick Harris?' they asked. 'We are two American basketball players living in Spain – can we please take a selfie?' I duly obliged and walked through the passport gate towards London – bound for flight BA 459 and home for good. As Valentino Rossi had told me the previous day, the nine-time World Champion would now be the oldest man in the MotoGP paddock.

I can't pretend that watching the 2018 season unfurl from afar was easy because it was not, especially at the start. I tried to immerse myself into the fortunes of Oxford United and enjoy actually being able to go to parties, weddings and various events I'd missed so often in the last 38 years – although it was more funerals and seventieth birthday parties than weddings this time round.

I could not turn on the television to watch Dovizioso's victory at the opening round in Qatar. I didn't want to watch the second race either, but my friends sent me a text about Jack Miller's amazing pole in Argentina. The same friends who'd met the Aussie in the bar in Valencia just as the end of season party was kicking off many years ago and later saw him being carried out. I switched on the telly, swallowed my stupid pride and enjoyed the racing.

It's so easy to commentate sitting on the sofa at home, and you can spot everything that is going on much more than when you have the microphone in your hand. I really thought Dovizioso was going to win the title, so enjoyed watching the smooth Lorenzo at last winning on the Ducati, but when it came to the crunch it was Márquez with that win in Motegi that did it again. I'm sure he was just as professional and patient as he had been previously after the race, but I bet there was one hell of a party in Phillip Island a week later.

I so wanted Valentino Rossi to win that penultimate round in Malaysia to complete the absolute perfect day for a rider who has experienced so many in that amazing career. Four laps from the finish of the MotoGP race and Rossi was on course to experience a day that most sportsmen at any level can only dream about.

His step-brother Luca Marini had just won his first grand prix with victory in the Moto2 race. Marini's team-mate Francesco (Pecco) Bagnaia clinched the Moto2 world title after finishing third in the same race and both riding for Rossi's Sky Racing Team VR46. Could it get any better? Yes was the answer, because Vale himself was leading the MotoGP race as they flashed across the line at Sepang with four laps remaining. Just over 14 miles to go on the red hot tarmac before the 39-year-old Italian would be celebrating his first win of the season to end a perfect day even by his incredible standards.

Nine world titles and 115 grands prix wins in 22 years of grand prix racing had taught Vale never to count his chickens, never presume in any circumstances in a sport that has a habit of wrecking the party just as you are putting up the decorations and the guests are about to arrive. Less than ten seconds after racing past his pit board telling him Marc Márquez was closing he went down at turn one in front of a sea of yellow flags in the Rossi grandstand.

That perfect day may have been ruined but this should take nothing away from the Sepang experience that was the perfect illustration of why the man from Tavullia has had a bigger impact and influence both on and off the track than any other rider in the 70-year history of the sport. Who else, at 39 years old, could lead a MotoGP race for so long in such sweltering conditions around one of the most demanding race tracks in the 19-race calendar? Who else would form his own team after being dismayed at the lack of young Italian talent on the world scene and then build a dirt track and ranch to train with the youngsters who have gone on to become World Champions? Who else could deal with the publicity the arrival of his step-brother in the World Championship generated, protect him and then help him become a grand prix winner? Who else would have already announced his plans to carry on racing for at least two more years as he approaches that dreaded fortieth birthday? Who else would just relish the fact that his protégés are now lining up to take him on, not on the dirt track, but in the ultimate MotoGP test?

I missed that wonderful breakfast at Ducati where the staff called me Uncle Albert from the *Only Fools and Horses* television programme. I missed watching the football with a beer and discussing the fortunes of Cornish Pirates rugby team with Jerry Appleton in the Alpine Stars Hospitality Unit. I missed the commentary-box banter which too often involved lavatory humour. I missed being asked white or pink champagne on a rare business class Qatar Airways flight. I missed finding out on my phone that Oxford United had been promoted in the middle of a Jorge Lorenzo qualifying press conference. I missed Dylan trying to explain to me just what his beloved winglets were all about. Most of all I missed the friends I'd made on this incredible journey and especially that moment on a Sunday morning when those red starting lights changed.

The British Grand Prix just up the road at Silverstone from my Oxford home was always going to be difficult for me, as I would not actually be involved for the first time in 38 years. So instead I decided to embark on a 'Last of the Summer Wine' world tour to the Classic TT on the Isle of Man during the grand prix weekend. I did go to Silverstone on the Thursday before practice to meet up with old friends and colleagues, which is never easy for them. They are busy and focused on the weekend ahead and so it was a brief hello before catching the flight to the island the next day.

I've been there so many times before. Stuck in the commentary box with nothing to talk about but having to talk about something to keep the producer and more important the dwindling number of viewers happy. I've never been on the other side until that Sunday morning at Jak's Sports Bar on the very wet and windy Douglas Promenade as the Irish Sea pounded the beach on the Isle of Man. The savvy manager opened up early at 11am with the MotoGP race at Silverstone due to start early at 11.30 because of a bad weather warning. The place was jam-packed with race fans from all over the world on the island to watch the TT Classic races.

The big screens that adorned the walls showed that weather warning was justified as the rain poured down at Silverstone and the new track surface got more and more flooded. Some customers started with coffee while others were straight onto the ale – after all they were on holiday. Like everybody we sat, drank, waited and drank, waiting for something to happen. More and more people arrived but despite the disappointment at each announcement of more delays nobody moaned about riders not risking their lives to go out there; it was those sodden spectators that everybody raised a glass to, toasting their dedication.

Around 2.30pm, the rain had stopped outside. The three ex-TT riders on the 'Last of the Summer Wine' tour and I decided to relieve the boredom and make our own lap of the TT circuit in a Ford Mondeo. They wanted to relive their memories, which they did, telling some scary old stories.

Roger Cope told us how he'd crashed at Creg-ny-Baa and was disappointed not to get a ride in the helicopter to Noble's Hospital. Cliffy Jones recounted his 85mph lap on a 125cc BSA Bantam. Dave 'Locktite' Lock how Ángelo Nieto had crashed in front of him at the bottom of Barregarrow in the last 50cc TT and I even threw in a couple of stories from my sidecar lap. We stopped at a pub in Ramsey and, to the annoyance of the customers, asked the landlord to switch over from Premier League football coverage to MotoGP. The pictures from the studio with the rain pouring outside told their own story and the customers cheered as they switched back to the football.

Back at Jak's plenty of alcohol was still being consumed because everybody knew what the news from Silverstone was going to be. The announcement of the cancellation came as no great surprise. We were the lucky ones in the warm and dry and all the sympathy was for those spectators who'd braved it out.

My thoughts turned to the television presenters and commentators. Our pit-lane reporter Ian Wheeler used to say they knew things were really desperate when Nick Harris reached the Milk Cup Final moment. When I had really run out of things to say I would recount the 1986 Milk Cup Final success of my beloved Oxford United. Then it was definitely time to switch off, not that there were many viewers still switched on.

As I was about to leave Jak's I raised my glass to those spectators at Silverstone and all the television commentators and presenters who did such an amazing job. The next day on Monday morning in the Isle of Man the start of racing was delayed because of the weather. Nothing changes.

Grand Prix motorcycle racing has never lost its basic principles in 70 amazing years. Some motorsports have forgotten that racing is all about what actually happens on the track. Of course, the infrastructure in place to support that principle has to be strong. Dorna came into the sport 25 years ago as the Spanish company nobody had ever heard of to run the show. They may have upset more than a few along the way but they have produced a World Championship worthy of its name – a championship that is spread throughout the world, yet encompasses all the beliefs that were shown on 13 June 1949 at the very start. They have provided a battleground for the riders and manufacturers to fight for glory in the safest and most competitive way. From dwindling grids, huge performance gaps and arguments about rule changes, the only debate now is whether the race will be close, or really close.

It's a battlefield that gives riders the opportunity to provide us with a spectacle none of us will ever forget. So many, especially in those early days, lost their lives chasing the dream. The riders are the real heroes of these 70 amazing years and, as Graham Noyce always told me all those years ago – when the flag drops, the bullshit stops.

That's when never say never takes over.

Acknowledgements

My wife Sheila and daughter Sophie.

Colin Fenton, John Brown, Barry Sheene, Mick Woollett, Peter Baker, Nicky Jennings and Marco Guidetti.

Dr Martin Raines, Lyn Shields, Dylan Gray and Jerome Sale who supported and encouraged me in some unsure moments.

Tony Rosser, Tony Adamson, Paul Fowler, Iain Mackay, Annie Bradshaw, Jerry Burgess, David Beck, Wayne Gardner, Manel Arroyo, Carmelo Ezpeleta, Eva Jirsenká, Judith Pieper Kohler, Frine Velilla, all my wonderful colleagues at Dorna (and sorry I never learnt Spanish).

Mike and Irene Trimby, Jeremy Appleton, Matt George, David Kent, Bradley and Allan Smith.

Everybody at Penguin Random House and especially to Lorna Russell for her enthusiasm, support and advice right from the start. Liz Marvin for her patience while editing my rambling copy. Michelle Warner for ensuring everything was on time and legal, Patsy O'Neill who made sure the world knew about the book and Matthew Wallace who guided an old fuddy duddy through the complexities of social media. A big thank you to David Luxton who believed in me and made it happen.

And finally, to all those riders who lost their lives chasing the dream over the last 70 years.

Index